Remnants of a Distant Past

A New Theory to Explain the UFO Phenomenon

www.kenjeremiah.com

Also by Ken Jeremiah:

Aikido Ground Fighting
Grappling and Submission Techniques

If the Samurai Played Golf…
Zen Strategies for a Winning Game

Christian Mummification
An Interpretive History of the Preservation of Saints, Martyrs, and Others

Living Buddhas
The Self-Mummified Monks of Yamagata, Japan

Remnants of a Distant Past

A New Theory to Explain the UFO Phenomenon

Dr. Ken Jeremiah

Copyright 2013 Ken Jeremiah. All rights reserved.

No part of this book, except for a brief review, may be reproduced, in whole or in part, by any means electronic or mechanical, including recording, photocopying, or by any information storage and retrieval system, without written permission from the author. For information, contact Ken Jeremiah at kjeremiah@pga.com.

REMNANTS OF A DISTANT PAST
A New Theory to Explain the UFO Phenomenon

Figures 4, 19, 21, 22, 23, 28, 29, 30, 31, 36, 42, 43, 44, 45, 46, 47, and 50 are © Ken Jeremiah
Figure 1 © Oilstreet, made available as part of the Creative Commons License on Wikimedia
Figure 2 © Roberto Arias (Wikimedia Creative Commons License)
Figure 3 © CarbonNYC (Wikimedia Creative Commons License)
Figure 11 © Crypto-Researcher (Wikimedia Creative Commons License)
Figure 16 © Davide Ferro (Wikimedia Creative Commons License)
Figure 24 © Ned Eddins. Used with permission.
Figure 25 © Thomas (Wikimedia Creative Commons License)
Figure 26 © Daein Ballard
Figure 27 courtesy of NASA and The Hubble Heritage Team (STScI / AURA)
Figure 32 © Masahiro Kaji (Wikimedia Creative Commons License)
Figure 33 © jpatokal (Wikimedia Creative Commons License)
Figure 37 © Marsyas (Wikimedia Creative Commons License)
Figure 39 © kallerna (Wikimedia Creative Commons License)
Figure 40 © Daniel Mayer (Wikimedia Creative Commons License)
Figure 41 © Ricardo Liberato (Wikimedia Creative Commons License)
Figure 49 © Ned Eddins. Used with permission.

Front and back cover image: Machu Picchu, Peru
(photograph by the author)

ISBN-13: 978-1484104309

ISBN-10: 1484104307

Contents

Figures viii

Acknowledgments x

Introduction 1

1. The UFO Phenomenon 18

   Strange Craft in the Sky 19

   A Historical Perspective 25

   The Modern UFO Phenomenon 30

   Reported Abductions 46

   Modern Sightings 60

2. USOs 73

   USO Sightings 74

   The Deepest Water 83

   The Bermuda Triangle 90

   The Pacific Triangle 97

   Underwater Bases 114

3. Underwater Cities 123

Underwater Homes of UFO and USO Pilots 124
　　The Yonaguni Monument: Japan's Underwater Pyramids 132
　　Dismissal of Anomalous Finds 136
　　The Legendary City of Dwarka 143
　　The Bimini Road 148
　　Underwater Ruins that Suggest a Global Flood 152
4. Cyclical Nature of Civilization 154
　　Many Worlds 155
　　The Hopi View of Creation and Destruction 157
　　The Beginning and End of the Mayan and Aztec Cycles 163
　　Hindu and Buddhist World Cycles 167
　　Planetary Disasters as a Natural Part of Earth's History 171
　　Mega-Disasters and Evolution 176
　　Refugia and Survival during Mass-Extinction Events 179
　　Periods of Glaciation 185
　　Destruction and Rebirth: Flood Stories and Survival 188
5. Advanced Ancient Civilizations 200
　　Mainstream View of Human History 201
　　Contradictory Archaeological Evidence 204
　　Archaeological Evidence of Advanced Civilizations 209
　　Ancient Anomalous Maps 214
　　Ancient Aircraft described in Judeo-Christian Texts 219
　　Ancient Indian Aircraft 222
　　Archaeology and Ancient Aircraft 229
　　Ancient Atomic Weapons 234
　　Other Ancient Civilizations 237
　　Megalithic Structures 240
　　Farming, Detoxification Processes, and Manna 254
　　Physical Evidence of Ancient Civilizations 258

Antediluvian Survivors 265
6. The Last Great Flood 268
　　Cycles of Destruction 269
　　Tebitu: Submarines in the Deep 279
　　The Development of Surface-Exploring Craft 284
　　Evolutionary Change and Intentional D.N.A. Modification 289
　　Exploring the Surface 295
　　Remnants from a Distant Past 299
Conclusion 302
Notes 309
Bibliography 319
Index 329

Figures

1. Jellyfish have shapes reminiscent of UFOs. (Kyoto, Japan) 20
2. UFOs glow like bioluminescent marine creatures. 21
3. Another example of jellyfish that resemble UFOs 22
4. Petroglyphs at Palatki, near Sedona, Arizona. 26
5. Woodcut by Hans Glaser (April 4, 1562). 28
6. Drawing of the UFO by Kenneth Arnold. 31
7. The Stealth Bomber 68
8. U.S. Airforce B-2 Stealth Bomber. 77
9. The deep-sea fish, Photostomias Guernei 84
10. Plesiosaur Skeleton (New Walk Museum, Leicester, UK) 86
11. Artistic reproduction of Ogopogo. 86
12. Coelacanth Model 87
13. Yureisen (Ghost Ship) by Hokusai 98
14. Woodblock carving of Utsurobune 106
15. Another carving of the Utsurobune event 107
16. Dogu Figure from Aomori, Japan 108
17. Dogu Figure from the Tokyo National Museum 108
18. Dogu Figure from the Musée Guimet (Paris, France) 109
19. Kachina (I) 110
20. Kachina (II) 110
21. Kachina (III) 111
22. Kachina (IV) 111
23. Kachina (V) 111
24. Petroglyphs at Barrier Canyon 112
25. Petroglyphs at Sego Canyon 113

26. What Mars once looked like 116
27. Mars seen through the Hubble Telescope 118
28. The Uros Islands 128
29. Taquile Islanders 129
30. Taquile Islanders 130
31. Lake Titicaca, Peru 130
32. Japan's Underwater Pyramids 133
33. Another area of the Yonaguni Monument, Japan 134
34. The Kensington Rune Stone 138
35. Lord Krishna playing the flute 144
36. Fresco of Apollo from the Augustus Period (Rome, Italy) 164
37. The Antikythera Mechanism 212
38. The Piri Reis Map 217
39. The Sphinx (Giza Plateau, Egypt) 241
40. Khafre's Pyramid and the Great Sphinx 242
41. The Pyramids at Giza, Egypt 244
42. The enormous stones at Sacsayhuaman 249
43. Close up of perfectly cut megalithic blocks 249
44. The ruins at Machu Picchu 251
45. Machu Picchu at sunrise 251
46. At the edge of a terrace at Machu Picchu 252
47. The Incan creator gods 270
48. Moai on Easter Island 274
49. Barrier Canyon Petroglyphs 277
50. Petroglyphs at Honanki 277

Acknowledgments

I need to thank various individuals for their assistance. This project involved a great deal of research, and as is the case with any major undertaking, the researcher can get lost in the research itself. Paul White helped me to sort through information, suggesting the elimination of some superfluous facts. He helped me to focus the text to expound upon the proposed theory. I am grateful for his help. In addition, thank you to Steve Pepe, who provided some initial insight regarding this project's direction. I would like to acknowledge White Bear Fredericks from Kykotsmovi, Arizona, for providing information about *kachina*. He is an accomplished artist, and has a studio in the Third Mesa (in Hopi Territory) near Tuba City. Thanks also to Kobi Chumash, Coordinator of Jewish Life and Advisor to Hillel at Colorado College, and to Joel Rosenberg from Tufts University for some translation assistance. Finally, I am grateful to Ned Eddins for allowing me to use some great pictures that he had taken of petroglyphs at Barrier Canyon, Utah.

Introduction

Much about the history of humankind and the history of this planet is unknown. However, some versions of history answer all questions. This is because human beings like certainty. They like to think that they know what happened on this planet; that they know their own origins. Leaving unanswered questions creates doubt, and individuals can live more comfortably without doubt.

Mainstream historical accounts provide a seemingly plausible story about the history of this planet, but such accounts do not consider any disconfirming evidence. There is evidence that contradicts the existing theories of human development, such as modern human footprints found in various countries that are millions of years old.[1] These finds suggest that human beings might be much older than suggested by the mainstream historical accounts — millions of years older. Other evidence supports this same conclusion. For example, archaeologists found a human skeleton in an undisturbed silver vein in Colorado along with an arrowhead made from copper.[2] It too was determined to be several million years old.[3]

Other archaeological evidence likewise disrupts the prevailing historical theory. An aeronautics text written in 400 B.C.E. by Maharshi Bharadwaaja contains specific instructions for building and flying machines called vimanas.[4] These instructions include electrical diagrams, explanations of their propulsion systems, and even what the pilots needed to wear and eat. The author also explained the weapons systems aboard. Other accounts from various civilizations likewise describe aircraft. There is evidence that ancient Egyptians were familiar with aerodynamics, and Judeo-Christian accounts such as the Old Testament and the Kebra Nagast likewise describe flying machines.

Evidence suggests that ancient civilizations had advanced tools used to cut and move heavy stone blocks.[5] Such civilizations may have also had electrical or other power sources.[6] Historical texts also seem to describe ancient atomic warfare. Besides flight, advanced weapons, advanced machinery, and electric energy, there is archaeological evidence that other new inventions, such as sparkplugs, batteries, and clocks are not new. Rather, they are ancient inventions that people once knew about. Archaeologists found a sparkplug in a geode that was determined to have been more than 500,000 years old.[7]

An example of an ancient battery is the so-called Baghdad battery, which archaeologists found during the excavation of a 2,000-year-old ancient city (near Baghdad). This battery was not unique. They found others in the same area. Most of the batteries that are currently on display in various museums date from 248 B.C.E. to 226 C.E.[8] However, the oldest intact batteries are more than 2,000 years old. It is likely that ancient cultures used the battery even earlier than this, however. They may have used it more than 4,500 years ago.[9]

Likewise, some people think that mechanical clocks are a modern invention, and mainstream historical accounts state that they did not appear until the 14th century in Europe. However, divers discovered a clock with more than 30 interconnected gears in the Antikythera shipwreck off the coast of Greece. It is the oldest known astronomical clock in the world, dating to c. 100 C.E.[10] This device is amazing due to the complexity of its design and the miniaturization of the gears used in its construction. How someone constructed such gears without machinery built to create them is unknown. However, it is quite possible that such machinery also existed. Sparkplugs, mechanical clocks, and batteries, which are generally thought to be modern inventions, are seemingly ancient. The technology (that once existed) had been lost, and it was only *rediscovered* in modern times. These archaeological finds are contrary to the existing theory of human history. Typically, anything discovered that disrupts the mainstream theory is discarded. It is not seriously considered nor used to rethink and change common historical accounts.

In 1880, geologist J. D. Whitney published information about advanced stone tools that were found in undisturbed layers of lava that were between 9 million and 55 million years old.[11] Critics were opposed to his findings, and some individuals immediately dismissed them as nonsense because they ran contrary to the existing theory. This is the prevailing practice. Any find that does not fit into the existing theory of human history is discarded. Historians do not update the existing theory based upon such new and contradictory finds. This is because people, as a whole, dislike considering evidence that is contrary to what they believe. It makes them uncomfortable. When they hear alternate theories about historical events or unusual phenomena, they typically dismiss them as nonsense. For this reason, incorrect historical accounts might exist.

There is an accepted theory regarding the history of this planet and the history of humankind. That theory is linear. In other words, human beings never take a step backward. Progress continues, and new inventions build upon older knowledge. Many dismiss the idea that ancient civilizations may have been just as advanced, (or even more advanced), as civilizations are today. However, the evidence seems to suggest that progress is cyclical. Knowledge is also cyclical. In the first century B.C.E., Posidonius had created a revolving model of the universe that accurately represented the planets orbiting around the sun.[12] By the end of the fourth century, the Roman Catholic Church banned this knowledge.

It became heretical to disbelieve that the Earth was the center of the solar system and God had placed the stars in the sky. Likewise, in the third century B.C.E. Eratosthenes determined the circumference of the planet, only to have the knowledge stamped out and discredited by the ruling religious organization.[13] It became known (as a fact) that the Earth was not round, but flat. The astronomical knowledge of the ancients was thereby lost. In modern times, it has been rediscovered, but evidence supports the idea that the ancients had more knowledge about the solar system than we currently possess. Perhaps some knowledge has not yet been rediscovered.

Things that are considered unarguably true have changed throughout history. The notion of what is fact compared to what is myth has also consistently changed. Until 1970, the ancient city of Troy did not exist. It was a myth alone, and the legends of the Trojan War immortalized in Homer's poems were just fanciful stories. German-American adventurer Heinrich Schliemann led an archaeological excavation at the site (in modern-day Turkey) in 1968.[14] Once unearthed, the mythological city was made real, and the stories described in *The Odyssey* and *The Iliad* were then interpreted as historical rather than fictitious.

Considering the legends of Troy alone indicate that historical knowledge is cyclical. Troy, founded in 2920 B.C.E., was destroyed and rebuilt eight different times. Up until the first or second century, people knew the city had been real, that it had actually existed. However, this knowledge was lost, and the historical city became a legend. In the 19th century, the knowledge was rediscovered and the city became historical once more. Other knowledge likewise had been lost in time, only to be recently rediscovered. In this way, knowledge is cyclical.

The rise and fall of civilizations may also be cyclical. This means that history is not linear, with the current civilization the result of historical human development. Rather, civilizations emerge and then disappear, and this current cycle of existence is just one of many that had existed before. Many religious and philosophical systems adhere to this view, including Hinduism, Hopi and other Native American religions, and some forms of Buddhism. Civilizations of the past developed, becoming increasingly more advanced, before worldwide disasters destroyed them. After, another age started, and civilization began anew. According to this view, there may have been previous civilizations that were as advanced as modern humans are today. However, worldwide catastrophes literally erased them from the Earth. Likewise, they were erased from human knowledge. However, there is still evidence that they once existed. There is also substantial evidence of a regularity of sudden, worldwide, natural disasters that nearly destroy all life on the planet.

Mega-disasters have been the culprit in three major extinctions on Earth. However, some creatures survived every extinction event. Those that did evolved. There is a correlation between natural disasters, such as global ice ages, and evolution.[15] Somehow, the disasters trigger changes in living creatures. They quickly adapt to the changing environments to survive. This type of mass-extinction of the majority of creatures and the adaptation and evolution of the survivors has occurred regularly. There have also been a number of smaller disasters caused by glaciation and massive floods. The last major period of glaciation began c. 19,000 B.C.E. and ended c. 8,000 B.C.E.[16] The peak of this period was in 16,000 B.C.E., and glaciers that were miles high covered Europe. Due to volcanic eruptions and other factors that mirror the end of the last ice age on a much smaller scale, the ice began to melt c. 12,000 B.C.E. Because of temperature variations on the planet, the ice melted at different times in diverse places. The breakup of glacial ice, mixing with the seas, created massive flooding. The flood stories of many of the world's religions refer to this flood, which occurred c. 11,000 B.C.E.[17]

Many of the world's religions have flood stories. Although more of them will be explored later in this text, three stories are important at this point in order to provide a general understanding of what occurred during this tumultuous event. Two stories explain preparations made to survive the Great Flood. The third describes preparations undertaken before the glaciation period's peak. It describes steps taken to survive the cold temperatures of the planet and the massive glaciers covering the land.

Before the flood began, and before the glaciers had expanded toward the equator, there were various civilizations on this planet. Some were highly advanced, making use of seemingly modern inventions such as aircraft and electricity. Others were primitive and ignorant of such technology. It is probable that some civilizations knew about the oncoming period of glaciation and the associated flood, while others did not. Evidence from multiple civilizations indicates that advanced civilizations informed less knowledgeable societies about the oncoming disasters. One example is in the Vendidad, a sacred Zoroastrian text from c. 800 B.C.E.

A man named Yima learned that a great ice age was coming. In order to survive this "evil winter," all creatures had to live underground. He built a large underground abode called a *vara* that would serve as a refuge for people. He also needed to save all animals upon which they relied. The Zoroastrian creator god Ahura Mazda told him to bring the seed of all kinds of animals and trees into the underground shelter. In addition, Ahura Mazda taught him how to transport water into the shelter and how to grow food in waterbeds, food that will never cease to exist. (Although this specific line will be discussed in more detail later, it is likely that this replenishable food source is a type of algae.)

Likely with hundreds of other people, he built this underground shelter. He partitioned off some water, as he had been taught, and carved out underground quarters for thousands of people and specific areas where he could keep livestock and other animals. Airshafts in this underground abode allowed humans and animals to breathe even in the complex's deepest recesses. These shafts also provided light. In addition to the natural light, artificial lighting was also used inside.[18] What these artificial lights actually were is an unanswered question. Some believe that they were electrical lights, but it is also possible that the inhabitants used torches to provide light, and they used gold to reflect the light into even the darkest parts of the subterranean city. According to the text, the complex was sealed with a circular door that was lined with a ring of gold. Perhaps they used gold throughout the entire complex. In many societies, gold held a prominent place due to its reflective capabilities. In castles and aristocratic homes in feudal Japan, for example, artists added golf leaf to paintings on the walls and ceilings. This was not for aesthetic purposes alone, but because the gold carried candlelight across rooms.

An underground complex, like the one described in the Zoroastrian text, has been found in modern day Turkey. In 1963, a resident of Derenkuyu, a town near Cappadocia, decided to renovate his home. He knocked down a wall, revealing an underground passageway. Exploring this lengthy road, he found himself in a large underground city. It has 13 stories, and it is more than 85 meters (280 feet) deep. There are thousands of ventilation shafts, and it has so many chambers that more than 20,000 human beings could have resided there for an extended period. The complex even included religious centers, food storerooms, wine presses, and areas for livestock. Mainstream archaeology dates the complex to c. 800 B.C.E. However, this structure cannot be accurately dated using any current archaeological or geological techniques. This structure matches up perfectly to the Zoroastrian account, which describes the completion of the facility's construction before ice covered the area. Therefore, this facility, properly called a vara, was likely created c. 17,000 B.C.E.

During the last glacial period, ocean levels were much lower than they are today. Glaciers more than three kilometers (two miles) high covered Europe. These ice caps began to melt approximately 14,000 years ago, and they finished melting approximately 12,000 years ago. The melting ice made the sea levels rise substantially, and more than 16 million square kilometers (10 million square miles) of land was submerged — a landmass the size of China and Europe put together. This is the Great Flood.

Melting glaciers and rising sea levels destroyed countless cities and towns. The devastation wiped out whole civilizations, and erased all traces of their existence. Technology was lost, and written historical records were destroyed. However, like all major catastrophes that have affected this planet, there were survivors. These survivors lived in various parts of the world, and they were part of diverse civilizations. The flood stories that appear in all of the historical and cultural traditions of these civilizations record the disaster and the way in which humankind managed to adapt and survive. They are true survivor stories, recounting the heroes of the past who survived an event so terrible that it killed the majority of living creatures.

The most familiar of these stories to the Western world is the biblical account of Noah. He was told to build a vessel to save living creatures, and he gathered animals and birds, both male and female, and brought them aboard. When the flooding began, he launched the vessel into the seas. It eventually came to rest on Mt. Ararat.[19] Once the floodwaters had subsided, Noah and his family led the animals down the mountain to repopulate the Earth.

The Epic of Gilgamesh is another flood story that should be reviewed at this point. Written c. 1800 B.C.E., it recounts another tale of survival during this mega-flood. The oldest version of the tale appears in Sumerian cuneiform, but there are also versions in Akkadian. In the Sumerian text, the hero (who built the vessel) is Ziusudra, while in the Akkadian texts it is Atrahasis. Other Babylonian accounts call the hero Utnapishtim. However, these tales refer to the same event, and feature the same person.[20] The hero abandoned his possessions and created a vessel capable of withstanding the oncoming deluge. After he had completed it, he gathered the seed of all living creatures. His family and friends came aboard the vessel, and they launched it. They sealed it and then headed into the deep. There they waited for the storm to end. Once it had ended, they rose to the surface and looked out into the distance. Like the biblical version, they could only see a mountain. The hero looked for land, but was unsuccessful. He only saw a mountain called Nisir in the distance. It was on this mountaintop that the vessel grounded. Similar to the biblical account, they waited on this mountaintop for the floodwaters to abate. Then they repopulated the Earth with the D.N.A. (i.e. seed) that they had collected.

     An important linguistic note should be explained. The terms used for "vessel" in both the Sumerian and the Akkadian accounts do not actually translate as "vessel." In the Sumerian version, the term was *magurgur*, a ship that can tumble and turn. The Akkadian version used the word *tebitu*, which translates to "submersible ship" or "submarine."[21] Therefore, when we accurately interpret these tales, they tell the story of individuals who survived the deluge in an underwater vessel, a submarine.

     There is another significant consideration regarding all three of these tales. The Zoroastrian account in which Yima built an underground safety zone was written c. 800 B.C.E., but the event that it referred to occurred c. 17,000 B.C.E. It is a written record of an event that happened 16,200 years earlier. Likewise, the Old Testament, which contains Noah's story, was written between 1313 – 450 B.C.E. The same is true with the Babylonian account, the oldest of the three. It was written c. 1800 B.C.E. The event that all three of these historical texts refer to occurred more than 9,000 years before they were written. These stories were about ancient civilizations, and the people who survived the flood did not write them. It is possible that the three accounts, (the Epic of Gilgamesh, the Old Testament, and the Vendidad), were based upon earlier texts or word-of-mouth, but it is clear that none of the authors of these texts were present when the actual events occurred. These stories refer to much more ancient civilizations — civilizations that were perhaps extremely advanced.

Evidence suggests there were highly advanced civilizations on this planet before the last glacial period. Plato refers to Atlantis in two of his historical texts, the *Timaeus* and the *Critias*. He wrote that it was a technologically advanced civilization that existed until c. 9,600 B.C.E., about the same time that the Great Flood ravished the Earth. Evidence supports the notion that other hitherto undiscovered civilizations of the distant past were likewise technologically advanced. Beyond historical tales of aircraft, electricity, and technologically advanced weaponry, some objects have been found and dated to periods in which mainstream archaeologists claim human beings did not exist.

Such objects include an artificially created grooved metal sphere found in a Precambrian mineral deposit. It is more than 2.8 billion years old.[22] Also preserved in Precambrian rock was a metallic vase found in Dorchester, Massachusetts. It is more than 600 million years old.[23] A perfectly formed, modern-looking shoe print was found in Cambrian shale in Utah, dated at over 505 million years ago.[24] Other human footprints or seemingly modern shoe prints have likewise been found preserved in various places, including Kentucky and Nevada. The one found in Kentucky dates to more than 286 million years ago, while the one in Nevada dates to c. 5 million years ago.[25] All of these are some of the oldest historical anomalies found on this planet.

When we approach the time immediately before the Great Flood, artifacts that clash with the mainstream view of human history become more numerous. Such findings, which will be presented later in this text, suggest that human beings are a much older species than generally thought. They also suggest there was at least one, if not multiple advanced civilizations in the distant past. Mainstream historians and archaeologists have ignored much of the evidence supporting this claim only because it does not fit into the current theory. However, the evidence is there, and one cannot easily dismiss it.

It is difficult for many individuals to change their preexisting beliefs. Many fight against it, as their beliefs, to a certain extent, make them who they are. This is not just the case with so-called conformists, who support the mainstream notion that human beings are a modern species, but also the case with some seemingly open-minded thinkers. These so-called thinkers get caught in a trap. Whatever the common belief might be that surrounds them influences their thoughts to such a degree that they might fail to see things clearly.

Throughout much of recorded history, witnesses have seen and reported unidentified flying objects. There was a sighting by Christopher Columbus on his famous voyage to the New World. Likewise, there were many reports by individuals during the Crusades that mention UFOs in the skies. UFO sightings seem to have increased in modern times. It is likely, however, that there are not more sightings than there were in the past, only that the means of communicating such sightings has improved substantially. In addition, many people who witnessed unexplainable sightings in the past likely believed that they had seen something religious, such as the appearance of angels, demons, or gods. For anyone to suggest otherwise might have been unthinkable. In time, however, the notion of what these craft are has changed. Now, the majority of people relate UFOs with aliens — creatures who are not of this world. Although there seems to be some evidence to support this theory, that same evidence can support a different theory.

There is a consistent connection between UFOs and water. In other words, in many sightings, UFOs are seen either emerging from the oceans or returning to them. Reports by U.S. service members aboard nuclear submarines support this connection, as do the sightings of strange phenomena in the areas of the Bermuda Triangle and the Pacific Triangle. These two areas are disaster zones, and reports of malfunctioning instruments and missing airplanes and boats suggest that there is a severe magnetic anomaly present at these two sights.

The Bermuda Triangle is an area covering more than 804 square kilometers (500,000 square miles) between Puerto Rico, Miami, and Bermuda. There have been so many reports of disappearing planes and ships that it seems like the area was swallowing them. One famous example occurred December 5, 1945, when the U.S. military sent five torpedo bombers on a training exercise. They took off from Ft. Lauderdale and all five planes disappeared soon after. When a rescue plane headed out to search for them, it too disappeared without a trace. As of right now, no one has been able to explain what happened.

Similar events happen in the Pacific Triangle. Also known as the Dragon's Triangle, it is the same size as the Bermuda Triangle. Located off the southeast coast of Japan, it too is a hot spot for strange phenomena. Like the Bermuda Triangle, located on the opposite side of the planet, ships and planes disappear within, and there are countless UFO sightings. In many of these sightings, people see craft either entering or leaving the water. For this reason, some have speculated that there are underwater bases at these locations. The notion of underwater bases is logical. Water covers more than 71 percent of the planet, and the deepest oceans are still unexplored. The scientific capability to reach many of the ocean floors does not yet exist. In fact, scientists know more about the moon and other planets in the solar system than they know about the deepest parts of the ocean.

Many individuals have accepted the most common theory regarding UFOs as an unquestionable fact. Even the mention of the term UFO will cause many individuals to think of flying saucers and gray humanoid figures with large heads, large black eyes, and smaller bodies. This common belief holds that alien beings pilot UFOs. Some refer to them as "the grays." They supposedly enter the Earth's atmosphere, coming from another planet, and they quite possibly have two or more undersea bases in the deepest parts of the planet's oceans. However, the evidence presented in this book supports a different theory: that these craft are not alien at all. Modern human beings have not created them either.

The shape of the craft as described by witnesses is generally spherical. They resemble the descriptions of vimanas in ancient Indian texts. This shape is not conducive to interstellar travel.[26] It is therefore unlikely that they are extraterrestrial. Rather, they are terrestrial — from this planet. In addition, a review of the descriptions of the craft sighted throughout the last 600 years indicates something strange. The earlier drawings and explanations by witnesses depict larger craft that are seemingly not as technologically advanced as modern UFOs. This indicates that there might have been some technological advancements throughout the last millennia or more in which designers and pilots of the craft have improved them. This book supports a theory that the pilots of these craft are not aliens, but humans. However, they are not modern humans, but ancient humans — remnants from an advanced civilization (or multiple advanced civilizations) in the distant past.

Although the idea may sound outlandish now, enough evidence will be provided throughout this book to back up the claim. There is more evidence to support this conclusion than there is to support the extraterrestrial theory. In order to explore this, let us return to the three glacial period flood stories previously presented. In the Zoroastrian account, Yima constructs an underground city that can house more than 20,000 citizens along with livestock and other animals. The city has running water, ventilation shafts, and both natural and artificial lights. It also has a food source that will replenish itself. This same food possibly sustained Moses and his followers throughout 40 years in the desert. Called *mana* in the Dead Sea Scrolls, it likely refers to a type of algae that proliferates in the correct environment. This technology had been lost for many years and is now being rediscovered, as NASA and other organizations are exploring the use of chlorophyta algae alone to sustain human beings for long periods.[27]

It is necessary to remember that the writers of these tales (as they have been passed down to the present) were not present during the Great Flood. This event happened thousands of years before any of these accounts were written. It is therefore possible, if not probable, that the story of the creation of one or two vessels was recorded, but that many more were actually created. It is also possible that future generations did not fully understand the technology of the ancients. If not, they would have rendered misunderstood terms into their own language using the (limited) understanding and vocabulary that they had.

The biblical version tells the story of a group of people who gathered some animals and other humans into a large covered boat. They rode out the deluge along its surface. However, the Babylonian account states that they gathered up the D.N.A. of living creatures and brought it aboard a submarine. They intended to travel underwater to escape the planet's volatile surface. This flood occurred just after the peak of the last glacial period, and there were glaciers everywhere. The ocean's surface was extremely cold. Snow and ice covered any land that was exposed, and little food was available. To escape the harsh, cold conditions on the surface, the civilization to which this tale refers sealed their submarine and headed underwater.

In every mass-extinction event that has occurred on this planet, there have always been survivors. To escape the devastation and harsh climates that these disasters bring, animals and other creatures travel to *refugia*. This term, used by paleontologists and ecologists, refers to zones that are more hospitable to life. Human beings, faced with the same worldwide disasters, would likewise seek out such shelters. In a world covered in ice, they would head deep into the oceans, toward the underwater volcanoes that constantly erupt.

Based upon the tale recorded in the Babylonian account, it is possible that an ancient, technologically advanced civilization launched various submarines. Not knowing how long they would actually need to remain in their vessels, they may have headed toward a warmer underwater environment, where volcanic activity provides natural heat. It is here, in this location, that the submarines waited. They had a sustainable food source, the food called manna that seems to have been commonplace in ancient civilizations. They also had the D.N.A. of various creatures aboard. This indicates that they had knowledge regarding genes and gene manipulation, knowledge that had been lost in time and only rediscovered in the present.

During this worldwide disaster, malfunctions might have occurred. Communication links could have been disabled, and power might have been lost. One or two of these submarines might have even been trapped underwater, never to return to the surface. Try to imagine this situation. Trapped in an underground environment with many other human beings, quarters were tight. The only food available was a type of green algae, and the darkness was palpable. The planet's surface raged. Chunks of ice cracked and slipped into the expanding oceans, burying cities and towns forever. Meanwhile, deep below the surface, a group of unfortunate people waited, afraid, in the darkness of the abyss. Trapped in this underwater environment, they made decisions. They had to take action. The submarine was out of commission. Limited power could be gained from the ocean water itself, but plans were underway to create some type of craft that could take them back to the surface. Unfortunately, this was not as easy of a task as it might seem.

Years passed. Decades turned into centuries. The people aboard continued to breed, but their offspring looked different. There is a correlation between ice ages and evolutionary change. In a new, stressful environment, all creatures adapt and adjust. Underwater in their new, small home, they may have even altered their D.N.A. intentionally to improve their situation. As trials for the creation of a new craft in an inhospitable environment continued, repeated generations of these undersea humans also continued to change genetically. Surviving on algae alone, in a dark, high-pressure environment, the humans eventually looked radically different. After

11,000 years, the deep water had become their home. Even when they finally created ships to explore the surface, knowledge of it was not firsthand. It was a distant idea, a story passed down orally through the last 150 generations, but it had no real relevance to those who heard it. The surface had become an alien, inhospitable world, and their new bodies were not equipped to deal with it for long periods. They needed to remain in their exploratory ships, which approximated the high pressure and darkness to which they were accustomed.

Upon reading this for the first time, it might seem like a fanciful story with no basis in reality. Certainly, there is an imaginative leap involved. However, it is important to create a theory that deals with all historical evidence. Anomalous evidence that does not fit into the current theory should not exist. In other words, a theory should explain all archaeological and historical evidence discovered. If a hypothesis is suggested, but it ignores or trivializes unusual archaeological finds, it must be discarded, and a new theory proposed. The theory presented herein explains many historical events without discarding any evidence. It also clarifies modern phenomena that have not been adequately explained.

"All truth passes through three stages.
First, it is ridiculed.
Second, it is violently opposed.
Third, it is accepted as being self-evident."

— Arthur Schopenhauer (1788 – 1860)

1. The UFO Phenomenon

Strange Craft in the Sky

The mere mention of UFOs brings to mind for many a scene popularized in science fiction movies and books in which aliens pilot saucer-shaped aircraft. However, it is important to remember the true definition of the term. An unidentified flying object is any object in the sky that cannot be readily identified. And there are many such objects. Some individuals have researched orbs in the sky that can be seen with infrared goggles and spotlights. These orbs vary in size. Some large and others small, they seem to be living entities.

Author Scott Deschaine suggested that many UFOs are actually atmospheric creatures. To understand this, consider aquatic animals. Earth's oceans are a perfect habitat, home to some of the largest and some of the smallest creatures on the entire planet, and it is so immense that we might never know all the creatures that live in its depths. Every year biologists discover new creatures, and it might still house large animals that some believe are extinct. The atmosphere of the sky is not much different from that of the ocean insofar as its ability to maintain life. Deschaine wrote, "Tons of water in many forms moves through the sky at all levels. Minerals drift and drop in from space and swirl up from surface soil. Energy constantly crackles around the globe. Our atmosphere is a habitat."[1]

Some reports suggest that UFOs behave like living beings that are curious about people and other objects. Often these UFOs glow, just like some forms of marine invertebrates make use of bioluminescence. They also tend to move like sea creatures. Deschaine wrote:

> Jellyfish are living helicopters. They create their own fluid vortices to ride. Squid are living jets. They can rocket around, hover, and control their buoyancy. These two broad categories of life are perfectly adapted for fluid environments. In the fluid atmosphere, similarly shaped UFOs perform similar amazing movements. They change shape as they move. Some expand and contract. Many descend in a "falling leaf" motion typical of jellyfish. They hover almost motionlessly, then pulse and soar away with a whoosh. UFOs move like marine organisms.[2]

1. Jellyfish have shapes reminiscent of UFOs. (Kyoto, Japan)

2. UFOs glow like bioluminescent marine creatures.

The trace evidence that they leave can also be compared to trace evidence left by marine invertebrates. Some UFOs drop strange materials that resemble tentacles, and chemical analyses of the substances reveal the same minerals found in jellyfish. Every year, gelatinous materials fall from the sky. This substance seems biological in origin, and when a large amount of it falls over one area, the inhabitants become ill. There are other connections between aerial phenomena and marine creatures including group behavior.

Like marine creatures, UFOs generally appear in groups and their interaction is reminiscent of the interaction of living beings. And just like marine creatures, UFO sightings appear in cycles. The lifecycle of marine creatures such as jellyfish might be identical to the lifecycle of their sky-faring counterparts. Finally, the physical and neurological symptoms reported by individuals who have been exposed to UFOs are similar to the same symptoms reported when swimmers and divers encounter various invertebrates. These include skin damage, tingling or numbness, paralysis, and headaches.

3. Another example of jellyfish that resemble UFOs

It is quite possible, if not probable, that creatures similar to marine invertebrates live in the skies. These creatures have been seen by many, despite the fact that they are difficult to see. Think about jellyfish in the ocean. If you did not feel them while swimming and only tried to notice them from hundreds or thousands of feet above, they would be difficult to spot. Likewise, clear, see-through creatures who reside in the skies might camouflage in cloud canapés and the ever-changing colors of the atmosphere. When John Glenn orbited the Earth in 1962, he said that he traveled through a cloud that was composed of thousands of glowing particles. He compared them to fireflies. They behaved like insects, changed direction at will, and seem to interact with one another as though they were living creatures.[3] The atmosphere, like the oceans, is teeming with life. This life accounts for some of the UFO reports that witnesses have filed.

Other UFOs do not behave like living creatures. Some are described as huge aerial ships with lights and windows. On September 20, 1973, astronauts Allen Bean, Jack Lousma, and Owen Garriott reported a bright red flashing object outside of their shuttle. They watched it for ten minutes and took several photographs. It was between 8 – 9 meters (25 – 30 feet) away, and they estimated it to be approximately 244 meters (800 feet) in diameter. In some reports, witnesses claimed that such ships were even larger. One of the sightings took place on December 11, 1996, and multiple independent witnesses confirmed it. A large ship, approximately one mile in length, was reported by dozens of witnesses along the Klondike Highway in the Yukon Territory of Canada. The first sighting happened at Fox Lake. Six witnesses saw a smooth and solid craft pass silently over the frozen water. Thirty minutes later, the same ship appeared over Pelly Crossing. Then, it was seen over Carmacks. The appearance of these large ships is relatively rare in the UFO phenomenon. Reports of smaller craft are more common. Some people believe the size of the large ships makes it unlikely that they are from this planet, as it is unlikely, if not downright impossible, to hide a ship that big on this planet successfully. Therefore, some state that the extraterrestrial origin of the ships is likely. This has been the prevailing theory for many years, but just because an idea is commonplace does not make it true. It is possible that the large UFOs are a distinct phenomenon, unrelated to the smaller objects. If this is true, extraterrestrials might use the larger objects while creatures of this planet use the smaller objects. However, witness accounts often describe both large and small unidentified aircraft together in the same area simultaneously. For this reason, it is likely that the same species uses them both. Information in this chapter and the next will support this conclusion.

The most common type of UFO reported is a smaller, triangular craft piloted by humanoid figures with large heads, smaller bodies, and big black eyes. Some call these pilots "the grays." People claiming to have been abducted have described them in detail, and both military and civilian pilots, as well as a multitude of other individuals, have described their ships. The ships have appeared on radar, left trace evidence, and have even been caught on camera. It is unlikely that these smaller ships originate from outside of this atmosphere. The evidence suggests that earthlings pilot these machines, and that they have been here longer than modern human beings have. Before getting into the specifics of this theory, let us look at the history of the UFO phenomenon.

A Historical Perspective

Ancient civilizations consistently turned their attention toward the skies. Heavenly patterns were seemingly more important than terrestrial events. Of course, perhaps they recognized the connection between heavenly movements and things that occur on Earth: a connection that we might not completely understand yet. Before the widespread use of electricity, people who gazed at the night sky were likely to see much more than we currently see. They mapped planetary movement, movement that would be nearly impossible to map today with the naked eye. They understood the rotational nature of not only planets in the solar system but also of the Earth itself. And while looking up at the skies, it is certain that they would have seen UFOs. Historical texts provide many examples in which unidentified flying objects were seen in the skies. Some of these objects have been interpreted as divine in nature. Even today, many people think the orb-type UFOs are divine. In the past, they interpreted them as gods, angels, demons, fairies, and other supernatural creatures. In modern times, more nomenclature has been added; people call them mothmen and aliens. Whatever terms are used to describe these sky-traveling creatures, in all likelihood, they refer to the same species.

Evidence of these creatures' existence is found in some of the earliest human records. Cave paintings found in France, Spain and other countries represent what are clearly nonhuman entities. Some are depicted with large heads and large black eyes, while others appear to be wearing helmets or using advanced technology. Alongside these creatures are images that look like modern-day flying saucers or airplanes. Some of these depictions are more than 20,000 years old.

4. Petroglyphs at Palatki, near Sedona, Arizona. A humanoid figure appears to be wearing some type of helmet, while a flying machine, reminiscent of an airplane, is in the sky above.

The earliest texts also describe their existence. Texts from Sumeria, which existed 5,000 years ago, mention unidentified flying objects in the sky and the creatures that controlled them. Likewise, Indian texts describe flying machines in detail. Other UFO accounts are found in the sacred scriptures of many of the world's religions, including the Bible, Kebra Nagast, Bhagavad-Gita, and the Qur'an.

Besides pictures of UFOs found in cave paintings and other art forms, actual written reports of unexplained aerial phenomena date to more than 3,500 years ago. The Egyptian pharaoh Thutmosis III reported seeing bright circles in the sky, which he compared to the brightness of the sun. Initially there was only one. A few days later, there were many of them. Not knowing what they were, he still considered the event important, and he recorded it on a papyrus. Alexander the Great also reported a sighting. In 329 B.C.E., he and his soldiers witnessed a number of UFOs in the sky, which they described as shiny silver shields. The ships did not stay still. Instead, they drew close to the men, causing them and their horses to panic and run. This was not the last time that Alexander the Great saw unidentified aerial phenomena. About seven years later, while attacking the Phoenician city of Tyre, he again saw shiny silver shields in the sky. One of them fired a beam of light down onto a city wall, destroying it. Alexander made use of this fortunate occurrence. He led his troops through the opening and gained control of the city.

Some other famous sightings took place in medieval Europe. One of the most talked about occurred in 1463, when a large object surrounded by light glided over several cities. A man named Hermann Schaden illustrated the event. In his depiction, the object's lights appear to be flames. Perhaps not knowing anything about electricity and artificial lights, he interpreted the glow as the light issued by a fire.

5. Woodcut by Hans Glaser documenting the aerial battle in Nuremberg, Germany (April 4, 1562).

A similar sighting occurred over Nuremberg, Germany on April 4, 1561. Witnesses described what they thought was a war in the heavens involving different types of aerial craft. They described some as spear-like, others as cylindrical. Still others were described as crosses or plates. These UFOs seemed to fight each other for over an hour. Some smaller, spherical UFOs emerged from the cylindrical objects. At the end of the so-called battle, a large, black, flying ship appeared, which ended the event. A woodcut created by Hans Glaser documented the event. There was another by an unknown artist that also depicted the same occurrence. Interpreting the event as divine, the following appeared in a local newspaper:

> The God-fearing will by no means discard these signs, but will take it to heart as a warning of their merciful Annunciation with St. Emidius Father in heaven, will mend their lives and faithfully beg God, that he avert His wrath,

including the well-deserved punishment, on us, so that we may, temporarily here and perpetually there, live as His children.[4]

An almost identical event occurred four years later in Switzerland on August 7, 1566. In the morning, witnesses reported numerous black spheres in the sky that were fighting. The local newspaper reported it:

At the time when the sun rose, one saw many large black balls which moved at high speed in the air towards the sun, then made half-turns, banging one against the others as if they were fighting a battle out a combat [sic.], a great number of them became red and igneous, thereafter they were consumed and died out.[5]

There have been many historical UFO sightings. Even Christopher Columbus reported one on his journey to the New World. On October 11, 1492, from the deck of the Santa Maria, he saw a light shimmering in the distance. He summoned another member of the crew, Pedro Gutierrez, and both of them watched as the mysterious light moved up and down. At times, it traveled underwater near the ship. Then it broke the surface of the water and flew into the sky. He wrote about this sighting in his journal and it later almost got him killed, for Columbus had compared the light to that reflected from the Jewish menorah. When the intolerant Church found out about his comparison, they accused him of being a heretic and brought him before the Inquisition. He talked his way out of punishment, but the lights that he saw have forever remained an enigma. The UFO phenomenon is nothing new. These craft and the creatures who pilot them have been with human beings for as long as historical records have existed. The so-called modern UFO era began after World War II had ended, while the U.S. still occupied Japan.

The Modern UFO Phenomenon

The modern UFO phenomenon began June 24, 1947 when Kenneth Arnold, flying in a single-engine plane, reported nine metallic craft flying in a straight line near Mt. Rainer in Washington. He stated that they were flying at incredible speeds, and that they resembled saucers, if someone skipped them over the surface of water. This description led to others calling the craft, somewhat erroneously, flying saucers. After his report, the floodgates opened. Hundreds of reports, from all over the world, indicated that what Mr. Arnold had seen was not unique, that this phenomenon was widespread.

Mr. Arnold had been on his way home to Idaho after a business trip. It was a sunny day with perfect visibility, so for more than an hour on his return trip, he searched for a plane that had crashed several days before. He saw a flashing light in the sky, which he soon determined was sunlight reflecting off flying craft in the distance. They were traveling south from an area near Mt. Ranier toward Mt. Adams, and he followed them during the 47-mile flight to clock their speed. He determined that they were flying in a linear formation at approximately 2,897 kilometers (1,800 miles) per hour. Knowing that no known craft could fly at this speed, he considered that no one would believe him. So when he reported it, he claimed that they were moving at about 1,931 kilometers (1,200 miles) per hour. Still unbelievable, but it may have softened the news for an incredulous public. A local newspaper published the story, and then the national news picked it up. Shortly after, stories flooded in. Within weeks, people from all over the world filed more than 3,000 reports.

6. Drawing of the UFO by Kenneth Arnold. This is within a statement that he handed over to Army Air Force Intelligence on July 12, 1947.

On July 7, 1947, only 13 days after Mr. Arnold's sighting that initiated the "flying saucer" frenzy, the U.S. Army issued a press release regarding a downed craft in Roswell, New Mexico. Frank Joyce, a reporter at the KGFL radio station, received the release from a public relations officer named Walther Haut. He reported, "The Army Air Force has announced that a flying disc has been found and is now in the possession of the Army."[6] The story appeared in the Roswell Daily Record the next day:

RAAF Captures Flying Saucer on Ranch in Roswell Region

> The intelligence office of the 509th Bombardment Group at Roswell Army Air Field announced at noon today that the field has come into possession of a flying saucer. According to information released by the department, over authority of Major J. A. Marcel, intelligence officer, the disk was recovered on a ranch in the Roswell vicinity after an unidentified rancher had notified Sheriff George Wilcox here, that he had found the instrument on his premises. Major Marcel and a detail from his department went to the ranch and recovered the disk, it was stated. After the intelligence officer here had inspected the instrument, it was flown to higher headquarters. The intelligence officer also stated that no details of the saucer's construction or appearance had been revealed.[7]

The crash in Roswell actually occurred about a week before it was reported. After dark on July 2, Mac Brazel, a foreman at the Foster Ranch near Roswell, heard a loud noise like an explosion, but he could not determine what it was or from where it issued. The next day, he found numerous metallic objects scattered across one of the fields. He picked up some of the pieces and shared them with one of his neighbors, Loretta Proctor, who suggested that he inform the sheriff. The ride into Roswell was approximately 121 kilometers (75 miles), so he took care of some chores on the ranch before making the trip. A couple of days later, he headed to the police station in Roswell, and showed the pieces that he had brought with him to sheriff George Wilcox, who immediately phoned the headquarters of the 509th Bomb Group at Roswell Army Air Field. This was the only nuclear strike force in existence at the time, and the *Enola Gay*, which dropped the bombs on Hiroshima and Nagasaki, Japan, was stationed at the New Mexico base. Shortly thereafter, the base intelligence officer, Major Jesse Marcel arrived with counterintelligence officer Captain Sheridan Cavitt.

  The two men looked over the debris and then called in their commanding officer, Colonel William Blanchard. He ordered them to take the supervisor back to the location of the debris to inspect the area. The three men got into their two automobiles and headed back to the site, but by the time they arrived, it was dark. They spent the night in sleeping bags in a shack, and then began their search early the next morning.

  While this was occurring, the sheriff's men headed back to the area Mac Brazel had described, hoping to find the debris field on their own. They could not locate it. Instead, they found a large, circular burn that was about the size of a football field. The sand had been exposed to so much heat that it had been fused to glass.

  The next morning, Marcel, Cavitt, and Brazel went out into the debris field and gathered up all the items they could find. The debris-covered area was approximately 250 yards wide and three-quarters of a mile long. The pieces were unlike anything that they had seen previously, so they were naturally excited. When they finally returned to Roswell that evening, they all stopped at Major Marcel's house so he could show his wife and son some of the items they had found. One piece that was of interest to his son was a "small rectangular piece, approximately a foot long and a half-inch wide. It was in the shape of an I-beam. What caught the boy's eye was a row of characters of some sort that appeared to run the full length of the beam."[8]

Other individuals also reported seeing and handling debris. Of particular note is the testimony of Frankie Rowe, who was at the Roswell firehouse when a state trooper, who had helped in the clean-up process, brought some objects inside. Mrs. Rowe reported that the trooper had "a piece of the material wadded up in his hand. It was just a tiny ball, and when he dropped it on the table, it spread out like it was liquid or quicksilver. And there was not one wrinkle in that. And I do remember that we all got to touch it…we all got to pick it up. You could bend it; it made no crinkle, no noise. It was very thin. Very shiny…very silvery color. It was about…maybe a foot square. And I have no idea what happened to it."[9]

Jesse Marcel also commented on this unusual material:

> It was something I had never seen before…But something that is more astounding is that the piece of metal that we brought back was so thin, just like the tinfoil in a pack of cigarette paper. I didn't pay too much attention to that at first, until one of the GIs came to me and said, "You know the metal that was in there? I tried to bend that stuff and it won't bend. I even tried it with a sledge-hammer. You can't make a dent on it." He said, "It's definite that it can't be bent, and it's so light that it doesn't weigh anything." And that was true of all the material that was brought up. It was so light that it practically weighed nothing."[10]

On the morning of July 8, a discovery was made that offered an explanation to the origin of the unusual metallic objects. It was this discovery that caused the Army to reverse its initial press statement and attempt to cover up the occurrence. A full week after Mac Brazel had heard an explosion in the sky above the ranch, a team of archaeologists was exploring the area nearby, looking for Native American artifacts. What they found instead was a circular craft, partially embedded into the wall of a ravine. Around the craft were the bodies of four humanoid figures. Standing nearby was a civil engineer named Grady Barnett, who stumbled upon the wreckage while surveying the area for a new irrigation project.

Barnett, (who was called Barney), spoke to a close friend, Vern Malthais about the experience, who later talked about it in a television interview:

> [Barnett] said I'm going to tell you something that I'm not supposed to divulge…he came across this object on the ground, which was the shape of a flying saucer, and it had split open. So he jumped out of his pickup and went down there. And there was four beings laying on the ground, and they were in a sort of a silver-colored suit, and they were about three to four feet high, and the suits were rather tight fitting…and the shape of the heads of the beings on the ground were hairless with a sort of pear-shaped head and the hands were exposed. He had just barely arrived and there was an archaeology team that had come up there…just a little bit after Barney, and then the military come in [sic] and surrounded the area and they called all those people that were there, the archaeology team and Mr. Barnett and they briefed them…that this was not to be divulged to anybody, that they were not to say one word about it…and forget that they had seen anything.[11]

The military warned many people not to divulge any information once an actual craft had been found, but these warnings were not given right away. As soon as they received the report, which indicated that it was, in fact, a craft of unknown origin, Colonel Blanchard sealed off all roads that led toward the crash site, and the Army secured the area. Civilians were not allowed anywhere near the site. This course of action was apparently not taken to hide information from the public, since the colonel issued a press release stating that a flying saucer had been captured. The local newspapers published the full story, and two local radio stations announced it, including KGFL, where Frank Joyce worked. He made the announcement, and then issued the story through the Western Union Line to the United Press, who picked it up and reported it as a bulletin. It was this same day, however, that some higher-ranked Army officers decided to stifle the media and keep the information as hushed as possible.

Joyce claimed he received a phone call from someone at the Pentagon who suggested that bad things would happen to him if he continued to air the story. Other reporters received similar warnings, and the next day, a new report on the findings was published. The *Roswell Daily Record* published the following on July 9, 1947:

Gen. Ramey Empties Roswell Saucer

Fort Worth, Texas, July 9 (AP) — An examination by the Army revealed last night that a mysterious object found on a lonely New Mexico ranch was a harmless high-altitude weather balloon — not a grounded flying disc. Excitement was high until Brig. Gen. Roger M. Ramey, commander of the Eighth Air Force with headquarters here, cleared up the mystery. The bundle of tinfoil, broken wood beams, and rubber remnants of a balloon were sent here yesterday by Army air transport in the wake of reports that it was a flying disk. But the general said the objects were the crushed remains of a ray wind target used to determine the direction and velocity of winds at high altitudes.[12]

The Army then took Mac Brazel into custody, the man whom initially found the debris. They put him under house arrest, and they made him undergo a physical examination and debriefing session that lasted hours. After this session, military officers accompanied him to the KGFL office, where Mac told reporters that he had been mistaken about some of his previous statements, and the things he had found could have been parts from a weather balloon. After this, the officers took him to an Army base, where he remained for about a week before they allowed him to return home. Other individuals who had information about the crash or wreckage had also been warned. Frankie Rowe, who handled some of the debris, declared in an interview that some military officers visited her and threatened harm if she did not remain silent. As a result, she did not talk about it for a full forty years.[13] Many individuals who had been threatened never spoke about it. They did as the military ordered: they forgot about it. However, years later, some Roswell witnesses' children came forward. They testified about what they had seen, or what their parents had seen and then reported to them. These individuals are collectively known as Children of Roswell.

Alpha Boyd was the son of Ervin Boyd, an airplane mechanic at the Roswell army base. On his deathbed, he told his son about the crash. He was taking a cigarette break in a hangar when troops arrived with wreckage and pilots' bodies. He saw them carrying what initially looked like a child's body. He said:

> They passed right by me and I looked down and knew it wasn't something from this world. It was child-size, four feet, maybe a little more, and had a head that was larger than normal. The eyes were walnut-shaped and larger than normal. From my angle, it didn't look like it had much of a nose. The arms were a bit longer too, and the skin was ashy, gray, and kind of scaly. I don't know for sure, but I believe it was alive when I saw it.[14]

William Brazel, Jr. was the son of Mac Brazel, the ranch manager who initially reported the crash. His father showed him where the ship had crashed, and he scoured the area on horseback. Many pieces of wreckage that the Army had not confiscated were buried, but rain unearthed them. William picked up some pieces that he found. Some were tan. Others resembled tinfoil. He crumpled one of these pieces in his pocket. When he returned home, he pulled it out of his pocket and laid it on his workbench. It flattened on its own. Curious, he folded it up and watched it flatten again. No matter what he did, he could not keep it from flattening out. Among the other items that he collected were debris pieces that resembled wood chips, but they could not be cut or burned. He kept all these items in a cigar box for some time, and when people asked if he had ever found anything, he told them about the items. Eventually, word got out, and some air force officers showed up asking for the items. He related that they were nice; they simply asked for the items, stating that it was a matter of national security.

Glenn Davis was a mortician in Roswell. He claimed that Army personnel called him after the crash and asked if he had any coffins that were three and a half or four feet in length. He had some in stock, but the Army asked him to procure more. After about an hour, someone from the Army called back. This time, he asked Mr. Davis about embalming solutions and mummification techniques. He also asked about transporting bodies.

That same day, Glenn received a phone call requesting an ambulance for an aviator who had been hurt in a motorcycle accident. The man was not critically injured. He could walk, but he needed medical attention. He headed out to pick up the man, and drove him directly to the base. When he arrived, there were three Army ambulances parked where he normally parked, so he parked on the other side of the lot. As he passed them, he looked inside. Debris filled the first one. One large piece resembled a canoe, and others resembled broken glass. Some of those pieces and the canoe looked as though they were made out of metal, and markings on the pieces resembled hieroglyphs. Similar debris filled the second ambulance. The third had its doors closed, so he could not discern what was inside.

He followed the aviator into the hospital, and saw people everywhere. There was a lot of commotion. From bits and pieces of conversations that he overheard, and the debris that he had seen outside, he thought that there might have been an airplane crash. Glenn asked a captain if this was the case, and if he needed to get ready for the deceased. The man looked angry, asked who he was, and then told him to remain exactly where he was. He walked away and came back with some MPs, who escorted Glenn off the base. On his way out, he saw that a nurse whom he knew looked frantic. When she saw him, she told him to leave as soon as possible. She looked like she was having difficulty breathing; two men behind her also looked like they were gasping for air. According to Mr. Davis, the nurse called him later that afternoon, stating that she wanted to talk. He suggested that they meet at the Officers' Club, at which time she explained everything that had transpired.

Apparently, she was not supposed to come into work that morning, but she did not get the message and showed up anyway. Once there, officers asked her to take notes as they examined bodies recovered from the crash. She described them to Glenn:

> She said a hand was severed from one of the bodies, and they turned it over with a long forceps. There were only four fingers. They had little pads on the tips with what looked like tiny suction cups. Their mouths were only slits, about an inch wide. There were no teeth, only a firm piece of tissue-like cartilage. They had no earlobes. The nose was concave, with two orifices, but no bridge. The eyes were very large and sunken so far back in you couldn't tell what they looked like. She said the heads were disproportionately large, and the doctors noted the skull structure was like a newborn baby's.[15]

Frank Kaufman, also known as Steve Arnold, a pen name that he initially used when discussing the Roswell crash with the press, was a sergeant in the CIC division at the Roswell Army Air Force Base. He claimed that on the night of the crash a motorist traveling on U.S. 285 saw what appeared to be a glowing ball that crashed to the ground. The military sent a detail to locate and secure the area. The initial scouts located the site and removed civilians, securing the area before Kaufman's detail arrived.

He claimed that they approached the craft, which emitted an orange glow, and they stopped about 100 yards away. The vehicle's bottom was a grayish white color, and it emitted a white light. The craft itself was triangular, and the front end, which had impacted the ground, was crumpled. From one side of the triangle to the other, which he interpreted as being a type of wing, the craft was about four meters (twelve feet) long. From front to back, it was about 7.6 meters (twenty-five feet) long. There was an opening on one side of the craft where it had split open upon impact.

Searchlights illuminated the craft, and individuals with chemical suits and devices to measure radiation and other unknown properties approached first. It was then that Kaufman noticed two non-human bodies. One of them was hanging from the ship's hole. He reported, "As I remember it, they were somewhere around five feet in height and well-proportioned for people that size. They had fingers like ours, but the head and eyes were larger, although not a lot. Their skin appeared human-like to me; ashen in color like dead people."[16]

Phyliss McGuire was the daughter of Sheriff George Wilcox, who knew about the non-human crash. Her father had told her about the debris that Mac Brazel brought into the police station. He told her that it looked like tinfoil but was not: when you crumpled it, it just straightened itself. Her mother told her that her father had even seen the bodies from the crash site. She claimed there were three. Two of them were dead. One was still alive. They had large heads with large eyes but the bodies were small.

Frankie Rowe, whose father was a Roswell Firefighter, also reported what her father had said about the famous crash. Her father was in one of the first teams to reach the crash site. He told her they received a call that there was a fire about forty-eight kilometers

(thirty miles) to the north, near Black Water Draw. They instantly headed to the site and were shocked to realize that a saucer-like craft had crashed. He related, "We all got off the truck and just stood there, not believing what we were seeing. It was a flying saucer. Two of the crew were dead, but one was still alive."[17] His descriptions of the creatures matched those given by other witnesses.

Frankie was also at the fire station when a police officer showed up with a piece of the wreckage. It was the tinfoil-like debris previously described. She too related that some of the men present crumpled it up, but it kept straightening itself. They also unsuccessfully tried to cut and burn it. The testimonies of the children of Roswell witnesses, although not first-hand accounts, provide great secondary sources to back up their parents' claims.

The Roswell crash debris was flown to Fort Worth, and then to the Pentagon. It was given to Benjamin Chidlaw, the commanding general at Wright Field, which was later called Wright-Patterson Air Force Base. It is believed that the wreckage of the craft was kept at this location in Hanger 18.

The Roswell crash is likely the most well-known UFO crash, but it is only one of many. Another is the so-called Berwyn Mountain Incident, also referred to as the Welsh Roswell. On January 23, 1974, a UFO crashed near Cader Bronwen Mountain in Llandrillo, North Wales, United Kingdom. People heard a loud noise and looked outside, and they reported orange and blue lights emanating from the crash site. Soon after, the ground nearby shook as though an earthquake was occurring, and locals reported that objects inside their homes fell to the ground. This shaking lasted for several minutes. The police were first on the scene, followed by the military, which secured the area. One witness worked at a nearby hotel in Bala. According to her, several men came to the area and stayed at the hotel for a few days while they were working at the crash site. Another witness was driving on B-4391 with her daughters. As she drove up the mountain, she saw a large, glowing, circular craft that was relatively intact. They were approximately 91 –

121 meters (300 – 400 feet) away, but she noticed some military personnel who were much closer. They approached her car, told her that she had to leave, and then escorted her away.[18]

The Coyame UFO Event is known as the Mexican Roswell. On August 24, 1974, U.S. Air Defense detected an unknown object traveling at 4,000 km / hr. on radar. It was headed toward Corpus Christi, Texas. Mid-air, it suddenly changed directions and flew toward Coyame, Chihuahua, Mexico. En route, it crashed into a small plane that had taken off from El Paso, Texas and was headed to Mexico City. The U.S. military captured both aircraft on its radar, and there was no doubt that the two had crashed into each other. The Mexican government sent a team to recover the plane and its passengers, who were soldiers. They included Captain Rogelio Arguelles Gonzalez, Sergeant Teófilo Margarito Puebla, Corporal José Trinidad Meráz, and Corporal Ricardo Velazquez.

The U.S. sent a 15-person recovery team to the site as well via four Huey helicopters. Captain Lawrence Merley, Lieutenant Randall Bishop, Lieutenant Eduardo Ramirez, Lieutenant Jerome Smit, Lieutenant Benjamin Rodes, and Sergeant Terence Miles were all part of the recovery team. When they arrived, they found a round metallic disk that had apparently crashed into the plane. It displayed frontal damage. The burned plane was nearby, and its passengers had been loaded into a Mexican military vehicle. The U.S. military wasted no time in securing the downed UFO for their own research. They took possession of it, and a Huey helicopter transported it to the Wright-Patterson Air Force Base.[19]

On January 29, 1986, a UFO allegedly crashed in Dalnegorsk, Primorsky Krai, Russia. At approximately 8 P.M., inhabitants reported a glowing red ball of light flying parallel to the ground at approximately 15 meters per second with no sound. It was 700 – 800 meters (2,297 – 2,625 feet) above ground. Suddenly, it fell with a flash of light. The light emanating from the craft made it seem like the trees in the area were on fire. Three days later, some investigators went to the location. They noted that the entire area had been affected by high temperatures. Rocks were blackened, and a felled burned tree lay near the crash zone, which was a depression in the Earth measuring approximately three-square meters. A silvery metal also covered some of the rocks. This metal was a type of lead typically not found in the area. Alongside these deposits were mesh particles and another black substance. One of the mesh samples was composed of gold, scandium, lanthanum, samarium, and sodium. Another sample contained gold, silver and nickel. After being heated in a vacuum, molybdenum and rhenium were detected. To this day, the origin of these deposits is unknown.[20]

Many UFO crashes have been reported. One of the earliest in the modern era is the Aurora UFO Incident. It is also one of the most interesting cases other than Roswell. Witnesses reported a "space ship" moving slowly through the sky that ended up crashing into a windmill in Aurora, Texas on April 17, 1897. It broke into pieces. Local residents sorted through the debris and came upon a small humanoid body. They instantly dubbed this creature a "Martian pilot." Near the body, they found some pieces of metal-like material covered with hieroglyphs. They gathered some of the debris and put the humanoid in a small coffin, burying it in a local cemetery.

News of this event spread, although not as quickly as it would spread today. One newspaper article written by S. E. Haydon for the Dallas Morning News still exists:

> About 6 o'clock this morning the early risers of Aurora were astonished at the sudden appearance of the airship which has been sailing around the country. It was traveling due north and much nearer the Earth than before.
>
> Evidently, some of the machinery was out of order, for it was making a speed of only ten or twelve miles an hour, and gradually settling toward the Earth. It sailed over the public square and when it reached the north part of town it collided with the tower of Judge Proctor's windmill and went into pieces with a terrific explosion, scattering debris over several

> acres of ground, wrecking the windmill and water tank and destroying the judge's flower garden.
>
> The pilot of the ship is supposed to have been the only one aboard and, while his remains were badly disfigured, enough of the original has been picked up to show that he was not an inhabitant of this world.[21]

Another publication referenced this article in 1973, and after the story was released, an old woman from Aurora came forward, claiming to be a witness. She had forgotten about the incident until the newspaper article jarred her memory. Her parents had been to the crash site, and they told her that the remains of the pilot, a "small man," were buried in the Aurora cemetery. The Associated Press then published a related story about some unusual debris found near Denton, Texas:

> A North Texas State University professor had found some metal fragments near the Oates gas station (former Proctor farm). One fragment was said to be 'most intriguing' because it consisted primarily of iron which did not seem to exhibit magnetic properties. The professor also said he was puzzled because the fragment was "shiny and malleable instead of dull and brittle like iron."[22]

There are other alleged UFO crashes, but they are all similar. Sightings of flying UFOs are much more common than reported crashes, and people see them nearly every day in various parts of the world. Only some sightings are reported; it is believed that 90 percent remain unreported. Sightings are known as "close encounters of the first kind." If sightings are reported along with side effects or physical evidence, they are called "close encounters of the second kind." Close encounters of the third kind refer to sightings of (non-human) animated beings. The fourth category is a relatively rare phenomenon. It has been the subject of many movies, mostly in the horror genre, including the film *The Fourth Kind*. Although a work of fiction, it was based on actual case studies. "Close encounters of the fourth kind" is the lexicon used to describe instances of alien abduction.[23] Case studies documenting this phenomenon are rare compared to UFO sightings, but hundreds of individuals claim to have been abducted at least once, if not multiple times, throughout their lives. These cases, if they are believed, might be the most provocative evidence available, pointing to possible reasons behind the appearance of UFOs and their pilots. This information might help us to understand what these creatures want, and what they are doing here.

Reported Abductions

Most UFO sightings are nothing more than unexplained lights in the sky. Some people report being close enough to discern the shape of the craft. Among these, some claim to have seen creatures through some kind of windows. A rarity is the discovery of downed UFOs and the pilots' bodies. However, this contact between (possible) aliens and human beings does not only take place when accidents occur. There is a much more commonly reported interaction between humans and these otherworldly creatures. Many people claim that these creatures have abducted them, and that they were subjected to various experiments or treatments. Such claims must always be considered with caution, since researchers rely primarily on the testimonies of the claimants, but sometimes evidence supports their stories. This evidence includes unusual injuries, objects embedded under the abductee's skin, unexplained time loss and other inexplicable phenomena. Mr. Hatzopoulos summarized this phenomenon:

> The abduction phenomenon is an umbrella term used to describe a number of assertions stating that alien beings take humans against their will, to an unknown environment (which they may perceive as a UFO), for "medical testing"

with a focus on reproductive issues, after which they are returned to the same place they were taken from, with their memories clouded or erased (hence the "missing time"). The history of abduction reports seems to start in the 1960s. The 1980s brought a major degree of mainstream attention to the subject in the U.S.A. Stigma and self-doubt may be obstacles to more widespread study and/or reporting of the phenomenon, whatever its origins or explanation. Several abduction reports have been quite detailed and there is a persistent structure (what follows what) to them. Typically, such memories are recovered under hypnosis, which has been the main point of contention. However, according to T. E. Bullard, Ph.D. folklorist, "abduction reports bear extensive similarities to one another, no matter who investigates, how abductees recall the encounter and in what year or country the story originates." (src: MUFON Journal Jun-1998) The mixture of social patterning, medical effects, the evident post-traumatic stress syndrome and the remarkable consistency of abduction reports all argue for a complex phenomenon, which cannot be reduced to simple perceptual contagion or individual psychopathology.[24]

Whitley Strieber, who claimed to have been abducted numerous times in his home in upstate New York, filed one of the most well-known reports of alien abductions. A best-selling author, he reported his experiences in a book entitled *Communion*. Initially, he claimed the book was a novel, but later admitted that the events had actually occurred. After the success of his first book, he wrote other alien-related texts, including *Transformation, The Secret School, The Grays*, and *Hybrids*.

In his first, tell-all alien abduction book, *Communion*, Mr. Strieber related that on the evening of December 26, 1985, non-human entities secured his home and abducted him while he lay in his bed. He awakened to a strange sound issuing from his living room, and saw a small figure in his doorway. It was approximately three and a half feet tall, and its eyes looked like two dark holes, its mouth a straight line. It rushed into the room, and Mr. Strieber reported a state of paralysis, in which he could neither move nor feel anything. He felt like they were moving him, and he blacked out. When he awakened, he was sitting in the woods with his legs bent and his hands in his lap. He could see a small creature to his side wearing a grayish suit that also sat on the ground with its arms around its legs. Looking at the face gave him the impression that it was a mask. The eyes, mouth and nose seemed unreal.

After noticing this creature, he became aware of others that were also present. One of them was doing something to the side of his head. He still could not move, as the sense of paralysis had not ceased. In addition, his eyes were not working as they normally do. However, one of the creatures impressed him. He somehow understood that it was female. She explained something to him that he could not understand, and then he was swept up into the sky. Somehow, he ended up on a gray floor in a round room, where he noticed many of these creatures hurrying about, apparently busy with something. Eventually, one of them showed a box to Mr. Strieber. The creature slid it open, revealing a long needle, which he believed they intended to insert into his brain. He was petrified and began screaming. One of them asked, "What can we do to help you stop screaming?"[25] He was certain that he actually heard this question rather than sensing it. Describing the voice, he stated that it had a Midwest accent with a subtle electronic tone. He then made a strange request. He asked to smell the visitor, and the visitor acquiesced. Mr. Strieber reported that the creature on his right held its hand against his face, and it smelled something like cardboard. Immediately after, there was a loud noise and a flash of light, during which they performed the intended procedure.

He looked around the room, which he interpreted as being an operating room or theater, and noticed some creatures watching.

They did not all look the same. Some had round eyes, while others had slanted eyes. He described them:

> I was aware that I had seen four different types of figures. The first was the small robot-like being that had led the way into my bedroom. He was followed by a large group of short, stocky ones in dark-blue coveralls. These had wide faces, appearing either dark gray or dark blue in that light, with glittering, deep-set eyes, pug noses, and broad, somewhat human mouths. Inside the room, I encountered two types of creatures that did not look at all human. The most provocative of these was about five feet tall, very slender and delicate, with extremely prominent and mesmerizing black slanted eyes. This being had an almost vestigial mouth and nose. The huddled figures in the theater were somewhat smaller, with similarly shaped heads but round, black eyes like large buttons."[26]

As though it could not get any stranger, the creatures continued their tests. They picked up a foot-long instrument with wires on it and showed him the end of the device. He had the impression that they were warning him about something, but he never found out what it was. Then, they cut his finger. He did not feel any pain at all, and this was all he could remember. An owl appeared in his memory, and he even told his family about it. However, he knew deep down the owl did not exist, that the owl was either a planted memory or a psychological mechanism put into place to protect him from realizing that creatures had abducted him. Eventually, the trauma of the experience began to affect his life and the people around him. Still not fully able to recall what had happened, he went to a researcher who asked him about other unusual events in his life. Mr. Strieber related that a strange incident had taken place at his country home in October of the same year.

Like the incident in December, he had pushed it out of his mind. Whether this was a psychological effect or an intentionally induced reaction is unknown. Other possibilities must always be kept in mind: that this entire scenario never occurred. This is not to cast doubt on the narrator's conviction that the events did occur as explained, but there is so much that is unknown about the brain, and the generally untapped power of the mind, that one must always retain some degree of doubt when considering such personal experiences. However, in October some friends stayed with him at the cabin. During the night, something happened. He remembered a loud noise, like an explosion, along with a bright flash of light. Later, he recalled a huge crystalline object in the sky above his home from which emanated a bright blue light. Since there were other people present, he asked them what they remembered, hoping once and for all to determine if the events unfolding in his life were psychological or otherworldly in nature. His houseguests reported that they remember bright lights outside the house. His son, upon being questioned, referred to the incident as the "night of the bang," and although he did not have any conscious recollections of the evening's events, when asked about his dreams he stated, "I dreamed that a bunch of little doctors took me out on the porch and put me on a cot. I got scared and they started saying, 'we won't hurt you' over and over again in my head.[27]

After this confirmation that the events unfolding in his life were perhaps not psychological in nature, he was hypnotized to reveal repressed memories. The hypnosis sessions did more than bring forth some repressed memories of those two incidents. They revealed that the visitors had been a part of his life, and the lives of his family members, for as long as he could recall. They had visited and abducted him many times. During the course of his alleged abductions, he experienced some things that are common to abduction testimonies worldwide. One of them is the insertion of something either under the skin or into the nose. He related that in March, while lying in bed, he had the impression that something was inserted into his left nostril. He awakened during the night and found that he was unable to move, as though he had been given an injection to paralyze him, the same type of injection that is given to patients by doctors before some types of surgery. He felt that this object was inserted far up into his left nostril, and he then experienced a type of popping, crunching noise between his eyes. On another occasion, the visitors cut shapes into his arm. There was a period of missing time, which is another common factor in abduction scenarios. Many abductees report thinking that only a minute or two had gone by, only to realize later that hours had passed. Mr. Strieber likewise described this missing time phenomenon. He was reading in bed, wearing pajamas, when he suddenly realized that four hours had inexplicably past, and he was naked. He looked at his left arm, which had two triangular shapes cut into the flesh. He wrote, "The larger triangle was quite straight, delicately incised in just the outer few skin layers as if by the work of a skilled master surgeon. The outer triangle, very tiny, was pointing at the larger one."[28] In other abduction scenarios that he wrote about, he described the visitors as bug-like, with large heads, slanted eyes, and a slit for a mouth.

Mr. Strieber's account is similar to many others. The so-called "abduction phenomenon" is widespread, and it affects a large number of people from countries all over the world. Brazilian farmer Antonio Villas Boas reported the earliest known case in 1957, when he was 23 years old. In an effort to escape the heat during the day, he was plowing fields near São Francisco de Sales (in Minas Gerais) when he saw an object in the sky that resembled a red star. This light approached him. As it neared, he realized that it was an oval ship with a red light on the front and a dome on the top. Three legs extended from the bottom of the craft and it landed in the field. Frightened, Mr. Boas fled as it was coming down. He got onto his tractor and took off, but the engine and lights stopped functioning, forcing him to continue on foot. He jumped to the ground and began running, but he was restrained. One of the creatures, a five-foot-tall gray humanoid, grabbed him from behind. According to Boas, the creature wore clothing that resembled overalls and a helmet, and it had small, blue eyes. It made noises comparable to the barks or yelps that an animal might make. Other creatures joined their companion, and they all dragged Boas aboard the ship.

Once inside, the creatures stripped him and covered his entire body with gel. They led him through a doorway crowned with red, indecipherable letters, and into a circular examination room. Here, the creatures took samples of his blood before leading him into another room. Leaving him alone in this room, the humanoids disappeared into another area of the ship. They slowly filled the room with some kind of gas that made him feel ill, and he remained there for approximately thirty minutes. As if the story thus far were not strange enough, Boas explained that something weird happened next. Another humanoid walked into the room. This one was female, and she was naked. Long, white hair cascaded from her head, and she had large blue eyes. Boas found her attractive, and the two of them had sex. She did not kiss him, only pecked his chin. After it had ended, she smiled at him, touching her stomach. She pointed at the ceiling of the ship, which he interpreted as her telling him that she was going to raise their child on another planet, where she was from. It was to be a half-breed, both human and whatever they were. The female seemed relieved that her task was over, and the other creatures returned his clothes. Once he had put them on, they gave him a tour of their ship. He tried to take something on board that resembled a clock as proof that this event had taken place, but they saw him and prevented him from leaving with it. They escorted him off the ship, and he watched as it departed the same way in which it had arrived. When he returned home, he discovered that four hours had passed.[29]

Following this experience, Boas felt weak and nauseous. He had headaches and skin lesions. After several months, Boas saw a newspaper advertisement in which local journalist Jose Martins was looking for individuals who had seen UFOs. He contacted Martins, who put him in touch with Dr. Olavo Fontes of Brazil's National School of Medicine. Dr. Fontes examined Mr. Boas and concluded that he suffered from mild radiation sickness. Researcher Bruce Rux wrote the following:

> Reluctant to tell his story, Boas was convinced by Dr. Olavo T. Fontes, Professor of Medicine at the National School of Medicine of Brazil and also an APRO representative, to publicly relate what happened, which he did on February 22 of the following year to Fontes, journalist Jose Martins, and a Brazilian military intelligence agent. Boas had been found to be suffering from radiation poisoning, and Fontes was curious. Among the symptoms were "pains throughout the body, nausea, headaches, loss of appetite, ceaselessly burning sensations in the eyes, cutaneous lesions at the slightest of light bruising, which went on appearing for months, looking like small reddish nodules, harder than the skin around them and protuberant, painful when touched, each with a small central orifice yielding a yellowish thin waterish discharge [sic]." The skin surrounding the wounds presented a "hyperchromatic violet-tinged area." The military intelligence man interrogated Boas, and he was subjected to a battery of physical and psychological tests. The most conservative of UFOlogists accept his abduction as an actual occurrence.[30]

This story was first revealed to selected individuals in 1958, and it was first mentioned in print in 1962. At this time, Boas revealed much more specific information about what the creatures wore, what they looked like, and details of their ship. For example, here is a description of what the creatures were wearing:

> All...of them wore a very tight-fitting siren-suit, made of soft, thick, unevenly striped gray material. This garment reached right up to their necks where it was joined to a kind of helmet made of a grey material that looked stiffer and was

strengthened back at nose level. Their helmets hide everything except their eyes, which were protected by two round glasses, like the lenses in ordinary glasses. Through them, the men looked at me, and their eyes seemed to be much smaller than ours, though I believe that may have been the effect of the lenses. All of them had light-colored eyes that looked blue to me, but this I cannot vouch for. Above their eyes, those helmets looked so tall that they corresponded to what the double of the size of a normal head should be. Probably there was something else hidden under those helmets, placed on top of their heads, but nothing could be seen from the outside. Right on top, from the middle of their heads, there sprouted three round silvery metal tubes (I can't tell whether they were made of metal or of rubber) which were a little narrower than a common garden hose. The tubes, which were placed one in the middle and one on each side of their heads, were smooth and bent backward and downward, toward the back. There they fitted into their clothes; how I cannot say, but one went down the center, where the backbone is, and the other two, one on each side, fitted under the shoulders at about four inches from the armpits — nearly at the sides, where the back begins. I didn't notice anything at all, no hump or lump to show where the tubes were attached, nor any box or contrivance hidden under their clothes.[31]

Later in life, Boas became a lawyer, married, and had four children. He died in 1992. Throughout his life, he never changed his story. He always claimed that this event actually occurred. For this reason, many believe it. Others find that it is too strange to believe, and despite the corresponding evidence that supports its veracity, they do not believe his tale. This is common in all abduction scenarios. Many individuals who come forward are not believed. Some are blatantly mocked. For this reason, there are likely more individuals who believe they have been abducted but who have never come forward to reveal their story.

Many abduction reports seem unbelievable. Some people, hearing such tales for the first time, would dismiss them as nonsense. Boas's story in particular seems so far-fetched that it is difficult to take any part of it seriously. However, many of the abductees, including Boas, did not initially tell their stories. They kept the information to themselves, so it might indicate that these stories were likely not publicity stunts. In addition, if such people wanted others to believe them, the stories would probably not be so outrageous. In other words, if I wanted to write a humorous and interesting science fiction story, I might make it as outrageous as possible in order to entertain and interest readers. But if I wanted others to believe that the event occurred in real life, I would tone down my storytelling. I would make it more ordinary, and hence more credible. Keeping this in mind, what makes this story more credible could be the fact that it is so outrageous. Many of the abductee stories are as bizarre as this one. What is more significant is that most of them are similar in nearly every regard.

According to different studies, 0.3 percent to 2 percent of people in the United States have experienced this kind of abduction.[32] Besides stories of individuals who experience this phenomenon, there is often physical evidence that such events had actually occurred. Scoop marks, for example, are areas of the body in which layers of skin had been allegedly removed by alien abductors. In addition, there are often unexplained scars where abductees recall being cut, missing pregnancies, foreign implants found under the skin, and remnants of a gel-like, sometimes fluorescent substance found on the skin. Some of the abductees are seized at different ages, as though the abductors were curious about the process of growth and aging. In addition, there is a curious connection with UFO abductions and water.

John Velez considers himself an abductee.[33] He reached out to other individuals who have gone through the same traumatic event, and over the course of six years, he had been in touch with more than 600 people who also claimed to have been abducted. Many of these individuals lived near water, or their actual abductions occurred near water. Even more interesting is the fact that many of the abductees specifically remember being brought underwater. [34] A relatively well-known abduction case that involved being brought underwater was the report of Filiberto Cardenas. According to his testimony, on January 3, 1979, his car stalled on a highway near Hialeah, Florida. The electrical system also stopped functioning. Along with three passengers, he exited the car to see what was wrong. Once outside, they heard a buzzing sound. A blue beam of light appeared on Cardenas, and he could not move. It pulled him into the sky, where a UFO hovered. It sucked Cardenas inside while his friends watched dumbfounded from the ground. Then, it flew off.

Two hours later, he reappeared and told his friends what had occurred. He stated that the UFO had traveled for some distance before diving into the ocean. Water rushed passed the windows of the ship. Although his memories were not perfectly clear, he recalled that the beings that brought him underwater were small humanoids who wore one-piece jumpsuits. They took him to an underwater base, and they showed him images of the past, present and future of humankind. He was greeted by one particular creature who stated that it was from Earth.[35] The next thing he knew, he was returned to his shocked friends. Later, it was determined that hundreds of people at the Miami International Airport had witnessed one large UFO and two smaller UFOs in the same area in which Cardenas was taken. The underwater base that he described could have been located in the Bermuda Triangle, or at least near it.

His description of being underwater during an abduction scenario is not unique. Another person, who claimed to have been abducted, described flying through the sky inside a semi-translucent UFO. She claimed that the walls appeared solid while in flight, but they became transparent when in water. Eventually, she felt the vessel stop. When it did, she noticed that she was in water. It was well-lit outside, and she saw fish and aquatic plants. She specifically remembered a yellow fish with a blue stripe that was next to the outer wall of the vessel. After some time, the craft slowly exited the water, and it appeared more opaque.[36] Abductees who assert that visitors had brought them underwater typically report visiting oceans, but some abductees claim that the UFOs entered freshwater lakes and streams. Two hotspots for such phenomena include Lake Erie in the United States and Lake Titicaca in Peru, but witnesses have also described other unlikely locations, such as the East River in New York.

    In late November 1989, multiple independent witnesses observed a red colored, glowing UFO in the sky over Manhattan. They were amazed to see a woman being pulled through the window of her apartment building and into the craft by an apparent beam of light. Once she was inside, it sped away. Some of the witnesses, including police officers and a U.N. official, reported even more detail. They too saw her being pulled from her window in a beam of bluish, white light, but they also claim to have seen small humanoid figures that took control of her and physically pulled her into the vessel. Once the woman was inside, the object regained its original reddish white color and dove into the river near the Brooklyn Bridge. Obviously curious, the witnesses investigated, and the woman told her tale. She claimed that at approximately 3:00 A.M., she awoke to find that her body was numb. She saw a small figure with a large head and enormous black eyes moving toward her. Her recollections were fragmented after this point, but she did recall a sensation of floating through her window. Sometime later, she was hypnotized to remember more. She said that the creatures had performed medical operations or experiments on her. Then, she remembered that the craft dove underwater. She believed that it finally stopped at the bottom of the East River. "Through a large window she could see the murky bottom of what she took to be the East River. Garbage and even a soft drink bottle were visible in the UFO's lights."[37]

One must always be skeptical when weighing abduction reports. Some people might blatantly lie. Others might have psychological problems. However, abduction reports are widespread, issuing from countries all over the world, and they are surprisingly similar. Whether one believes they have occurred in the manner described is irrelevant; no one can deny that something is happening. Certainly, it could be some sort of mass-induced psychological condition, but no matter what, questions remain. It is an area of inquiry that needs to be pursued. Right now, there are no answers. If we assume that there are actual abductions occurring, perpetrated by non-human entities, we can make a generalization: These visitors have a specific purpose, and they actually need human beings. They perform surgeries, and many of these operations involve human reproduction. Some pregnant female abductees claimed that the visitors had taken their unborn babies. In other, more bizarre scenarios, some women report two distinct abductions. During the first experience, the visitors artificially impregnated them. During the second abduction, the visitors removed the fetuses. Such procedures, allegedly conducted by the visitors, are not confined to women. Operations involving reproduction and D.N.A. are also carried out on men. In other words, the visitors seem to need men's sperm.

Whitley Strieber wrote:

> In recent years many of the taken have reported having sexual experiences with the visitors. Currently among them this is a source of great disquiet. It is terrifying, of course. But reflect also that mankind has had sexual relations with the fairies, the sylphs, the incubi, the succubi, and the denizens of the night from the very beginning of time. Nowadays men find themselves on examining tables in flying saucers with vacuum devices attached to their privates, while women must endure the very real agony of having their pregnancies disappear, a torment that I, as a man, doubt I can really imagine.[38]

Considering these facts alone, it seems that these creatures are somehow manipulating D.N.A. In the Boas case, he was forced to have intercourse with a female entity. In other alien abduction scenarios, the visitors removed sperm from the abductees. Likewise, some pregnant women reported that their unborn babies were taken from them. All of this leads to one basic conclusion: For some reason, these creatures are attempting to alter either their own D.N.A. or the D.N.A. of human beings for some unknown purpose. It is almost as if they are trying to combine the D.N.A. of both creatures, so that a hybrid being is created. However, the real reasons behind these so-called experiments might be much more logical, and they might point to a sad and unfortunate scenario, one that will be explored in more detail later in this text.

Although there are thousands of reports of so-called alien abductions, and dozens of reports of crashed UFOs, these two phenomena are rare compared to UFO sightings. By reviewing some significant cases, we can gain a better understanding of the complete nature of this phenomenon.

Modern Sightings

UFO sightings have been reported from diverse countries. Witnesses have been both civilians and military personnel, and the evidence collected beside testimonies includes radar reports, photographs, and trace evidence. UFOs seem to be drawn to military bases, and they have an apparent fascination with nuclear weapons. In 1967, a few guards reported a craft with strange lights in the sky above the Malmstrom Air Force Base in Great Falls, Montana. It was maneuvering in impossible ways. It made sharp turns, accelerated quickly, and came to complete stops in the sky. Eventually, the craft hovered in front of the main gate. All of the facility's missiles shut down, and warning lights in the control center activated. This same thing happened a week earlier at another nearby base.[39]

UFOs commonly visit different military bases in the same area within a short timeframe, but there are cases in which UFOs visited the same location decades apart. One famous case occurred near the Royal Air Force Base in Lakenheath-Bentwaters, England. UFOs visited twice, once in 1956 and again in 1980. On August 13, 1956, radar detected some unidentified craft traveling at approximately 4,023 kilometers (2,500 miles) per hour. Tower controllers reported bright lights in the sky. Another pilot stated he had seen the same thing. Soon thereafter, one of these objects hovered outside the base. A Venom night-fighter investigated. As the jet approached, the UFO accelerated to supersonic speeds, stopped mid-flight to change directions, and continued to outmaneuver the approaching aircraft. Eventually, the jet ran low on fuel and had to return to base. A second pilot headed out in another jet to continue the pursuit, but it had a problem. There was an instrument malfunction, and it too had to return to base. The UFO remained in the vicinity for some time after this investigation, and then it disappeared. If this were the only sighting in the area, it would likely not be well known, as many similar interactions between military personnel and UFOs have been reported. The second visit made this area famous.

On December 26, 1980, the ships returned. People who lived near the base reported glowing objects that fell from the sky and into the Rendlesham forest. The objects also appeared on both British and American military radar. Civilian radar also picked them up. Some U.S. Air police officers saw lights heading toward the forest and decided to investigate. They expected to find debris, but were shocked to discover instead a bright, hovering craft. The men phoned the base, and some units from the security division were dispatched. The craft disappeared beneath the treetops, and the men headed into the forest. They were surprised to find that it had landed, and it was resting on three landing struts. The craft had a glass-like surface and was covered with strange symbols. The men approached the object, and it quickly withdrew its landing gear and returned to the sky. Once it cleared the treetops, it accelerated at an incredible speed and disappeared. The men returned to the base and reported what had occurred. The next day, an investigation revealed depressions in the Earth where the landing struts were, and the area had a high radiation level. This was just the beginning of the encounter, however. The next night, lights once again appeared over the same forest and then descended beneath the treetops.

Lieutenant Colonel Halt and other officers led patrol teams into the forest to investigate. One of the teams reported that the lights changed colors as they drew near, and the area was marked by a yellow fog that blanketed the forest floor. When they approached the craft, it slowly floated away, as though repositioning itself. As it moved it emitted a pulse of energy, and all present felt their hair stand on end, as though it were static electricity. The men in this patrol received a radio transmission. They were ordered to withdraw and join Lt. Col. Halt's patrol, which was approaching the repositioned craft with giant lights that would illuminate the entire area.

Once Halt's detail had secured and illuminated the area, more security personnel arrived. A staff car transporting senior officers also pulled up. As it approached, a floating orb-like object emerged from the UFO's side. The security personnel noticed apparent humanoid figures inside the orb. It floated in front of the officers, and the small creatures inside, which were observed wearing silver colored suits, seemed to be trying to communicate with them. However, no one could hear any sounds from them. Whether or not there was actually some kind of communication that took place is unknown. The British Office of Official Secrets recently declassified and released the only written documents of the events, but researchers generally believe that they have been sanitized.[40]

Lieutenant Colonel Halt described what occurred in detail:

> It appeared to be like an eye. That's the best way I can describe it. It had a dark center and appeared to be dripping something molten, so it was something like steel from a crucible. The object came even closer. It moved through the trees, going horizontal, up and down a little bit as it went. We were really in awe at this time, so we tried to get closer. We moved toward the object itself. The object receded out into the field. We watched it there in the field for a few minutes and then it very silently exploded and broke into... I

believe it was five white spheres…small spheres, and they just disappeared. While we're standing there in awe, one of the party members looks up and says, "look in the sky." We looked up, and there to the north were several objects: three objects that were elliptical and they had multi-color. They were moving at high speeds at sharp angular movements and so they were doing a grid or something; I really can't say what, for sure, but they were moving about quite rapidly. We noticed to the south there were several objects there. One particular one approached us at a very, very high speed, probably three or four thousand feet high, maybe a little more, stopped almost directly overhead and sent a beam down to our feet. The interesting thing about the beam was that the beam didn't radiate out. It was a steady beam about 10 – 12 inches in diameter. Not like a flashlight beam that spreads out as it goes, so obviously, it was not normal lighting. Something more like a laser. And we stood there in awe, quite concerned, but you know, if it's signaling us, warning us, trying to injure us… we really weren't sure what it was trying to do, but we were really concerned at that point. And just as suddenly as it appeared, it disappeared.

Most of the witnesses were military personnel. Markings were found on the forest floor, and the area had a high radiation level. Several years later I started running into people who were involved and I didn't realize were on the edge or picked up bits and pieces from here. For instance, one of the radar operators in the tower at the eastern radar who had air defense responsibility for that sector told me that they actually picked up objects on the screen that night. They had them on tape, but someone took the tape. Then a couple of the young troops came forward and said, "you know, after the incident the three people who were involved, who went out and approached the craft, were taken into a room and pumped full of drugs and given…hypnotized and debriefed, so to speak." Then I found out a mysterious C1-41 landed soon thereafter with an unusual crew and all sorts of things.[41]

Sergeant James Penniston was also present during this incident. He was the senior officer in charge of base security at Woodbridge. He held top-secret U.S. and N.A.T.O. security clearances, and was in charge of war resources at the base. He reported that after midnight on Christmas night Staff Sergeant Steffens had told him that lights were seen over the forest. Steffens told him that whatever caused the lights did not crash; it landed. Penniston initially dismissed that statement as nonsense, but headed to the location to determine the cause of the lights. He explained, "There was a bright light emanating from an object on the forest floor. As we approached it on foot, a silhouetted triangular craft about nine feet long by six and a half feet high came into view. The craft was fully intact, sitting in a small clearing inside the woods."[42] The craft had blue and yellow lights, and the air seemed electrically charged. It made their hair stand up. The craft was silent. It did not make any sound. Penniston determined that it was not hostile, and his men and he approached to examine it more thoroughly. He reported what he had seen:

> On one side of the craft were symbols that measured about three inches high and two and a half feet across. These symbols were pictorial in design; the largest symbol was a triangle, which was centered in the middle of the others. They were etched into the surface of the craft. I put my hand on the craft, and it was warm to the touch. The surface was smooth, like glass, but it had the quality of metal, and I felt a constant low voltage running through my hand and moving to my mid-forearm.[43]

After approximately 45 minutes, the ship's lights brightened, and it lifted off the ground without sound. It slowly maneuvered through the trees. Once it was free, it shot into the sky at an incredible speed.

They headed back to the base to report, and the next day they returned to the site to catalogue physical evidence. In the daylight, they found broken branches where the craft had landed, and some of the trees had been burned. There were also indentations in the ground, three of them, where the landing struts had touched down.

This incident at Rendlesham Forest is one of the most famous UFO sightings, but there are many others that involve the military. Military pilots not only reported seeing UFOs, but also actually engaged them in aerial pursuit. These unidentified craft showed up on radar, and some of them left trace evidence of their existence.

On November 2, 1982, Captain Júlio Miguel Guerra of the Portuguese Air Force flew a DHC-1 Chipmunk near Montejunto Mountain in the proximity of Ota Air Base. It was a clear and cloudless day. He was out there to train, and he had planned to climb to 1,829 meters (6,000 feet) to work on aerobatic exercises. When his craft reached a height of approximately 1,524 meters (5,000 feet), he noticed another aircraft to his left at a lower altitude. This unknown craft did not seem to have wings or a fuselage. It was oval. He turned his plane to the left so that he could get a better look at it. He wrote, "Suddenly, the object climbed straight up to my altitude of 5,000 feet in under ten seconds. It stopped right in front of me, at first with some instability, and then it stabilized and was still — a metallic disk composed of two halves, one on top and another on the bottom, with some kind of a band around the center, brilliant, with the top reflecting the sun. The bottom half was a darker tone."[44] First, it moved as Guerra moved his airplane, but then it flew at an impossible speed in a large elliptical orbit to his left between 1,524 meters (5,000 feet) to the south and 3,048 meters (10,000 feet) to the north. It kept repeating this same pattern.

Guerra phoned the tower and told them he was witnessing a UFO. Right away, some other pilots gave him a hard time over the radio. Someone at the tower suggested that it was some kind of balloon. He invited the other pilots to fly toward him if they did not believe him, so that they could see it for themselves. They asked for his location, and two other officers, Carlos Garcês and António Gomes approached. They also saw the craft. They watched it repeat the same pattern from north to south. Guerra waited for about ten minutes, and then decided that he wanted to get a closer look. He decided to intercept it: he would head right at it, forcing the object to alter its flight pattern. The UFO's speed was much greater than his own, so rather than fly straight at it, as he would do versus a standard human-piloted aircraft, he picked a point on its course and headed for that. It came directly at Guerra's plane. Then it flew over the airplane and stopped directly overhead, breaking all known rules of aerodynamics. It remained approximately 4.6 meters (15 feet) over his plane, without wavering, as Guerra continued flying straight ahead. Then, it disappeared with a flash in the direction of Sintra Mountain. All three pilots returned to the base and filed reports, but nothing ever came of them. There was no military investigation of the incident.[45]

Armed forces are naturally interested in UFO technology. UFOs maneuver in ways considered impossible based on our current understanding of aerodynamics. If they could procure one and reverse engineer a prototype, they would have a substantial advantage over other countries in war. For this reason, when UFOs crash, military personnel show up. The event is kept as quiet as possible so that other countries cannot gain access to the technology. This is all logical, but unidentified, highly advanced craft flying around at will in restricted airspace is also a major concern. It is an issue of national security. For this reason, pilots in various countries have engaged and fired upon UFOs.

In 1976, General Parviz Jafari of the Iranian Air Force was ordered to take down a saucer-shaped UFO. He described it as a "thin rectangle with a light at each end and one in the middle."[46] He could also see a "round dome over it with a dim light inside."[47] Piloting a Phantom F-4 II jet, he chased the glowing object and attempted to fire a Sidewinder missile at it. He approached the object and prepared to fire, but his equipment malfunctioned. It did not return to normal until after he had moved the plane away from the UFO. This chase was recorded on radar and observed by many individuals from the base.[48] A similar event happened in 1980 in Peru, which is known as a UFO hotspot. Lieutenant Oscar Santa María Huertas was ordered to intercept an unknown flying object. At first, he believed it was some kind of spying device and fired at it with machine gun shells. They had no effect. As he got closer, he realized that this was an unknown aircraft, perhaps not made by humans. He described it:

> It was an object that measured about 35 feet (10 meters) in diameter with a shiny dome on top that was cream-colored, similar to a light bulb cut in half. The bottom was a wider circular base, a silver color, and looked like some kind of metal. It lacked all the typical components of aircraft. It had no wings, propulsion jets, exhausts, windows, antennae, and so forth. It had no visible propulsion system.[49]

The object was stationary, so he tried to lock onto it. When he did, it shot upward. He locked onto it two more times with the same result. He realized that the attempt to shoot it out of the sky was futile. More than 1,000 soldiers were on the ground watching this event at the La Joya base.

Besides the sample cases listed herein, on many occasions military pilots have interacted with UFOs. In some cases, they have just witnessed the objects; in others, they engaged the craft and even fired upon them. And most likely, there have been various UFO crashes in which the military collected debris. Through reverse engineering, it is possible that the U.S. government, in particular, created aircraft based upon their findings, aircraft such as the Stealth Bomber.

7. The Stealth Bomber

Initially created at Lockheed and Northrop, the shape of this plane is supposedly similar to the craft that crashed at Roswell. It "may even utilize some form of electrogravitic generator culled from the Roswell saucer."[50] The Stealth Bomber does not show up on radar, just as UFOs sometimes do not show up. The top-secret Aurora aircraft might also be the result of such reverse engineering. It is thought that the propulsion system is a pulse engine fueled by cryogenic methane. It has been seen over Area 51 in Nevada and in California. Supposedly, this craft can travel at over 9,656 kilometers (6,000 miles) per hour, but it is difficult to control. This difficulty has resulted in several crashes and fatalities.[51]

Reports of unidentified flying objects by civilian airlines are more common than military reports. On many occasions, pilots and passengers reported seeing unidentified objects in the sky that posed a direct threat to the safety of those on board. These objects, referred to as unidentified aerial phenomena (UAP), have caused pilots to maneuver their airplanes quickly to avoid crashing into them. Dr. Richard Haines, chief scientist for the National Aviation Reporting Center on Anomalous Phenomena (NARCAP) noted that in-flight collision was generally unlikely because USPs are seemingly able to maneuver in unexplained ways. However, the appearance of these unidentified flying objects can cause dangerous pilot reactions. Only by legitimately investigating this phenomenon and training pilots how to deal with them can safety truly be maintained, but pilots who report such sightings are often ridiculed. Dr. Haines wrote:

> This attitude serves no one and in fact puts all of us at greater risk while traveling in airplanes. It prevents the scientific community from acquiring the data necessary to investigate the origin of these UAP, and it also keeps airlines and pilot organizations from taking action or providing their pilots with specialized training and safety protocols. Despite all this, these unusual aerial phenomena have continued to plague commercial military and private flight operations over many years.[52]

On August 22, 1968, two pilots were traveling from Adelaide to Perth, Australia. They were in a Piper Navajo single-engine airplane traveling at approximately 2,538 meters (8,000 feet), when they noticed what they described as a cigar-shaped craft surrounded by five smaller flying objects. These UFOs maintained their formation and followed the airplane for approximately 10 minutes. The pilots contacted air traffic control, which replied that there was no known traffic in the area. Then, their radio communication failed and the objects following them disappeared.

This is the most common type of interaction between UFOs and airlines, but other types of interactions have resulted in death. On October 21, 1978, Frederick Valentich rented a small airplane for a short flight. Just after 9:00 P.M., he made a distress call to the Tullamarine Airport while he was over the Bass Strait. He claimed that an unidentified flying object was orbiting his airplane. At times, the object headed straight for him. Then it appeared to be chasing him. He described this object as a large aircraft with four bright lights. One of the lights was green. The craft was metallic and shiny. Eventually, Mr. Valentich stopped speaking. There were some unusual metallic noises on the tape, and then silence. He was never heard from again.[53]

Many collisions and near collisions have been reported. Pilot Thomas Preziose crashed into an unknown object in flight on October 23, 2002 near Mobile, Alabama while traveling from Mobile to Montgomery. Another collision was nearly avoided on August 8, 1994. A commercial flight from Acapulco Guerrero to Mexico City had to take action to avoid colliding with a UFO that emerged from behind a cloud cover. Likewise, a Boeing 737 was traveling from Okinawa to Tokyo when two UFOs suddenly appeared in front of it. They were described as two large lights that separated quickly. The pilot had to dive to avoid the objects.[54] UFOs in the skies are not rare, and there is a good chance that a high percentage of pilots will one day see one; they might even have to maneuver their craft to avoid a mid-air collision. For this reason, Dr. Haines believes aviation safety experts should seriously study UAPs, and that it should be a subject breached in pilot training courses. However, the mention of the term UFO or UAP currently provokes ridicule, and many pilots and airline employees do not come forward to report sightings for fear of losing their jobs.

When one or two pilots witness a UFO, they can keep their mouths shut, and no one else will know about the sighting. This gets more difficult when multiple independent witnesses have seen the ships. On November 7, 2006, for example, a UFO appeared over the

United Airlines terminal at the O'Hare Airport in Chicago. It hovered over gate C17 for approximately five minutes, where many individuals, both airline employees and passengers, saw it before it flew into a cloud, leaving a circular hole where it entered. A pilot first announced the sighting, and then other pilots looked up and confirmed it. Taxi mechanics and management also spotted the object. The story appeared on the front page of the Chicago Tribune about two months later, and many television networks then picked it up. Certainly, some airline passengers might have been nervous, as the existence of such craft at an airport could cause some serious accidents. Perhaps for this reason, the airline officially claimed that nothing extraordinary had occurred; they said it was an unusual weather phenomenon. The pilots and other witnesses are sure that what they saw was not an unusual weather event. This idea is laughable. They are sure that they saw an unidentified aircraft that was not from the known world.[55]

Five months later, another object was reported by pilots and other aviation personnel near Normandy over the English Channel. Captain Ray Bower wrote, "On April 23, 2007, my passengers and I witnessed multiple, as yet unidentified objects over these islands while crossing the English Channel. They were very, very large. The objects were picked up on radar at two locations, and one was witnessed by another pilot from a totally different vantage point."[56] He saw a light in the distance, which he first mistook as the sun reflecting off something on the ground. But since the distance between his plane and the object remained constant, he knew it was something different. With the autopilot engaged, he looked through binoculars. He found that it was shaped like a cigar or a CD on its edge with a slight protuberance in the center. He also described it as having a flattened disk shape. It also emitted a light. He approached the object, and another of the same shape and size appeared. Passengers noticed both of these objects, and some of them were nervous. Bower too was a bit nervous. He continued on his course and was able to land the plane. Once on the ground, he filled out a report and filed it with the Civil Aviation Authority (CAA). For a while, there was a great deal of publicity, and people interested in UFOs contacted him, but that has died down now. As he puts it, "People have other things on their minds now, and concern about something otherworldly when the mortgage payment is due falls firmly into second or third place."[57]

UFO sightings continue today. Whatever this phenomenon is, it is certain that it is a part of our civilization. Reviewing historical reports of unidentified aerial phenomenon provides some evidence that their appearance is nothing new, and that these ships have coexisted with human beings for at least the last several thousand years, if not before. The creatures that pilot these machines might even predate the rise of human beings. If so, they could be the first intelligent beings to inhabit this planet. When Filiberto Cardenas was abducted, one of the beings that greeted him explained that it was from Earth. If this is true, it is quite possible that UFOs are not extraterrestrial ships. The shape of these round, saucer-like ships does not seem conducive to interstellar travel. But if the pilots are not intelligent beings from another planet, where are they coming from? And if they are from this planet, where do they reside?

2. USOs

USO Sightings

Many UFO reports indicate a connection to water. One such UFO sighting occurred at Shag Harbor, located on the southern tip of Nova Scotia. On October 4, 1967, local residents spotted lights in the sky. After watching for a bit, they determined that the lights belonged to an unidentified flying craft. Shocked, they watched it moved through the air. Then, they saw it dive into the water at a forty-five degree angle. After its initial dive, it resurfaced and seemed to float on the ocean's surface approximately a half mile from shore. Many people saw this and called the police station. Three officers investigated. They reported the same thing: orange lights floating on the ocean's surface. The police officers gathered on the shore with other residents to watch. The lights changed colors from orange to yellow, and the object, which had a flat base and a domed top, begin moving across the surface of the water. As it moved, it left a glowing trail in its wake. Eventually, it disappeared beneath the surface. None of the witnesses could follow it further with their eyes. For this reason, local law enforcement called in the military, which tracked the ship underwater on their sonar. It traveled approximately 40 kilometers (25 miles), until it stopped at a place called Government Point, where the United States military had a base used primarily for tracking submarines. As they watched the blinking dot on its screens, which showed them the location of the craft, another dot appeared, indicating another craft. Initially the two were separate. They were no longer UFOs because they were not flying. The proper term for these objects is USOs: unidentified submerged objects. The U.S. military tracked two individual USOs interacting with each other. Soon a strange thing occurred. The objects seemed to mesh. Once joined, they broke the surface of the water at an incredible pace and then disappeared into the sky.

This famous UFO sighting is one of the best examples when looking for a standard, as the majority of unidentified flying objects are seen either beginning or ending their travels in water. More than fifty percent of all sightings occur over water, or witnesses report the ships either entering or leaving water. The actual terms UFOs and USOs are typically treated as distinct. Books and television programs about the subject do not generally combine the two, but the fact is that these two classifications refer to the same phenomenon. The so-called "alien spacecraft" usually begin or end in water, but no witness has ever seen an entire UFO flight. Witnesses always see UFOs while in flight. Sometimes, they see the flight beginning, and many of them begin in water. Others have seen UFOs as they were landing, and in some cases, those landings occurred over water. Considering that no witness has ever watched an entire UFO flight, it is possible that all these craft originate and end in water.

The most common phenomenon witnessed involves both travel underwater and into the sky. However, USOs alone have also been reported. One famous example occurred in 1963 when the U.S. Navy was conducting submarine exercises off the coast of Puerto Rico. An aircraft carrier, destroyer, and numerous submarines were participating in the exercises. Some airplanes were also present, flying at a low altitude. The submarines were all stationary and they were linked by communications systems. Initially, everything went smoothly. Then one of the submarines broke formation. A sonar operator on the destroyer reported this occurrence to the bridge. He told them that the submarine appeared to be in pursuit of an unknown object that was also detected by sonar. This unknown object was miraculously traveling at over 150 knots. The fastest submarines in the world only travel at 45 knots. Therefore, this object was more technologically advanced than any known underwater craft in existence, both military and civilian. Similar reports came from the involved aircraft, the other surface vessels, and even the other submarines. Ivan Sanderson explained what happened next:

> It is said that the technicians kept track of the thing for four days, and that it maneuvered round about, and down to depths of 27,000 feet. The record dive for a standard submarine is 6,200 feet, achieved by the U.S. Aluminaut on 12 November 1967, 20 miles off the West Coast of the Gran Abaco Island in the Bahamas.[1]

This unidentified craft, whatever it was, had technological capabilities that surpassed all known submarines at the time. Pressure would crush a human-made submarine at a depth of 2,134 meters (7,000 feet). In addition, this object moved at speeds three times faster than the top military submarines are capable of moving. Finally, the object was tracked on sonar for several days before disappearing. This capability is not unheard of in modern military technology. For example, Stealth technology effectively hides both aircraft and seafaring vessels from enemy radar. (Radar is short for "radio detecting and ranging." It locates an object by transmitting ultra-high frequency radio waves, and then measuring the amount of time it takes for these waves to transfer back to the transmitter. This indicates the location, speed, and size of objects. Stealth technology makes use of specially designed contours that can deflect radar. It also uses construction materials that can absorb or track radar waves.) It becomes clear, by looking at this one incident alone, that the unknown craft also made use of Stealth (or similar) technology. This assertion is supported by ample sightings.

**8. U.S. Airforce B-2 Stealth Bomber.
Its contour helps to eliminate radar detection.**

There are many other USO reports. In 1965, at approximately 10:00 P.M., passengers and crewmembers aboard a Norwegian ship called the *T. T. Jawesta* reported an unidentified craft. Some people aboard first spotted it in the sky. It was glowing as though on fire, and it moved in ways that conventional aircraft could not. It flew at an incredible speed, zigzagged, and even came to complete stops. A witness on the port side of the ship, Hernandez Ambrosio, saw that the craft had emerged from the ocean.[2] Two years later, in 1967, the Argentinian ship *Naviero* had a similar interaction with a UFO – USO. On July 20, the ship was approximately 193 kilometers (120 miles) off Brazil's coast, when those aboard saw a glowing object in the ocean approximately 15 meters (50 feet) away from the starboard side. Like many other UFO reports, witnesses stated that the object was cigar shaped and just over 30 meters (100 feet) in length. It had both blue and white lights, and it moved silently. After traveling alongside the ship for approximately 15 minutes, the craft dove deeper and passed underneath. Then it disappeared completely. Chief Officer Carlos Lasca described it as "a submergible UFO with its own illumination."[3]

USOs are commonly reported today, but such sightings are nothing new. For more than 1,000 years, people have reported strange craft in the oceans that seem identical to unidentified objects seen today. The earliest known USO report was by Alexander the Great in 329 B.C.E. He saw numerous objects resembling metal shields that emerged from a river in India. This sight was so unusual that he became obsessed with finding them. He spent the last six years of his life searching for them, even making use of an underwater diving bell that some describe as the world's first submarine. Some believe that ancient Egyptians also recorded similar sightings. This is because objects resembling modern, technologically advanced machines, such as submarines and helicopters, appear in wall carvings beside hieroglyphs. One of the most famous of these depictions is found in the Abydos Temple.

As mentioned in the previous chapter, Christopher Columbus also spotted a USO. It was a glowing object that followed alongside his ship for some time before breaking the water's surface and exiting into the sky. He had described it as resembling the flickering flames of Menorah candles being moved up and down. His diary records this incident. It also indicates that this sighting was not the first that he and his crewmembers had experienced. Other unusual phenomena were recorded, and the crewmembers described their sightings by relating them to objects to which they were familiar. Two of them reported birds flying through the sky while they were out at sea and far from land. The birds they reported seeing could not have been there, since they did not stray far from shore. They also reported stars and other heavenly bodies moving across the sky.

Even older texts indicate similar observations. One is in the French text *L'Histoire des Anglais*. In 1067, witnesses reported a flame-like object in the sky. It moved up and down until it eventually descended into the sea.[4] Reports grow even more numerous after

Columbus's sighting while *en route* to the Americas. Many from the 1800's describe glowing meteors that flew through the sky and then crashed into oceans. Some of these reports describe the opposite: "meteors" that began underwater and then flew into the sky. Although the nomenclature was different, these reports clearly refer to the same phenomenon, which today would be called either UFOs or USOs.

Andrew Bloxam described an event that occurred on August 12, 1825. In the middle of the night, everything on deck was suddenly and inexplicably illuminated by a large, round, unidentified object that rose from the sea. It was reddish in color, and it moved up and down repeatedly before disappearing into the clouds above. Another example from 1887 was recorded in the logbook of a Dutch ship. Captain C. D. Sweet wrote, "In a fierce storm; two objects were sighted in the air above the ship, one luminous, the other dark. They fell into the sea with a loud noise."[5] A similar occurrence was recorded in the *S. S. Fort Salisbury's* logbook:

> The lookout observed a huge dark object several hundred feet off to starboard. He called second officer A. H. Raymer, who hurried on deck and joined the lookout and the helmsman. "It was a little frightening," Raymer said later. "We couldn't see too much detail in the darkness, but it was between five and six hundred feet in length. It had two lights, one at each end. A mechanism of some kind — or fins, maybe — was making a commotion in the water." The officer reported that the object seemed to be slowly sinking. He didn't believe it was a vessel that had turned turtle. Its surface was not smooth, but "appeared to be scaled."[6]

Another object was seen in January, 1956, off the coast of Pusan, Korea. It was first seen in the sky and was reported to have been the size of a large washtub. It had a bluish, grayish glow. It dropped down onto the surface of the water approximately 50 yards offshore near Heunde, and remained in this location, seemingly floating, for approximately an hour and a half. Then it sank into the sea, leaving a glowing trail in its wake. USOs often leave glowing trails when they move. Another report from December 1956 was filed by a Swedish ship, which radioed the La Guaira, Venezuela harbor control. They reported a brightly-lit, cone-shaped object that had fallen vertically into the ocean. When it hit the surface of the water, witnesses heard a sound like an explosion. The water instantaneously took on the colors emitted by the object. As it descended underwater and out of view, the colors remained and the water's surface also moved rapidly for some time. This is another phenomenon common with USOs. The water moves in unnatural ways, as though the ships themselves were creating vortices. In 1957, the Japanese fishing vessel *Kitsukawa Maru* described the same phenomenon. They saw two silver objects descend into the ocean. Their entry points became instantaneously turbulent, and the movement endured for some time after their disappearance beneath the surface.[7]

Another interesting case involved a sighting in Kaipara Harbour, New Zealand. On January 12, 1965, a pilot, first officer, and operations officer were traveling from Whenuapai to Kaitaia, a flight that took just over an hour. When they approached the harbor, just north of Helensville, they dropped 152 meters (500 feet). At the time, it was low tide, so they could easily see what was underwater. In an estuary, they spotted a large gray-white object, which at first glance they took to be a whale. They flew directly over it to get a closer look, and realized that it was a metallic craft. It was symmetrical in shape with no external protrusions. They estimated the length of the object to be 30 meters (100 feet), with a diameter of approximately 4.5 meters (15 feet). It rested in only 9 meters (30 feet) of water and could therefore be easily seen.[8]

The majority of USO and UFO sightings do not last for many days, but there have been some interesting cases in which the objects were tracked for not just one or two days, but for weeks.

One of these occurred on November 11, 1972. The Norwegian Navy, using sonar, detected a fast-moving submarine-like object of the west coast of Norway. Believing it to be another country's military vessel, they dispatched submarine seeking helicopters and surface vessels to hunt. After a couple days, they located it in the Sonja Fjord and tracked it for more than a week. It was first seen visually on November 20, nine days after its initial sonar detection. Witnesses described it as a large cigar-shaped object. The Navy ships immediately fired their weapons at it. First, they attacked with torpedoes; then with depth charges. Having no success whatsoever, they sealed the fjord so that nothing could get in or out, thereby trapping it inside. However, after more than two weeks of tracking its movement, it disappeared completely. It was at this point that they determined the object was not made by human beings, and should therefore be classified as a USO.

Certain bodies of water are USO hotspots. Lakes in which such objects are commonly sighted include Lake Erie in the United States, and Lake Titicaca in Peru. Certain oceanic areas also have an abundance of UFO and USO sightings. These include the Bermuda Triangle off Florida's coast, and the Dragon's Triangle off the coast of Japan. They also include deep-sea trenches. One of these is the Santa Catalina Channel, which stretches 41 kilometers (26 miles). Located off California, the water is more than 9,144 meters (30,000 feet) deep. Numerous unidentified craft have been reported in this area. One of the most famous reports occurred on June 14, 1992, when approximately two hundred USOs were seen emerging from the water at once. According to witness reports, they quietly emerged and hovered for approximately two minutes before disappearing into the sky. The police and Coast Guard received numerous witness statements, but they were not surprised, as this was not the first time that something like this happened. Three years earlier, a large USO was seen resting near the ocean's surface. This was reported by divers, people on boats, and more on the shore. Six or seven smaller USOs were seen emerging from this large craft.

They too silently exited the water, hovered for a moment, and then flew off into the sky. Once they were gone, the larger craft re-submerged and could not be located.

Besides USO sightings, there is other evidence of their existence in the deepest oceans. This evidence includes the issuance of signals, perhaps an attempt to communicate. One recorded example of this involves a scientific organization experimenting with a new form of underwater communication. Long distance communication under the surface of the sea was an evasive technology. One scientist set up antennae approximately a mile apart along the continental shelf. This shelf stretches out 160 kilometers (100 miles) from the eastern coast of the United States before dropping into some of the deepest waters of the Atlantic. A research ship lowered its instruments into the water to pick up potential signals. They were attempting to transmit signals from one of the antenna to the other. The individuals aboard the research vessel were shocked to hear not only the initial signal, but a repeat of that sound followed by an indecipherable code. They were certain that an unidentified form of intelligence had copied the signal and added its own sounds to it. It is likely that these supplementary sounds were intended as a form of communication, but just what they meant is still unknown. And whom or what made these sounds also remains unknown. Strangely, they tracked the source of the signal and discovered that it emanated from one of the deepest parts of the Atlantic. This sound came from a depth of approximately 8,839 meters (29,000 feet).[9]

The Deepest Water

The oceans comprise 99 percent of all living space on the planet, yet we know little about them. With all our current technology, we have only explored about three percent of them.[10] We cannot reach the deepest areas, and we do not know what kinds of creatures live in their depths. We know more about the moon than we do about the oceans. Perhaps this is because humans tend to look up, rather than look down. In the twentieth century, oceanic trenches were discovered. These are deep topographic depressions on the ocean floor caused by convergent plate boundaries. The bottoms of these trenches are usually more than three kilometers (two miles) below the water's surface, but some of them are even deeper; some trenches in the Pacific are nearly ten kilometers (six miles) deep. We cannot even sound the entirety of such trenches. The deepest area ever sounded was the Mariana Trench, 10,911 meters (35,797 feet) below sea level. Therefore, almost nothing is known about what is down there. What kinds of creatures live in such an environment? Although we do not have the scientific capabilities to answer this question adequately, we can make some intelligent guesses based on some unusual creatures that have been discovered in incredibly deep water.

Some creatures found in water approximately 4,877 meters (16,000 feet) deep, (less than half the depth of the Mariana Trench), include types of bioluminescent squid and jellyfish, and unusual fish with large black eyes — eyes that appear too large for their heads. Larger fish that look like skeletons are also found at this depth, fish that have long, slender teeth and look prehistoric. Some fish actually have glowing eyes. Many of the creatures at depths like this use bioluminescence to scare away potential predators. Others use it to hypnotize both prey and predators alike. When used for such purposes, their bodies do not light up uniformly. Instead, glowing patterns emerge that captivate and mesmerize other creatures that see them. Such creatures are interesting. They seem so removed from the natural world with which we are familiar that they appear alien. And if these creatures can make their home in depths of 4,877 meters (16,000 feet), one must wonder what types of creatures live in depths greater than 9,144 meters (30,000 feet).

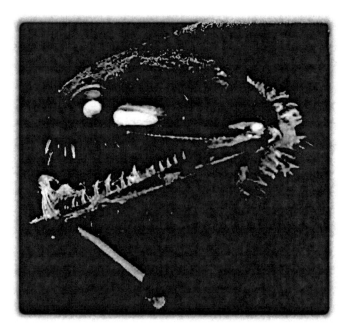

9. This deep-sea fish, called Photostomias Guernei, uses a built-in, bioluminescent flashlight.

Besides the aforementioned creatures, they are likely much larger animals that reside in the deepest oceans. Tales of sea-dwelling dragons can be found all over the world. They are especially common in Chinese and Japanese historical accounts. Although many chalk up such tales to myth, the stories themselves are probably historical in nature. This can be deduced from numerous factors, such as the inclusion of dragon teeth and bones in medicinal recipes. It is clear that the ancient Chinese used items for medicinal purposes that they believed came from the bodies of dragons. In addition, sightings of dragons or other types of sea monsters continue today. Such sightings have taken place in the twentieth century, and unidentified large creatures that resemble dragons have been spotted in the Indian, Pacific and Atlantic Oceans. These stories might sound bizarre to individuals who view dragons as mythological beasts alone. However, the term dragon was applied to many large creatures — living dinosaurs that were thought to have been extinct. These creatures include the plesiosaur, which was thought to have become extinct sixty million years ago, until a Japanese angler caught one in the area of the Pacific Triangle in 1977. Similarly described creatures have been seen in waters off the coast of Alaska, and in large lakes all over the world, including Lake Erie, Lake Okanagan, and Loch Ness.

Besides the plesiosaur, the coelacanth is another creature that supposedly became extinct more than sixty million years ago. However, they have been seen and caught in the Indian Ocean and in various parts of the Pacific Ocean. Berlitz posited, "Perhaps the plesiosaur and the coelacanth, as well as other living fossils, were shielded from the theoretical Cosmic Ray Extinction of Cretaceous times by living in or adapting to the ocean depths."[11]

10. Plesiosaur Skeleton (New Walk Museum, Leicester, UK)

11. Artistic reproduction of Ogopogo, the "monster" of Lake Okanagan (British Columbia), based upon witness accounts. It is believed that this creature is a plesiosaur.

12. Coelacanth Model
(Houston Museum of Natural Science, Houston, TX)

This is a logical assumption. When disasters ravished the surface of the planet, creatures headed to more hospitable zones. These areas, called *refugia*, are safe places that sustain life. When the planet's surface was riddled with ice, sea creatures with bodies that could withstand a high-pressure environment in the ocean depths would have descended. Typically, we think of such deep areas as cold and dark, but there are some locales in which undersea volcanoes constantly erupt, thus providing heat and limited light. If creatures can withstand the pressure, these areas might seem like palaces. We know that smaller creatures can live in deep oceanic areas, creatures like bioluminescent cephalopods, which live alongside prehistoric looking fish.

They find comfort in areas of the ocean in which others cannot survive. It is therefore likely that larger creatures can survive in even deeper water. They might spend their entire lives in the deepest trenches. There they mate, give birth, and then die, with no one on the surface ever knowing of their existence. This is probably the most common lifecycle of these creatures. It is a rarity when one of them surfaces for unknown reasons, perhaps looking for food when the seabed supply has waned. These large creatures likely live together with other unknown creatures in the deepest parts of the world's oceans. There are approximately 50,000 kilometers (31,000 miles) of convergent plate margins, most of which are located in the Pacific Ocean. Trenches exist along such margins, some of which are miles deep.

The Mariana Trench, for example, is nearly eleven kilometers (seven miles) deep. Other trenches of similar depth include the Tonga, Kuril-Kamchatka, Philippine, Kermadec, Atacama, and the Japan Trench in the Pacific. The Atlantic has one trench that is almost as deep: the Puerto Rico Trench, with an average depth of almost ten kilometers (six miles). Many other trenches exist that are not as deep. There are also four ancient oceanic trenches. One is the Intermontane Trench, located between the Intermontane Islands and North America. Others are the Insular Trench and the Farallon Trench, both located in Western North America, and the Tethyan Trench, which is south of Turkey, Iran, Tibet and Southeast Asia.

Any creature that escaped extinction and continues to exist relatively unnoticed by surface-dwellers likely lives in such deep trenches. If technologically advanced creatures also wish to remain unknown, they would similarly hide their craft in such places. Adding support to this notion are the numerous reports of unidentified craft entering and leaving bodies of water in which large sea creatures have also been seen. There is another reason such locations would be favorable to advanced creatures. Energy sources are located near venting sites within the trenches.

Fluids escape from subduction zones along plate boundaries. This fluid is primarily composed of water, but also includes dissolved ions and other organic molecules like methane. Methane is abundant in deep oceanic trenches. It typically remains in a solid form similar to ice (called methane clathrate) that breaks down over time. The destabilization of this solid form adds to global warming. However, it is also a potential energy source. (Many believe that the top-secret Aurora aircraft, mentioned in the previous chapter, is powered by methane.) Other energy sources are also accessible in these areas. Underwater volcanism provides geothermal power, and subduction zones in deep trenches release large amounts of electromagnetic energy due to the tremendous pressure on rocks there. Intelligent beings that need energy may make use of such prolific and potentially powerful sources.

Their location in underwater trenches has an added benefit: they can remain unseen while repowering their ships. They could even establish underwater cities there powered by methane, geothermal, or electromagnetic energy that would remain unknown to surface-dwelling creatures. We can imagine such nonhuman-piloted craft hidden on ocean floors or embedded in caves and crags in trench walls, watching large, prehistoric creatures swim past their windows. Unfortunately, we cannot verify this hypothesis, as human beings do not yet have the technological advancements needed to explore such regions. We can only make educated guesses based upon the existing evidence. Intelligent beings may very well reside in some of the deepest trenches on the planet. And although we cannot get down there to see such a spectacle with our own eyes, their existence causes side effects that humans can see and feel, sometimes with tragic consequences. Pockets of gas escaping from the ocean depths have destroyed boats and ships. One ship, which experienced this phenomenon yet survived, reported the event. Gas bubbles burst against its hull, making a large noise like an explosion while nearly capsizing the vessel. It was later determined that a deep-sea underwater volcano had erupted directly beneath the ship.[12] If gas bubbles released in undersea volcanic activity can cause such damage, underwater power plants, designed to harvest energy from two or three different sources, would cause more devastation. Destruction is commonplace in the Bermuda and Pacific Triangles. Not surprisingly, these areas contain two of the planet's deepest oceanic trenches.

The Bermuda Triangle

Both the Bermuda Triangle and the Pacific Triangle are mysterious areas, although neither of them can properly be called a triangle. The so-called Bermuda Triangle, also known as the Devil's Triangle, refers to an area of water approximately 805 square kilometers (500 square miles) in size, which is located between Florida, Bermuda, and Puerto Rico. The Pacific Triangle is sometimes called the Dragon's Triangle or the Devil's Sea. It is located between Japan, Guam, and Taiwan, and strangely, it is the same size as its counterpart in the Atlantic: 805 square kilometers (500 square miles). To people in the West, the Bermuda Triangle is, without doubt, the most infamous. Countless ships, boats, and airplanes in the area have gone missing.

Such vessels have disappeared all over the world. Things like rogue waves, freak storms, attacks by pirates, and even human error might account for most missing vessels. However, such occurrences in the Bermuda Triangle are often accompanied by other strange phenomena. Pilots flying through the area have reported things like luminescent clouds, a complete malfunction of instruments, missing time, or impossible speed variations. One famous case of missing aircraft had been briefly mentioned in the introduction to this text. It involves five torpedo bombers that flew out of Fort Lauderdale

Naval Air Station in Florida on December 5, 1945. Experienced pilots, who had life jackets, inflatable life rafts, and other safety equipment operated each plane. Before heading out, each plane was inspected and found to be in perfect working condition. They headed into the air at approximately 2:00 P.M. They intended to fly approximately 257 kilometers (160 miles) east into the Atlantic, then turn north for 64 kilometers (40 miles), before returning. At 3:35 P.M., the base received the first radio communication from one of the pilots. He said the following:

> Calling tower this is an emergency... We seem to be off course... We cannot see land... (Repeat)... We cannot see land." Asked by the tower for their position, the astonishing reply came back: "We're not sure of our position. We can't be sure just where we are. We seem to be lost." Advised by the tower to head due west, the even more astonishing reply came back: "We don't know which way is west. Everything is wrong... strange. We can't be sure of any direction. Even the ocean doesn't look as it should."[13]

After radio silence that lasted for about a half hour, a different pilot radioed the base. He said, "We don't know where we are. We think we must be about 225 miles northeast of base... It looks like we are..."[14] This is the last thing anyone ever heard from these pilots. They truly disappeared. Within minutes, two rescue planes headed out in search of the missing aircraft. It headed to the last known location of the five planes, and kept in constant radio communication with the tower for the first 15 minutes. Then, people at the tower asked the pilot for an update and received no response. They tried multiple times, but still received no response. Alarmed, they alerted the Coast Guard, which sent another plane to scout the area. He reported no sign of any of the airplanes, and found that the ocean and the sky were clear and calm. After this report, the Navy joined the Coast Guard in a search for the missing pilots. They continued all night, but found no trace of them. An aircraft carrier was called in, and all 30 planes aboard were dispatched to assist in the search. While this was going on, search parties on land looked for wreckage. Other boats and planes also helped. In all, more than 20 seafaring vessels and 300 planes aided in the search. But it was to no avail. Nothing was ever found. The disappearance is still a mystery.

In the last 35 years, more than 120 planes have disappeared while in the area known as the Bermuda Triangle. Many pilots reported flying through something that can be described as electronic fog. It has this name because it seems to affect the proper functioning of electronic devices. In 1980, a pilot headed from St. Thomas to Miami. Hours after takeoff, he reported that he was just off the coast of Miami. He told the tower that he was disoriented because of the unusual clouds in the sky, and his equipment was no longer functioning properly. His engines too were cutting out. He said he was running out of fuel and going down. This confused the tower, because the sky was cloudless. It was a clear day, and those on duty could not see the plane at all. After this initial call, there was radio silence. The pilot had truly disappeared without a trace. Then, eleven hours later, something remarkable happened. A radio tower 966 kilometers (600 miles) from Miami received a call from him. He said he was approximately 10 minutes away, and wanted clearance to land. They granted it, but he never arrived. He was never heard from again.

Only one pilot experienced this same phenomenon, yet survived. Pilot Bruce Gernon, who first coined the term "electronic fog," traveled through a cloud that resembled a tunnel. He believes something inside the cloud allowed him to time travel. He stated:

> There are still many unanswered questions. I realized that I had experienced something that no one had ever done [sic.] before. The radar controller was yelling as loud as he could that he had an airplane directly over Miami Beach. Now I look at my watch, and we had only been flying for just over

30 minutes. [The flight should have taken an hour.] There was a rip or cut in the fabric of time. Everything sort of had an electricity to it. That is when I thought of [the term] electronic fog.[15]

It is unknown what this phenomenon is, whether an atmospheric condition or something truly inexplicable, but it might be the cause of all of the missing airplanes in this area. If so, what causes it? Some think there is a connection between this singularity and unidentified submerged objects. The Bermuda Triangle, besides a graveyard of the Atlantic, is also a UFO and USO hotspot. Countless craft have been reported in the skies above, and inexplicable lights have been seen beneath the water's surface. There may be a connection between such otherworldly craft and missing airplanes and ships.

There also could be a reason why UFOs and USOs commonly appear in this area. A military research facility exists in this location called the Atlantic Undersea Test and Evaluation Center (AUTEC). It was initially created as a U. S. and British submarine testing facility, but today, it is likely used for the testing and evaluation of experimental vessels. It has been called the Area 51 of the seas. Some even think that crashed UFOs have been brought to this location for further study. This could explain the high percentage of sightings in the area. However, UFOs and USOs seem to be generally interested in military endeavors. They are commonly seen exploring military facilities and transports. They are especially common around nuclear facilities. There may be a connection between this military base in the Atlantic and sightings of inexplicable objects.

The constant activity of UFOs and USOs may also be the cause of the so-called electronic fog, which is thought to be responsible for downing airplanes. Besides affecting aircraft, this fog also might have caused the disappearance of many seafaring vessels. Many ships and boats have gone missing in the area. In the last 35 years, more than 700 boats and ships have been lost.[16] Some of them left no trace — no clues as to what might have happened. One of these unfortunate ships was the *U. S. S. Cyclops*, a 542-foot Navy cargo ship headed to Baltimore, which disappeared in 1918. It was last seen off the coast of Barbados in perfect condition. Hours later, it disappeared along with its crew of more than 300 people. Like other disappearances in this area, there was no distress call.

Sometimes, the reappearance of ships is stranger than their vanishing. Some of these cases, which will be shared next, are creepy. They seem like mysteries taken directly from shows like *Twilight Zone* and *X-Files*, only they are completely true. To this day, most of the mysteries involving this area have not been solved. Sometimes, ships were reported missing, and search parties found no clues as to what had happened. Weeks or even months later, the ships reappeared and seemed to work perfectly. However, all those aboard were missing.

One example of this involved the *Mary Celeste*, a large ship about 31 meters (100 feet) in length and weighing approximately 280 tons. In 1872, it brought alcohol from New York to Italy. It did not travel alone. Another ship called the *Dei Gratia*, captained by David Morehouse, set out behind it. The *Mary Celeste* traveled for approximately 18 days, with the *Dei Gratia* following behind. At a point between the Azores and Portugal, Morehouse noticed that the ship's canvas was shredded. It was swaying listlessly over the ocean waves. He pulled up beside it, and called to those on board. There was no response. Therefore, he launched a boarding party.

Everything was silent on deck. They searched the quarters, and could find no sign of any person, living or dead. Checking the logbook, they found a chart that indicated the ship had passed the Azores 10 days earlier. There was no sign of a struggle aboard, and there was ample food and water. The standing rig was also in working condition, but all of the small boats were missing, and the wheel was left unsecured. The chronometer, sextant, and some other important papers were also missing. The captain and crew have never been found, this case remains a mystery.[17]

This unsolved mystery is not unique. Many ships were found in similar condition. In some cases, there was no sign whatsoever of crewmembers, but the animals aboard, (such as dogs), remained. They were alive and healthy.   It is difficult to surmise rational explanations for what could have happened. Typically, there were no storms or rogue waves reported, and the ships themselves were in working order. It is unknown what would force a captain and his crewmembers to abandon their ship.   And even if they had abandoned ship for some reason, why was there no sign of their bodies, their emergency boats, or anything else they might have brought with them? It is truly a puzzle.

In rare cases, people aboard these mystery ships have contacted others before disappearing forever. The *S. S. Ourang Medan* was not in the area of the Bermuda Triangle or even the Pacific Triangle when something strange occurred, but considering the circumstances might help us to understand this seemingly inexplicable occurrence better. It was going to Jakarta, Indonesia through the Straits of Malacca, near Sumatra, when it began issuing S.O.S. calls. Other boats in the area headed out toward the ship, and the *S. S. Ourang Medan* continued to repeat its calls for help. Soon, the distress calls stopped. There was a moment of silence followed by this eerie message: "All officers including captain dead, lying in chartroom and on bridge… Probably whole crew dead."[18] A series of indecipherable symbols followed this message. It was as though the crewmember was attempting to convey some sort of message via Morse code but no longer had the ability to do so. However, a moment later he issued one final message: "I die."[19]

This story already sounds like something right out of a horror movie, but believe it or not, it gets even stranger. Rescue vessels located the ship within a few hours.   It seemed to be in good condition, but no one aboard answered when called. The rescue workers boarded the ship and found the captain and all of the crewmembers dead. The captain was on the bridge, and other bodies were found in the wheelhouse, the chartroom, and on the deck. Another was in the radio room. According to a document called the *Proceedings of the Merchant Marine Council*, "Their frozen faces were upturned to the sun. The mouths were gaping open and the eyes staring."[20] A dog on the deck was in a similar condition, its lips drawn back exposing its teeth.[21]

The rescue party discussed the situation on the deck, and they decided to tow the ship back to shore. Before they had a chance to, however, a huge fire that had apparently begun beneath deck blasted through the hold. Smoke spilled out across the deck and into the sky, and flames stretched out as far as they could to claim anything in their path. Unable to stop the fire, the rescue party left the ship and returned to their own vessels, where they could safely observe the destruction from a distance. After they had left, the boilers exploded, jolting the ship onto its side and then pulling it down into the deep. What transpired aboard is still an unsolved mystery.

Such stories naturally spark the imagination, and numerous theories have been proposed to explain such occurrences. Unfortunately, we might never know what happened to ships like this. The Bermuda Triangle is quite possibly the most dangerous area in the Atlantic, but it might not be the most dangerous on the planet. Its counterpart in the Pacific, called the Devil's Sea and the Dragon's Triangle, is even more treacherous.

The Pacific Triangle

The oldest name for this area is the Dragon's Triangle. It stems from a legend that a great dragon lives under the sea at this location. From time to time, it emerges to take possession of boats on the surface. People in ancient times concocted this story to explain countless missing boats and unusual lights. For thousands of years, people have reported strange, unidentified objects flying out of the water in this area. The objects have almost crashed into ships and airplanes, and they might be responsible for the large number of missing boats, ships, and planes. Since World War II, over 1,500 vessels and hundreds of aircraft, both civilian and military, have disappeared without a trace in the Triangle.[22] Since 1949, an amazing 632,000 tons of boats and ships have disappeared, leaving no indication whatsoever of what had occurred.[23] More than 1,200 individuals who were on board likewise vanished.[24] It is unknown what really happened to them, although they are all presumed dead.

Hundreds of other pilots, ship captains, and crewmembers have reported strange occurrences while in the Pacific Triangle. These include instrument malfunctions and missing time. In other words, the strange events in the Pacific Triangle are the same as those that occur in the Bermuda Triangle. The only difference is that such events are more common in the Pacific. Boats and airplanes have been moved far off course by inexplicable means. In addition, ghost ships have been reported alongside unidentified, subsurface lights.

13. Yureisen (Ghost Ship) by Hokusai

Ghost ships are unusual, and real witness reports have been used as fodder for fictional horror stories. They are large phantom-like ships floating at sea that randomly appear and then disappear without a trace. The ships seem like they are in working order, but have no signs of human beings aboard. How an entire crew might disappear without a trace is unknown. It is such an unusual phenomenon that people who see the ships are terrified. Some readers unfamiliar with these reports might instantly dismiss witness statements as fictionalized tales. However, a large number of ghost ships, sometimes weighing more than 1,000 tons, have been spotted in the area. For example, on June 11, 1881, a British ship encountered a legendary ghost ship called the *Flying Dutchman*. A prince aboard, who later became King George V, wrote about the encounter in the ship's log. He wrote:

> The Flying Dutchman crossed our bows. She emitted a strange phosphorescent light, as if a phantom ship all aglow. She came up on the port bow where also the officer of the watch from the bridge saw her. But on arrival, there was no vestige or any sign whatever of any material ship to be seen either near or right away to the horizon. The night became clear, and the sea calm.[25]

Similar to cases in the Bermuda Triangle, some boats and ships were discovered floating listlessly with no signs of human beings. In rarer cases, dead bodies were aboard; there were no signs of a struggle, nor had anyone aboard radioed for help, despite the fact that the radios worked. In 1989, a Japanese whaling ship approached a small fishing boat moving erratically through the Triangle. The captain's dead body was found aboard, but there was no sign of any crewmembers.

Another bizarre case occurred in 1989. A whaling ship was traveling north of Ogasawara Island when crewmembers spotted a sailing vessel headed toward it. The ship continued on its course, expecting the ketch to veer off course to avoid impact. However, the sailboat continued toward the ship, and they almost hit it. They stopped and called out to those aboard, but received no response. Tying the ship to the sailing boat, they boarded and found something disturbing. Berlitz described the scene:

> They found that the helmsman was a partially decomposed corpse, half standing and loosely fastened to the wheel. He appeared to have been dead for several weeks prior to the time that the crewmembers of the whaler came aboard. No other members of the dead man's crew were found, although the ketch should have had a crew of four or five.[26]

The body was skewered by a cutlass, and the scabbard was on the deck next to a single word written in blood: depths. The men who found it alerted the Japanese authorities, who looked into the case, but no explanation was ever proffered. There are several other similar cases, in which dead crewmembers were found aboard ships and boats in unusual positions — scenes reminiscent of movies like *Pirates of the Caribbean*. However, such cases in the Dragon's Triangle are rare. When something strange happens to ships in the area, they are usually not found; nor are any crew members found. Instead, they simply vanish.

A Japanese pilot disappeared during World War II, which is not saying much by itself, since Allied Forces shot down many planes. However, this pilot contacted his commander right before his disappearance, and did not mention any enemy aircraft. His message was strange. He sounded confused when he reported, "Something is happening to the sky...the sky is opening up —."[27] This was the last thing anyone ever heard from him.

Many other planes have disappeared in the area after this, and since they vanished without indications of what happened and during peaceful times, the disappearances cannot be attributed to enemy fighters. For example, a KB-50 with a crew of eight vanished on a routine flight between Wake Island and Honshu (Japan's main island) in 1957. There were no distress calls, and no wreckage was ever located. That same year, other U.S. planes likewise disappeared, including a JD-1 Invader and a C-97 U.S. military transport with 67 people aboard. The former did not attempt to radio base. The last radio transmission received from the latter occurred when the transport was approximately 322 kilometers (200 miles) off shore. They reported that weather conditions were good and there were no problems.

Submarines have also disappeared in the Pacific Triangle, most of which were either nuclear powered or carrying nuclear weapons. Since 1968, thirteen submarines have vanished. Some were recovered from the ocean bottom, but others disappeared over the deepest areas of the Triangle, so they could not be salvaged. A few of them definitely malfunctioned, and in one case, an internal explosion occurred. However, the majority of these submarines were disabled by unknown means. And it is only assumed that their wreckage is on the ocean floor. This information cannot be known for sure. The only statement that can be made definitively is this: submarines, like planes and ships, have disappeared in the Pacific Triangle, and it is unknown what caused their disappearance.

The most common type of maritime disasters in this area is the disappearance of ships. In 1975, the 227,912-ton *Berge Istra* disappeared over the Mindanao Trench. Just before it vanished, the captain contacted his wife and told her that everything was going smoothly. The weather was fine, the sea calm. A short time later, the ship was gone and only two of thirty crewmembers were ever found. They were above the deck painting when the incident occurred, and they were knocked off the ship and into the sea. They were not sure what caused this, or what happened to the ship and the other crewmembers, although they had heard some kind of explosion. Investigators looked into this possibility, but an exploding ship would have left wreckage. Something would have been found floating on the water's surface, but nothing was ever found.[25] Strangely, the *Berge Istra's* sister ship, *Berge Vanga* similarly disappeared without a trace in the same area three years later.

Often, none survive such events, but the *Berge Istra's* fate is not unique. Another disappearance in which there were some survivors was the *Bolivar Maru*. Before the ship vanished, it reported problems. A hatch was damaged and water was pouring in. This did not seem like a matter of life and death to those aboard, and the crewmembers gathered their belongings and important papers. The two survivors described what happened next: they heard a noise like an earthquake, and the ship instantly broke up and began to sink. When a rescue ship arrived shortly thereafter, the two men were seen treading water. There was no sign of anything else.

Other than these two cases, there have been no survivors of vanished ships. When the *Derbyshire*, a 169,000-ton British ship run by a crew of 44 people disappeared, there were no distress calls. It just vanished. Likewise, the *California Maru* disappeared along with three other large ships in 1969, and the *Sofia Pappas* vanished in 1970 along with the *Andrew Demades*. The disappearance of the *Kaiyo Maru Number Five*, a Japanese research vessel, is perhaps the most famous case, as it was in the Triangle investigating the disappearance of other vessels. On September 24, 1952, the ship was conducting research to determine if some sort of atmospheric phenomenon was to blame for missing boats, ships and airplanes. Unfortunately, the crewmembers may have learned firsthand what was happening.

The ship vanished. There were no distress calls. She just disappeared, along with nine scientists and twenty-two crewmembers. Like most other disappearances, search teams did not find any flotsam. Today, a shrine in Tokyo honors the missing. The disappearance of the *Kaiyo Maru Number Five* is similar to the disturbing event that happened seven years earlier in the Bermuda Triangle, when five naval planes disappeared. The next plane that went to investigate also vanished. No trace of any of them was ever found. When rescue planes and ships disappear while searching for other vessels that had previously vanished, it indicates that there is a real and threatening phenomenon at work in these areas. Just what this phenomenon is has not been adequately investigated. A theory needs to be proposed that takes into account all uncovered evidence.

Pilots and ship captains have reported traveling impossible distances in a short time while in the Pacific Triangle. Others move way off course without knowing what caused the deviation. Some people have even reported missing time. When they look at their clocks, they realize hours have passed, even though it only felt like seconds; they have no idea what occurred during the missing hours. People who claimed to have been abducted often report this missing time phenomenon. Sometimes, they see clocks literally roll backward.

The unusual phenomena reported by Pacific Triangle survivors include UFO or USO sightings. In the West, witnesses historically described such objects in religious terms, calling them angels or other similar creatures. Alternately, witnesses described them as supernatural or mythological creatures. It is only in modern times that the same phenomenon is described in terms of extraterrestrial beings. In Japan, a similar thing occurred. Today, many would describe these objects in terms related to alien-piloted spacecraft, but in the past, they described such sightings differently. They thought that the lights, which emerged from the ocean and flew up into the sky, were either dragons or demons. It appears that UFOs and USOs have been sighted all over the world for as long as human beings have been in existence. Sightings in the Bermuda Triangle and the Pacific Triangle are simply more common.

One important sighting occurred in 1981. A 165-foot ship called the *Taki Kyoto Maru* was approximately 322 kilometers (200 miles) off the coast of Kanazawa. More than thirty crewmembers were aboard. The sky was clear and the ocean was calm. Those aboard saw an unidentified glowing object emerge from the water, and the ship nearly capsized due to the turbulence caused by its appearance. The object was more than 15 meters (50 feet) in diameter. It hovered over the ship and instruments aboard instantly malfunctioned. The compass spun erratically, the radios would not work, and even the engines cut out. According to witnesses, the UFO slowly circled the ship for 15 minutes. Then, it dove back into the water, and the wake it created was even more violent than the previous one. The crewmembers braced themselves, and they waited for the turbulence to end. Once it had, the instruments aboard began to function again. This was when they noticed another anomaly. The times indicated by the crewmembers' watches compared to the time shown on the ship's instruments indicated that some time had inexplicably disappeared. They had lost 15 minutes, the same amount of time that the UFO had circled the ship.

There had been so many reports of UFO and USO sightings in the area that the Japanese government sent out one of its most technologically advanced research vessels to investigate. The *Kaiyo Maru* was the largest ship in the Ministry of Agriculture's fleet. It weighed 2,500 tons, and it attracted the attention of USOs and UFOs. Unidentified craft emerging from the seas have often been seen inspecting large vessels. They seem especially curious about ships carrying nuclear weapons. The *Kaiyo Maru*, although not carrying a nuclear arsenal, was a highly advanced research vessel. In 1984 and 1986, the captain and crewmembers reported that unidentified craft followed the ship. A scientist aboard, Mr. Naganobu, described what occurred. In December 1984, he was just south of the Falkland Islands, off the coast of South America, when he saw approximately 24 UFOs in the sky. He described them as floating lights. They were together and relatively motionless. Then, they suddenly split up, traveling in three distinct directions. In 1986, those aboard the *Kaiyo Maru* saw more UFOs, only this time they were in the Dragon's Triangle. Witnesses saw a large, cylindrical-shaped craft about 30 meters (100 feet) in diameter. It had a small red light that blinked intermittently. The craft approached the ship and then dove underwater. It appeared on radar while it was in the air, and the occurrence was reported in the Japanese edition of Scientific American magazine in September 1988. Although the government's findings were reported, exactly what the craft are and where they come from was not discussed. No theories were proposed.

Considering the evidence, it seems clear that UFOs congregate in both the Bermuda and Pacific Triangles. Individuals from different countries have proposed theories to explain why. One theory involves visitors from other planets that use naturally occurring magnetic anomalies as directional indicators. Other similar hypotheses have also been proffered. However, sometimes the simplest explanation is actually the most logical. Perhaps the pilots of these craft actually live underwater in these locations.

There have been near misses just outside of the Dragon's Triangle, when USOs quickly emerge from underwater and almost hit both commercial and military airplanes. In many of these cases, the pilots had to take immediate action to avoid being struck. In some of these cases, the craft were not seen emerging from the water first. They emerged from clouds, traveling at incredible speeds toward airplanes in flight. One famous near miss occurred in Ikeda. A pilot witnessed a UFO and had to take evasive maneuvers to avoid contact. He reported this to the tower, and the tower in turn informed other pilots to be on guard, as a UFO was in the immediate vicinity. Another incident occurred on March 8, 1965. A pilot reported that an unidentified cylindrical object was quickly approaching his jet while he was over the Triangle. He made a quick turn to get away from it. The object also seemed to maneuver to avoid a collision. It stopped midair. Then it repositioned alongside the airplane and traveled beside it. The pilot reported that he was being tailed by an unidentified flying object. According to his description, it was 15 meters (50 feet) long and surrounded by a greenish glow. Several witnesses from the ground confirmed his description. The UFO kept up with the aircraft for a prolonged period before breaking away and heading back towards the Triangle.

If these unidentified craft are piloted by intelligent beings, it is unlikely that they would intentionally head toward other aircraft at incredible speeds. The near misses are likely not intentional. It seems that pilots of UFOs and USOs are occasionally blinded by outside conditions. When leaving the ocean, and while flying through clouds, their vision is obstructed, just as it is for human beings. Some pilots who made evasive maneuvers to avoid crashing into these objects watched them as they continued on their way. Many of the craft headed toward the Dragon's Triangle. Others were seen actually entering the water. It is as though they were going home.

Perhaps the creatures that pilot these objects *were* returning home. And maybe they have lived in this location for hundreds if not thousands of years. One of the earliest UFO stories is found in Japanese historical literature. It is called *utsurobune*, which translates to "hollow ship." According to the story, a woman who lived under the sea traveled to the surface in a metallic craft hundreds of years ago. Witnesses described the craft and even drew pictures of it. They resemble reports of modern UFOs and USOs. The craft was oval-shaped with various windows, and it came ashore at a beach called *Hiruto no Hama*. Witnesses approached and peered inside. They saw an apparent human woman wearing light-colored clothing. The interior walls were decorated with some sort of unknown writing, which was described as hieroglyphic.

14. Woodblock carving of Utsurobune by artist Nagahashi Matajiro (1844)

15. Another carving of the Utsurobune event by artist Kyokutei Bakin (1825)

Other evidence indicates that Japan is, and has always been, a hotspot for UFO and USO sightings. In modern times, airline pilots and ship captains have been warned when such craft are seen in order to avoid collisions. Interactions with unidentified flying or submerged objects are also described in Japanese historical texts. One of these took place in 1180. A glowing object resembling an "earthenware vessel" flew through the sky.[28] Other unidentified lights in the sky that traveled in unnatural ways were likewise reported in 1235. The samurai general Toritsune ordered an investigation of lights that were circling his encampment. Those responsible eventually returned with an unlikely explanation: the wind was moving the stars.[29]

Other evidence that pilots of UFOs and USOs have been seen throughout Japanese history include humanoid figurines carved by individuals in northern Japan during the Jomon Period (14,000 –

300 B.C.E.). Called *dogu*, the carvings depict creatures that look human, but have large heads and eyes. Some of them also appear to be wearing helmets, goggles, and pressurized suits or diving apparel. If the time of their creation were disregarded, most people would think that they were artistic representations of astronauts or deep-sea divers. The truth is, these may be both; they are quite possibly representations of creatures that pilot UFOs — creatures that call the Pacific Triangle home.

16. Dogu Figure from Aomori, Japan

17. Dogu Figure from Tokyo National Museum

18. Dogu Figure from the Musée Guimet (Paris, France)

Other ancient societies have created similar figures, such as the *kachina*, carved by Hopi Native Americans in the U.S. Southwest. Some figures wear helmets or goggles, like the Japanese dogu.

Others have large heads, large eyes, and unusual facial features that resemble descriptions of extraterrestrials by alleged abductees. The Hopi themselves claim that these images are representations of deities and spirit beings, but it is unknown why they are represented in such ways. According to White Bear Fredericks from Kykotsmovi, AZ (Third Mesa), these portrayals have been passed down from ancient times.[30] The reasons behind the way they are depicted have been lost and are now unknown. If one were to take these figurines out of context in time, they look like pilots of either aircraft or seacraft. The truth is, the Hopi's kachina and the Japanese dogu, like similar representations from other cultures all over the world, likely document actual creatures that have piloted advanced craft through the water and the sky.

Figure 19   Figure 20

Examples of Kachina figures,
representations of the ancient Hopi gods

Figure 21   Figure 22

Figure 23

More examples of Kachina, carved by the Hopi

Other representations of pilots, wearing helmets and other technologically advanced clothing, are found in petroglyphs all over the world, including the American Southwest. Some found in Arizona at the Canyon de Chelly, and at locations like Palatki and Honanki show humanoid figures with unusual devices attached to their heads. Others, found near Moab, in Canyonlands National Park, and Dry Fork Canyon, (all three sites are in Utah), depict humanoid figures with large, box shaped heads. It seems like they are wearing masks. The one in Canyonlands National Park, located at Barrier Canyon, for example, depicts a figure with unusually decorated clothing that has a large misshapen head; it is shaped like an upside-down eggplant. The face has large dark spots for eyes that are inlaid with smaller, white circles. Beneath these are two lines like vents that may be used in some sort of breathing apparatus. Other petroglyphs found nearby in Sego Canyon also show figures wearing masks that have large circular goggles and extensions like antennae protruding from their heads.

24. Petroglyphs at Barrier Canyon

25. Petroglyphs at Sego Canyon

Such evidence will be described more fully in subsequent chapters. At this point, however, it is important to note that UFOs and USOs have been seen for hundreds, if not thousands of years. Historical documents, along with carvings, drawings, and other artistic representations demonstrate that pilots of these craft have been interacting with human beings for all of recorded history. If so, it is likely that these creatures do not come from distant planets. It is probable that they are here on Earth. (Some previously described witness accounts support this conclusion; for example, abductee Filiberto Cardenas stated that he was greeted by one particular creature that said it was from Earth.) If so, where could they be? Looking at witness reports, there is an undeniable connection between such UAPs and large bodies of water.

Underwater Bases

Evidential analysis makes it impossible to deny a connection between unidentified flying objects and oceans. These craft clearly spend more time underwater than flying over it. This connection has caused some researchers to theorize that extraterrestrials have established bases in some of the deepest oceans. Some also believe that there are extraterrestrial bases in large lakes. However, there is no reason to assume the intelligent beings that use these locations are from another planet. The scientific community as a whole has a hard time buying into the idea that such craft are piloted by extraterrestrials. And based on our limited understanding of technological capabilities, creatures cannot travel back and forth between their home planets and Earth on a regular basis. Based on our current scientific understanding, even one trip would be impossible. However, the UFO phenomenon is a real thing, and it cannot be dismissed as nonsense.

It is difficult for anyone, no matter how skeptical, to believe that there are no unidentifiable aerial and aquatic craft piloted by intelligent beings. No one with a basic understanding of this phenomenon's history could think that they do not exist. The important question to be answered is, "Where do they come from?"

The overwhelmingly popular opinion is that these craft come from another planet, and that they are piloted by aliens — being who live on this other planet. Some have proposed that they reside on planets in this solar system, and that they remain hidden in apparently inhospitable zones that seem devoid of life. However, these beings are quite at home traveling through the water-filled planet Earth. Water is the basic building block of life on this planet. Oceans make up the majority of the planet's surface. Lakes and rivers make up more. Even the skies are filled with water, and all planetary creatures, including human beings, are primarily composed of water. Human infants are approximately 86 percent water, and as they age, this number decreases slightly. Based on our limited human understanding, water is a necessary building block. Without it, life could not flourish. Yet there are no similar habitats on other planets in this solar system.

New research has revealed that the planet Mars may have once had an atmosphere that was similar, if not exactly the same as Earth. McKay wrote, "Four billion years ago, Mars was a warm and wet planet, perhaps teeming with life. Spacecraft orbiting Mars have returned images of canyons and flood valleys — features that suggest that liquid water once flowed on the planet's surface."[31] So it is possible that these beings once inhabited the now red planet, and that they moved to the more hospitable planet Earth when their atmosphere began to fade. If this theory were true, these beings would have been on this planet for at least millions of years. This is possible. However, given the major cataclysmic events that have led to mass-extinctions, and the regularity of smaller yet world-changing events, (which will be discussed in more detail in subsequent chapters), this possibility is unlikely. In addition, if they had been here for so many years before the development of human beings, it is likely that some evidence of their homes and edifices would have been found.

26. What Mars once looked like

Let us explore this possibility a bit more. Let us assume the situation was reversed — that our planet was in trouble and that Mars had a suitable environment in which we could continue to live. If the atmosphere of Mars were once the same as it is on Earth now, the creatures that lived on its surface would be similar to those that live on Earth. Of course, there would be some differences; the human counterpart might look different, and of course, technology and language would have likely developed differently. However, if an intelligent civilization did reside on Mars, they would have had cities and transportation systems like those that we have today on Earth. If the situation was reversed and we moved to a nearby planet that had a similar atmosphere, it would only be a short time before we created cities and towns. We would also create streets for cars and airports for aircraft. In a short period, the new planet would become home. And even if there were worldwide disasters that led to the extinction of human beings, some evidence of our once having been there would still exist. It might be buried deep underground, or covered by miles of water, but it would exist. If Martians did in fact relocate to Earth in the distant past, there would be some evidence of their existence, and water would not cover all of it. This is because, based on analyses of how known creatures behave, they would not have instantly sought refuge in the deepest oceans. Rather, they would have established homes along the shores. If they had established such homes, it is likely that we would have found some evidence of their existence.

This holds true unless the creatures who pilot UFOs and USOs are much different from human beings. If their natural environment is in water, then they may have headed into the oceans upon entering Earth's atmosphere, without even considering the possibility of residing on solid land. However, if these creatures naturally breathe water and not air, it is probable that their exploratory ships would be filled with liquid. The pilots themselves might also use water-filled suits, which would approximate the environment in which they are most comfortable. As previously mentioned, we must be cautious when considering the testimonies of individuals who claim to have been abducted. But even if only some of them are truthful, these creatures do not breathe water. They seem to breathe air, just as we do.

Of course, there are creatures that live in the oceans yet breathe air, creatures such as dolphins and whales. In addition, there are sea creatures with gills that naturally breathe water, but can spend long periods outside of it. Therefore, it is still possible that these creatures choose to live in the water, as this environment is biologically natural. However, an analysis of UFO and USO reports, along with eyewitness testimonies in which both the interior and exterior of craft were described in detail, makes this an unlikely possibility. If such creatures came from Mars, they would have initially made homes on dry land near shores, just as modern humans continue to do. Permanently moving into a high-pressure environment in the deepest oceanic trenches would have resulted from a desperate situation. Such a move would only have been undertaken if there were no other options. There is seemingly no evidence whatsoever of the pilots of these ships once inhabiting the surface of this planet, so the theory of them being Martian refugees is unlikely.

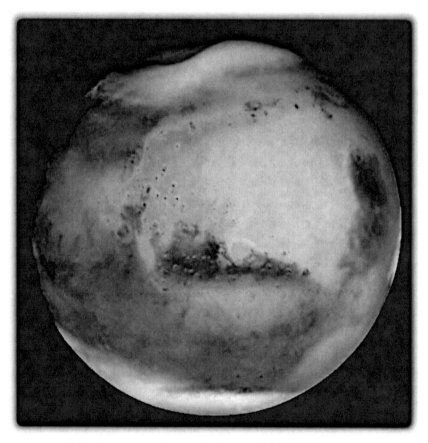

27. Mars seen through the Hubble Telescope

There is another problem with this theory. Although Mars may have had an environment similar to that found on this planet four billion years ago, Earth was different. It was devoid of life. Although it will be discussed in more detail in subsequent chapters, at about this time, there was no water or oxygen on the planet, and toxic gases covered Earth. The planet had only been recently created, approximately four and a half billion years ago, and it was regularly hit by cosmic debris. It was a turbulent place, not suitable for life as we know it. Considering that beings on Mars would have needed the same atmosphere that we have here now, the Earth would have been inhospitable.

Even if we skip forward in time to the Triassic Period, 245,000,000 to 208,000,000 years ago, the Earth had one large landmass called the Pangaea supercontinent. This period ended with a mass-extinction event that, put delicately, rocked the world, changing it forever. Other periods followed, such as the Jurassic Period (208,000,000 to 146,000,000 years ago) and the Cretaceous Period (146,000,000 to 65,000,000 years ago). Both of these periods ended with mass-extinction events. The Cretaceous Period saw the end of the dinosaurs as the continents continued to pull apart, becoming more recognizable as the globe we know today. It is unlikely that such creatures could have survived these tumultuous times without leaving any hint that they had not only been here, but are still here with us today. It is therefore probable that they did not come from Mars.

Assuming they did not come from Mars in the distant past, some might look to other planets outside our solar system. If they come from another galaxy, they had to have traveled more than two-million light-years to get here. Even traveling at the speed of light (300 kilometers per second or 186 miles per second), it would still take them two million years to arrive. This is unlikely. And although we could be wrong, all scientific knowledge makes this theory unlikely if not downright impossible. Even traveling from a distant star in our own galaxy is improbable. The nearest star is Alpha

Centauri. Let's assume for a moment that they resided on a planet circling this star. If they traveled 1,609,344 kilometers (one million miles) per day, it would still take them 70,000 years to reach Earth. This is hardly a minor trip, and unless they made use of hibernation devices or some kind of rip in the space-time continuum, it would not be possible. Even if they did have some kind of hibernation device, they would not be traveling 70,000 years just to pop in, look around, and then turn around and go home. If they made such a trip, it would be for the purposes of relocating permanently. However, all of this is highly improbable.

The scientific community is overwhelmingly skeptical when it comes to the possibility of aliens visiting this planet. Brigadier General José Carlos Pereira explained this:

> I'm a man devoted to science, a man with a scientific mind. If you present the hypothesis that extraterrestrials may be here and may be doing things that we can't understand, your idea runs contrary to conventional scientific reason. As far as we know, our own solar system does not contain life on any planet except Earth. I'm basing my ideas on knowledge that we have today, achieved by science as it currently understands the universe. This is the caveat to be considered. If we assume only current knowledge, I am forced to reject every possibility of anyone coming from outer space to Earth. And it gets more complex if we go further, because Alpha Centauri, the nearest star, does not seem to have a planetary system. We moved them to the portion of the universe astronomers call the "inhabitable zone," which is many light years from Earth.[32]

Of course, it is possible to theorize that our limited knowledge of the space-time continuum is wrong, and that such creatures could make their way here on a regular basis. However, it is important to seek out the most rational explanation for a phenomenon. Only after considering and then dismissing rational theories based on evidence unearthed should we move on to theories that are more outlandish. Sometimes, the best explanation is the simplest one. If these creatures do not come from another planet, then they must come from this one. They must be residents of Earth, just as we are. And it is only natural that we have not seen their homes. Human beings, with their limited knowledge, have only explored approximately three percent of the world's oceans. We lack the technology to probe the deepest parts. Such worlds are alien to us. The creatures found in extremely deep water display characteristics like bioluminescence, which again makes them appear alien. However, such creatures are not alien. They are Earthlings. The pilots of UFOs and USOs, although seemingly outside our realm of understanding, might also be Earthlings.

If they live in the deepest oceans, they can live peacefully without interference by human beings. Humans by nature are violent creatures, constantly killing not just other species, but also each other. It seems that for as long as human beings have recorded historical events in texts or through pictures, there have been unidentified flying objects. And although these craft have observed human beings possibly for millennia, it is only in recent times that interaction between these objects, their pilots and human beings has increased. The largest rush of witness reports occurred during World War II, when submarines first began exploring the deep, and nuclear power was rediscovered. The awesome power of nuclear energy might make such creatures curious. It might worry them. Perhaps for this reason they have emerged, and for years, they have been seen near nuclear-powered submarines, aircraft carriers, and other nuclear testing facilities on land and in the sea.

Human beings are careful to avoid predatory animals in the wild. This is a matter of safety. When such animals begin to encroach on human developments, they are seen as a threat to safety. Action is taken to protect the humans who live therein. If these creatures have watched human beings for millennia, they know that we pose a threat to their safety. UFOs have been attacked while flying over military airspace in various countries. From their perspective, human beings are violent and unfriendly creatures. It is only natural that they would want to avoid us. So far, our technological capabilities prevent us from exploring the depths of the seas. But maybe our baby-steps over some oceanic trenches have alerted these deep-sea creatures. For this reason, they are appearing more frequently, especially in areas like the Bermuda and Pacific Triangles.

A thorough analysis of the evidence, coupled with what we know about scientific and technological capabilities, points to the extraordinary conclusion that UFO and USO pilots are not aliens. They live on this planet, as they have for thousands of years. It is likely that they have been on this planet longer than modern human beings have existed. They have most likely been here for more than 14,000 years. Some evidence to support this theory is found underwater.

3. Underwater Cities

Underwater Homes of UFO and USO Pilots

Unidentified ships piloted by unknown entities have been seen entering and leaving large bodies of water all over the world. If UFOs truly wish to remain hidden, it is logical that they would head into the deepest parts of the world's oceans. At such locations, they could establish bases, even small cities, and remain completely undetected. Human beings are not technologically advanced enough to completely explore oceanic trenches. As our technology advances, we might develop the capability to explore such areas. Even then, the discovery of bases might prove difficult. After reviewing hundreds of UFO sightings, it becomes clear that at times, these craft are visible, but other times they seem to disappear. Witnesses report seeing airships that are stationary for up to 15 minutes. Then, the craft fly away quickly, moving out of sight. Other reports indicate that witnesses perceived the craft as disappearing.

Obviously, disappearing is not the correct word. They might seem to disappear to observers. But we all know from magic shows that the hand is quicker than the eye. Human vision cannot always detect fast motions, so is possible that these craft simply move too quickly for human beings to follow their movement. These craft also have the ability to blend into the background; they are able to camouflage themselves and thus hide. Many creatures on this planet have similar abilities, such as the octopus. It can change its skin color and texture to blend into the background. Cuttlefish likewise change colors and even the shapes of their bodies to blend into the surrounding environment. They back their bodies into holes in coral or rock, and then change the color and shape of their tentacles to blend seamlessly with seaweed swaying in the ocean current. Although modern human beings are only beginning to explore such technology, it is likely that UFOs and USOs have been built using biological, rather than mechanical, principles. If so, they have the ability to camouflage themselves.

UFO and USO witnesses have described craft as semi-transparent and at times luminous. Sometimes they appear to change shape while in the sky or underwater. Other deep-sea creatures have such powers. In the darkest areas of the sea, some creatures, including cephalopods, create their own light. They are bioluminescent, and they use this skill either to avoid attacks by predators or to coax prey toward them. The similarities between abilities of deep-sea creatures and capabilities displayed by unknown craft piloted by humanoids provide more evidence that such craft originate from the oceans' depths. Such capabilities are also put to use in the sky, (which also has high water content).

Sometimes, UFOs appear on radar. Other times, they remain hidden, like the U.S. military's use of Stealth technology. This technology makes use of specific materials in the creation of both air and seafaring vessels. It also makes use of natural, yet specific, contours. The shape of jets and newer submarines makes them nearly invisible to radar. UFOs and USOs, whether built with mechanical or biological principles, (or a combination of the two), have the ability to remain hidden, just like military craft that make use of Stealth technology. For this reason, even if we had the ability to explore the deepest ocean trenches thoroughly, we still might have difficulty locating craft or bases, if they exist.

USOs have been seen in shallow water. Octopi are also sometimes visible. When their cloaking device is engaged, however, both USOs and octopi alike disappear. From witness reports, we can deduce that USOs burrow into lakebeds and seafloors. Many witness reports described craft entering lakes at high speeds. The water continued to gyrate at the entry point. In time, mud from the bottom surfaced. When search parties set out to find the craft, nothing was found. It is likely that UFOs and USOs burrow themselves into mud and sand under bodies of water to hide more completely from potential danger.

They may have learned a lot from sea creatures. Their technology may be based upon the biological principles of sea creatures adept at hiding, thus providing the ability to change color and shape to camouflage themselves. Observing the behavior of small fish, crustaceans, and cephalopods that burrow into sand or hide between rocks and corals may have helped the pilots of these unidentified craft to develop superior concealment techniques. These two behaviors, put together, make such craft nearly impossible to find.

Some might think this theory of UFOs and USOs concealing themselves in oceans and deep lakes makes sense when referring to small craft. But larger craft have also been described. Some witnesses have reported that large, so-called "mother ships" were over a mile in length. It would seem more difficult to hide a ship that size underwater. However, if vessels were able to hide in plain sight, in many ways it would be easier for a larger ship to do so. Let us assume for a moment that the giant USOs did not make use of any kind of cloaking device, but simply burrowed into the ocean floor, so that only the top half of them were visible. The sheer size of the objects would make their appearance on sonar unlikely. They would appear as raised portions of lakebeds or sea floors. Thus, they could truly remain hidden in plain sight. This ability, coupled with cephalopod-like concealment skills, would make any sized ship nearly invisible to human beings.

UFOs, USOs, and underwater bases may exist in some of the deepest oceanic trenches; two of which are located within the infamous areas described in the previous chapter: the Bermuda and Pacific Triangles. Other lakes are also potential sites, as numerous UFOs and USOs have been spotted nearby. One is Lake Titicaca, the highest navigable lake in the world, which is located on the Peruvian and Bolivian borders. This lake has a surface elevation of more than 3,658 meters (12,000 feet), and a surface area of 3,232 square miles (5,201 square kilometers). The deepest parts of the lake are more than 274 meters (900 feet), and the average depth is about 107 meters (350 feet).

Numerous islands are in Lake Titicaca. On the Bolivian side are Suriqui, Isla del Sol (Island of the Sun), and Isla de la Luna (Island of the Moon). The Isla del Sol is off the coast of the tourist town Copacabana, and it is one of the lake's largest islands. The majority of its inhabitants are farmers, but they also fish. More than 180 ruins are on the island, and numerous archaeological sites are in the surrounding water. A local legend holds that the Incan Sun God was born at this location.

Other islands on the Peruvian side of the lake include the Uros, which is a collective term used to describe numerous man-made islands. An indigenous pre-Incan population called the Uros initially made them. They headed out into the lake to get away from attacking Incans, and they built large islands by tying reeds together to make a floating platform, then adding layers of reeds across the top. The houses and other community structures are also built using nothing more than reeds naturally found in the lake. Many of the Uros islands have an empty space in the center, which they use for fish cultivation. Sometimes, they also use this space to raise guinea pigs, which they eat. Island inhabitants who do this, so they always have meat, create a smaller island with a small home in which they guinea pigs can nestle, and then they float it on the water. They tie this tiny island to the larger island on which they live. By simply pulling on the rope, they can access the guinea pigs when needed.

The Uros headed into the lake and built these islands to escape from death. Eventually, word reached them that the Spaniards had defeated the Incans. Assuming that they were now safe, the Uros headed back to shore. They quickly realized, however, that these invaders were even worse than the Incans. As soon as they learned how dangerous these foreigners were, they returned to Lake Titicaca, where they have remained ever since. Today, families continue to live on these islands, but they have opened them to tourists. They knit blankets, make necklaces, and create other art to sell to visiting tourists, and they use this money to send their children to high school on the mainland.

28. The Uros Islands

Visitors who head into Lake Titicaca from the Peruvian side will first see the Uros islands after about 30 minutes of travel. If they continue toward the center of the lake, they will eventually come to other islands that are completely inhabited by indigenous populations like the Quechua and the Aymara. Amataní is home to about 4,000 people who speak Quechua. No machines are allowed on the island, so there are no cars. There are a few small stores, a health clinic, and several schools. Many of the homes do not have electricity. There are no hotels, and visitors are not welcome unless they arrange tours through licensed guides affiliated with the indigenous residents.

Taquile is another island in Lake Titicaca that has been virtually untouched by modern technology. It is inhabited by an indigenous tribe known as the Taquile, hence the island's name. They also speak Quechua, and like Amataní, visitors cannot just show up. Those who arrange visits using a tour company based in Puno can see pre-Incan ruins on the island's highest parts. In the main village square, at an altitude of 3,950 meters (12,959 feet), they can see natives dancing in brightly colored clothing. The Taquile make all of their own clothing, and due to their textile art, they were named a "masterpiece of the oral and intangible heritage of humanity" by UNESCO. The island's women weave and make yarn, and the men alone knit.

29. Taquile Islanders

30. Taquile Islanders

31. Lake Titicaca, Peru

Few buildings on the island have electricity, and almost none of the homes do. Therefore, islands like Taquile in Lake Titicaca are perfect locations for stargazing. The natives often report seeing much more than stationary stars in the sky. This area is a UFO hotspot, and strange lights are often seen moving across the sky, or diving down into the cold, deep lake water. For this reason, there might be an underwater base at the lake bottom, at a depth of approximately 274 meters (900 feet). Other things of interest at the bottom of this lake include an ancient submerged temple. Archaeologists discovered an underwater road near Copacabana. They followed it toward the lake's center, eventually finding a huge temple that is 201 meters (660 feet) in length. The structure's age is unknown.

Lake Titicaca, besides a UFO hotspot, also hides some missing pieces of human history in its depths. Many locations thought to hide USO bases also hide ancient ruins. It is almost as though there were a connection between the two — a connection between ancient underwater ruins and UAPs. One famous and controversial site is near the Pacific Triangle off the coast of Japan. It is called the Yonaguni Monument.

The Yonaguni Monument: Japan's Underwater Pyramids

Often referred to as Japan's underwater pyramids, the Yonaguni Monument is a large complex of underwater ruins. Located near the southern tip of the Ryukyu archipelago, it is approximately 120 kilometers (75 miles) off Taiwan's eastern coast. Marine geologist Masaaki Kimura from Ryukyu University has been diving in the area and mapping the site for more than 15 years. He found ten structures off the Yonaguni island coast, and another five related structures off the Okinawan coast. The total area of the ruins spans approximately 300 meters by 150 meters (984 feet by 492 feet).[1]

Local diver Kihachiro Aratake initially found them while looking for the breeding ground of hammerhead sharks. On one of his dives, he came across underwater megaliths. He saw what appeared to be a step pyramid, and to him the ruins looked like a ceremonial structure. They resembled similar structures found on the mainland. Kimura believes that the underwater structures are the ruins of an ancient and possibly unknown civilization. "The structures include the ruins of a castle, a triumphal arch, five temples, and at least one large stadium, all of which are connected by roads and water channels and are partly shielded by what could be huge retaining walls."[2] In addition, he has found quarry marks left in the stone megaliths, sculptures of animals, and even what appear to be pictographs and ideographs etched into stone structures. Toru Ouchi, associate professor at Kobe University, supports Kimura's conclusion. "I've dived there as well and touched the pyramid," he said. "What Professor Kimura says is not exaggerated at all."[3]

32. A structure known as "the turtle" at the underwater Yonaguni Archaeological Site

Kimura partially recovered animal monuments and characters from the site in his laboratory. An analysis of these figures leads him to believe that the culture that created them comes from the Asian continent. One example, which he describes as an underwater sphinx, is a carving that resembles a Chinese or ancient Okinawan king. The largest structure in the entire complex is the step pyramid, and it is this structure that has led to the site being referred to as Japan's underwater pyramids. Kimura said, "The largest structure looks like a complicated, monolithic, stepped pyramid that rises from a depth of 25 meters (82 feet)."⁴

33. Another area of the Yonaguni Monument, Japan

Graham Hancock dove at the site many times, and he describes it in his book *Underworld: The Mysterious Origins of Civilization*:

The first anomalous structure that was discovered at Yonaguni lies below glowering cliffs off the southern shore of the island. Local divers call it Iseki Point (Monument Point). Into its south face, at a depth of about 18 meters, an area of terracing with conspicuous flat planes and right angles has been cut. Two huge parallel blocks weighing approximately 30 tonnes each and separated by a gap of less than 10 centimeters have been placed upright side-by-side at its north-west corner. In about 5 meters of water at the very top of the structure there is a kidney shaped 'pool' and nearby is a feature that many divers believe is a crude rock-carved image of a turtle. At the base of the monument, in 27 meters of water, there is a clearly defined stone-paved path oriented towards the east. If the diver follows this path — a relatively easy task, since there is often a strong west-to-east current here — he will come in a few hundred meters to 'the megalith,' a rounded 2 tonne boulder that seems to have been purposely placed on a carved ledge at the center of a huge stone platform. Two kilometers west of Iseki Point is the 'Palace.' Here an underwater passageway leads into the northern end of a spacious chamber with megalithic walls and ceiling.[5]

The majority of scholars who dive the site return to the surface with the conclusion that the submerged objects have been made by human beings. This presents a problem for some closed-minded individuals, as the existence of this structure counters the known history of the world as presented in textbooks and taught in schools. If the pyramid, temples, arch, and stadiums were all created by human beings, then they must have been created when they were still on dry land. The last time these structures were above water was approximately 10,000 B.C.E. Many scholars claim that there were no advanced human civilizations at that time. For this reason, they state that they have been naturally formed.

Dismissal of Anomalous Finds

Many people are unwilling to consider evidence that is contrary to their pre-existing beliefs. This is especially true with some mainstream archaeologists and historians, who make a living off their assumptions. To admit that everything they know about history is quite possibly wrong is frightening. It takes a strong person to do such a thing. Most humans do not like to question their pre-existing beliefs. They live more comfortably without doubt. Therefore, historical accounts that answer every possible question are preferred. Anyone who is open to the idea of advanced civilizations during the last Ice Age will have no doubt that human beings created the monument at Yonaguni. Only those unwilling to question their pre-existing beliefs instantly dismiss it as something naturally formed. In other words, before even seeing the site, some will say it is a natural formation. This is a common human trait. They will do everything they can to fit anomalous evidence into their own preconceived notion of how the world works and what happened throughout history. Unfortunately, some have taken this a step further.

The Hypogeum is a large, mysterious site in Malta. Mainstream historical accounts place the construction of this stone structure to the Neolithic period, which began approximately 10,000 B.C.E. However, among the pictographs painted on the walls in red ochre was another in black manganese dioxide pigment. This depiction of a bison-bull contradicted the existing Maltese and world historical accounts, as its features were not Neolithic, but Paleolithic. This means that the entire structure must have been created before 10,000 B.C.E., before the end of the last Ice Age. Since there was no known culture capable of building this monument at that time according to mainstream accounts, it posed a serious threat to the generally accepted history of the planet and the development of humankind.

How was this dealt with? The former Director of Museums in Malta had it scrubbed off the wall.[6] "The result was the destruction of scarce physical evidence which potentially contradicts teachings about Malta's prehistory that are at the heart of the Orthodox world view."[7] Unfortunately, the destruction of artifacts that threaten prevailing belief systems is widespread. Another case of such appalling archaeological destruction occurred in the United States. In 1898, a farmer in Solem, Minnesota unearthed a 200-pound stone while clearing his land. He dug up the roots of a 30-year-old Aspen tree, exposing the stone. The tree's roots had grown around it. On closer inspection, he realized that the flat face of the stone was covered in runes. Not knowing anything about them, he called in some experts to examine it. It turned out that the inscription was medieval Swedish. It read:

> Eight Götalanders and twenty-two Norwegians on reclaiming, acquisition journey far west from Vinland. We had a camp by two [shelters?] one day's journey north from this stone. We were fishing one day. After we came home we found ten men red with blood and death. Ave Maria. Save from evil.[8]

On the side of the stone are these words: "There are ten men by the sea to look after our ships. Fourteen day's journey from this island. Year 1362."[9] As soon as this was translated, people who had never seen the stone nonetheless dismissed it as a hoax. They believed that they could not be wrong, (that their pre-existing beliefs could never be wrong), and that there was no way that anyone from Götland could have been in the Americas in 1362. As far as historians were concerned, no outsider reached the Americas before 1492, when it was discovered by Christopher Columbus, lost on his voyage to India. However, experts who examined the stone confirmed its authenticity.

34. The Kensington Rune Stone

"Independent testing by Newton Horace Winchell, a geologist at the Minnesota Historical Society, confirmed that the weathering on the stone's exterior indicated that its inscription was approximately 500 years old."[10] He claimed this in 1910. It was not until the twenty-first century that more advanced technological examination methods were used to confirm or debunk the stone's medieval origin. Scott Wolter conducted the modern examination:

> He began by using photography with a reflected light microscope, core sampling, and a scanning electron microscope. These tools revealed unmistakable signs of subsurface erosion requiring a minimum of 200 years to develop. In other words, the Kensington Rune Stone was buried for at least a century before Olof Öhman excavated it. Further examination of each individual rune through a scanning electron microscope revealed a series of dots engraved inside three rings for the letter "R." These dotted runes, never before noticed on the stone by anyone, have only been found in one other place: fourteenth-century headstones in church cemeteries on the island of Götland, off the coast of Sweden. The Kensington Rune Stone is inscribed with a fourteenth-century date, and its text cites eight crewmen from Götland. No less crucially, Wolter pointed out, "the rare, medieval rune called 'the dotted R' was not known to modern scholars until 1935, yet it occurs on the Kensington Rune Stone, found in 1898. Interpretation: The presence of 'the dotted R' indicates the Kensington Rune Stone inscription could only have been carved during medieval times.[11]

One would think that Mr. Wolter's discovery, which confirmed the conclusions of other experts that Norse explorers were in the United States 130 years before Columbus arrived, would have made newspaper headlines. One might think that historians would be excited by the idea of an unknown chapter in American history. However, the opposite occurred. Some ignored his claims, stating that such a thing was not possible: they cited the lack of carbon dating to verify the claim.

Wolter analyzed the stone's weathering patterns along with the runes themselves to date the monument. Since the stone was initially buried and protected by tree roots, carbon dating would have been possible. However, Newton Horace Winchell's initial determination, that the date of the stone was accurate, was so problematic that some overzealous historians took action to prevent such dating. The directors of the Smithsonian Institution scrubbed the entire stone with kerosene, removing all original dirt and roots, thus making carbon dating impossible. "Preservation of the artifact's original condition was crucial in affirming the authentic circumstances of its controversial discovery, something Smithsonian Institution scientists would have fully understood."[12]

The aforementioned cases are only cursory examples of a widespread desire to maintain one's existing notions about the nature of reality. People as a whole do not like change, and they therefore fight to keep hold of the illusion that they are omnipotent. Historically, people who thought outside the box were tortured, imprisoned, or even killed. At one time, it was common knowledge that the Earth was flat, and anyone who suggested otherwise was not just considered stupid, but heretical. The same is true regarding the nature of the solar system, history is a whole, and every other element of culture — those things that make us who we are.

The leaders of the early Roman Catholic Church shaped their own past. They eliminated documents that did not support what they were teaching, and they made it a crime to have contrary opinions. One example involves the history of Jesus of Nazareth. Various accounts describe him traveling extensively through Asia. For some reason, the Church determined that promulgation of this belief would undermine their authority. They therefore told their members that the destruction of any document that ran contrary to its teachings was a meritorious deed.[13] Hanson explained:

> By the second century C.E., the Church of Christ was destroying every piece of evidence of the life of Christ that did not support its doctrines, and the Church continued its purging with more or less fervor throughout the succeeding centuries. The activity continued at the turn of the twentieth century when the very question of Jesus's travels as a young man was raised first by Notovitch. Different Church authorities destroyed documents at the Himmis Monastery and later documents at the Tun-huang caves in central Asia. At stake throughout the centuries was the critical Church doctrine that Christ was a Jew who started his own religion as the Son of God. Any evidence not supporting this view was condemned as "apocrypha" and destroyed or rewritten. Even the four gospels were rewritten to provide the impression that Jesus never left Judea.[14]

The truth is, much of the history that people unquestionably accept to be true might not be. Rather than assume that we know what happened on this planet, we would be far better to remain open-minded. And if we truly view unusual archaeological finds with open minds, we will see evidence of advanced human civilizations that existed before the end of the last major glacial period.

Submerged cities are everywhere. Hundreds of cities have been discovered underwater in the Mediterranean. Others are found in various parts of the world, yet such discoveries are not controversial. It is common knowledge that cities and towns have been flooded by great storms, tidal waves, and other natural disasters. But the Yonaguni monument off Japan's coast is significant and controversial because of the date of its creation. Its existence, and many scholars' claim that human beings made the structure, forces a rewrite of history. However, if scholars began rewriting historical texts, there is so much that is unknown that full sections of textbooks would be empty. Either that, or statements would be added to tell (student) readers that certain parts of planetary and human history are unknown. This is a scary thing for historians to admit, and it is a difficult thing for publishers to keep in the texts that they publish. They generally edit such things out, as they edit out anything that might be considered controversial. For such reasons, books like this one in your hands will never be mainstream. They will be considered divisive or simply preposterous, and the majority of people will never seriously consider the ideas proposed within.

It is suggested that readers check out pictures of the Yonaguni monument online to make up their own minds. A great collection of these photographs are assembled at this site: http://www.tumblr.com/tagged/yonaguni. I suggest reviewing these pictures, and the conclusions of Masaaki Kimura, Toru Ouchi, and others, before rendering an opinion. The majority of people who dive this site believe that it was made by human beings. And since the site has been submerged for the last 12,000 years, it must have been made prior to 10,000 B.C.E. This is not the only structure found underwater that disrupts the prevailing understanding of world history. Another structure off the coast of India must have also been built more than 10,000 years ago.

The Legendary City of Dwarka

Dwarka is an ancient city that was swallowed by the sea. Also written as Dvarka, Dwaraka, and Dvaraka, it is mentioned in various historical and religious documents, including the *Mahabharata*, *Harivansha*, *Skanda Purana*, *Vishnu Purana*, and the *Bhagavata Purana*. In many cultures, it was commonplace to combine historical and religious texts. The Old Testament, for example, combines religious and mythological elements, such as the creation of humankind, with actual historical events. The New Testament does the same. In Japan, the Shinto texts *Kojiki* and *Nihongi* provide a historical record of the country's emperors, but the tales begin in the Age of the Gods. This combining of historical and religious teachings has sparked debates. Some believe everything in such texts. Others believe nothing, since even historical elements are tainted by mythological or religious overtones. Most pick and choose what they wish to believe based upon their pre-existing ideas of what is logical and what is not. As an example of this unusual phenomenon, take the writings of Marco Polo (1254-1324), the Venetian merchant traveler who traveled through Asia and recorded his adventures in a book. He described many places and events, which the majority of people believe as historical fact. However, he also described an island called

Andaman in the Bay of Bengal. He described the inhabitants of this island as having the heads of dogs. Many simply disregard this one statement as fiction, yet accept everything else he wrote as nonfiction. Selective beliefs plague many cultures because of the combination of historical and religious motifs.

Until recently, many people regarded Dwarka as a legendary city. Today, it is a city in Gujarat, India, but the name was also applied to an ancient city. Called Dwarawati in Sanskrit, it was one of the seven oldest cities in Indian history. According to legend, Dwarka was a city built by Lord Krishna. Krishna, according to Indian religious beliefs, is the Supreme Personality of Godhead. Although many outsiders claim that he did not exist, (just as some claim that Jesus did not exist), Indian tradition holds that he was an actual person who lived approximately 5,000 years ago. Based upon scriptural analyses, he was born c. 3228 B.C.E. and died c. 3102 B.C.E. During his life, he supposedly created a large city called Dwarka. A man named Vishwakarma built it according to Lord Krishna's specifications.

**35. Lord Krishna playing the flute
(Painting by Indischer Maler, 1740)**

On the western shores of Saurashtra, an ancient, holy city called Kususthali had once existed. Kususthali had been destroyed before Krishna was even born, but he wanted Dwarka built in the same location as this pre-existing, sacred city. The land near Saurashtra was reclaimed, and the city was built on the Gomati River shore. It had six sectors, encompassing both commercial and residential zones, which were connected by wide roads. The city had squares, plazas, and palaces, and the residents lived at ease due to public utilities. Public meetings were held in a place called Sudharma Sabha, and the city had a large harbor. Indian historical texts state that the city had 700,000 palaces, which were decorated with silver, gold, and precious stones. It also had beautiful gardens adorned with flowers and containing lakes. Dwarka is described as a paradise.

Like Kususthali before it, Dwarka also met its end. Approximately 36 years after the Mahabharat War (3138 B.C.E.), Krishna's disciple Arjuna headed to the city to bring Krishna's grandchildren and the Yadava wives to a place called Hastinapur for safety. After leaving, the city was swallowed by the sea. Arjuna's description of what occurred has been recorded in the Mahabharata:

> The sea rushed into the city. It coursed through the streets of the beautiful city. The sea covered up everything in the city. I saw the beautiful buildings becoming submerged one by one. In a matter of a few moments, it was all over. The sea had now become as placid as a lake. There was no trace of the city. Dwaraka was just a name; just a memory.[15]

The Vishnu Purana also describes the destruction: "On the same day that Krishna departed from the Earth, the powerful darkbodied Kali Age descended. The oceans rose and submerged the whole of Dwarka."[16] Because of the inclusion of some religious themes in tales about Krishna and his palatial city, many believed that tales about Dwarka were not historical. In addition, although stories of great deluges exist in the historical texts of many cultures, for some reason, human beings tend to disbelieve such tales of destruction. However, new discoveries have forced such disbelievers to rethink Indian history in its entirety:

> Ancient legends of Dwarka tell that the holy city was long ago entirely swept away by a great wave of water. This legend, disregarded by contemporary historians and archaeologists, has recently been given credence by findings of the new science of inundation mapping, which produces accurate models of ancient shorelines at specific dates. The legend has been given further support by oceanographic studies which have proven the existence of submerged temple structures off the coast of Dwarka.[17]

In 1983, the site was first discovered. Since then the Marine Archaeology Unit of the National Institute of Oceanography has been exploring and excavating the site, part of which is in an area presently called the Gulf of Khambhat. Artifacts discovered include stone structures, anchors, and wooden implements that were found at various depths. Numerous investigations took place between 1997 and 2001 before Murli Manohar Joshi, India's Minister of Science and Technology announced the discovery of the ruins on May 19, 2001. The main complex of structures is located approximately 9 kilometers (5.6 miles) off the coast of Gujarat at a depth of 40 meters (29.5 feet). Initially, researchers used acoustic technology to investigate the site. They also took pictures. After, they dove to recover artifacts. They also dredged for the same purpose. Many items, including pottery, were collected and sent to laboratories for carbon dating in Oxford, United Kingdom; Hannover, Germany, and more places. One piece of wood dated to 7500 B.C.E. This was the oldest artifact found, and due to its date, it has become highly debated. Other fishhooks and pottery shards dated to a less contentious period stretching from 1700 to 1400 B.C.E.

Among the submerged stone structures themselves, dates range considerably. Techniques like carbon dating do not work on stone structures. However, a simple yet reliable method narrows down the date of submerged ruins. Inundation maps reveal when certain areas of the sea floor were not submerged. Thus, although the date such structures had been created is not revealed, the era in which they were submerged can be determined. Looking at numerous submerged ruins off the coast of Kadaikadu and Poompuhur in the Bay of Bengal, some are located at depths of only 1 to 3 meters (3 to 10 feet). These are the most recent structures. They were on land approximately 2,000 years ago. Other areas were dated to approximately 3,800 years ago, between 1800 and 1700 B.C.E. The oldest structure was found at 23 meters (75 feet). Due to the depth of the water in which it was found, this site must have been used more than 11,000 years ago.[18] However, no known culture could have built such an object. For this reason, the discovery is highly controversial, like the pyramidal structures found off Japan's coast.

The Bimini Road

An underwater rock formation was discovered in 1968 near North Bimini Island in the Bahamas. It is often referred to either as the Bimini Road or the Bimini Wall. J. Mason Valentine was diving in water 5.5 meters (18 feet) deep when he noticed what appeared to be a road composed of rounded stones. He reported his discovery and archaeologists, geologists, and others later investigated. Initially, investigators thought that it was beachrock alone, and that the road-like structure had formed naturally. Then, some scientists who were exploring the Bimini site noticed that the beachrock was on top of other beachrock of approximately the same size, and that the two layers were separated with apparent balancing stones wedged between them. Of course, this does not occur in nature. Only humans could have built the road.

The largest of three linear features at the site, and the feature for which the site was named, is the road itself. It is 0.8 kilometers (0.5 miles) in length, and it stretches in a northeast to southwest direction. It has a pronounced curve at the southwestern end.

It consists of stone blocks measuring as much as 3 to 4 meters (9 to 13 feet) in horizontal dimensions with the average size being 2 to 3 meters (6 to 9 feet). The larger blocks show complementary edges, which are lacking in the smaller blocks. The two narrower and shorter, approximately 50 and 60 meters (164 and 197 feet) long, linear features lying shoreward of the Bimini Road consist of smaller tabular stone blocks that are only 1 to 2 meter (3 to 6 feet) in maximum horizontal breadth. Having rounded corners, the blocks comprising these pavements resemble giant loaves of bread. The blocks consist of limestone composed of carbonate cemented shell hash that is called beachrock. Beachrock is native to the Bahamas. The highly rounded nature of the blocks forming the Bimini Road indicates that a significant thickness of their original surface has [been] removed by biological, physical, and chemical processes. Given the degree that these blocks have been eroded, it is highly implausible that any original surface features, including any tool marks and inscriptions, would have survived this degree of erosion.[19]

Parts of this road are in shallow water only a few feet deep, but it stretches into the deep water of the Gulf Stream, 91 meters (300 feet) deep. If this road were truly built by human beings, then it might join underwater ruins. This road may have linked ancient, antediluvian cities. For this reason, many continue to explore the area, looking for remnants of the cities to which the road led. One of them may have been found within the area of the Bermuda Triangle, off the western coast of Cuba.

In 2001, Paulina Zelitsky discovered symmetrical stone structures while mapping the sea floor near Cuba. The structures were more than 670 meters (2,200 feet) underwater. It was too deep for human beings to explore. The next best thing, she and her research team sent down a remotely operated vehicle equipped with cameras, sonar equipment, and manipulators, which were controlled from the surface. The information obtained revealed that the structures were composed of large, rectangular stones, one placed atop another. They are defined by ninety-degree angles, and appear to be divided by lanes or avenues. Some of the structures are shaped like pyramids. Others are circular. The majority of structures are composed of huge stones almost five meters (16 feet) in height and weighing several tons each. They are megalithic constructions. This was reported through various news channels:

> ADC has also been exploring a string of underwater volcanoes about 5,000 feet (1,500 meters) deep off Cuba's western tip, where millions of years ago a strip of land once joined the island to Mexico's Yucatan Peninsula. Most intriguingly, researchers using sonar equipment have discovered, at a depth of about 2,200 feet (700 – 800 meters), a huge land plateau with clear images of what appears to be an urban development partly covered by sand. From above, the shapes resemble pyramids, roads and buildings. ADC is excited but reluctant to speculate until a joint investigation with the Cuban Academy of Sciences and the National Geographic Society takes place early this summer. "It is stunning. What we see in our high-resolution sonar images are limitless, rolling, white sand plains and, in the middle of this beautiful white sand, there are clear man-made large-size architectural designs. It looks like when you fly over an urban development in a plane and you see highways, tunnels and buildings," Zelitsky said. "We don't know what it is, and we don't have the videotaped evidence of this yet, but we do not believe that nature is capable of producing planned symmetrical architecture, unless it is a miracle," she added in an interview at her office at Tarara, along the coast east of Havana.[20]

Thirty total structures have been found, which appear to be the remains of pyramids, roads, tunnels, and other edifices.[21] It is estimated that this city had been submerged more than 6,000 years ago.[22] Some believe that this structure was part of the legendary city of Atlantis mentioned by Plato in his books *Timaeus* and *Critias*. But there are many submerged cities and lost islands. The fabled continents of Mu, Lemuria, and others disappeared without a trace. Today, many do not believe they were real; they think they were mythological cities alone, devoid of historicity.

Underwater Ruins that Suggest a Global Flood

Historical accounts from multiple worldwide civilizations describe cities that were destroyed by great deluges. Other stories talk about complete islands or continents that the seas swallowed. Advanced civilizations of the distant past, including Atlantis, Mu and others are said to have been wiped out by massive floods, literally destroyed by the seas. Many consider such stories to be myths alone, but the evidence available indicates that many established civilizations *had* been destroyed by huge inundations. The names of certain civilizations have been carried to the present, but it is likely that many other civilizations were likewise destroyed by devastating floods. The pyramidal structures off the coast of Japan may be the remnants of the fabled continent of Mu. They may also be the remains of an ancient yet unknown civilization. The ruins off the coast of India, which many now believe was the city of Dwarka, where Krishna lived, are controversial because the oldest structures must have been created before the end of the last Ice Age, more than 10,000 years ago. For this same reason, the ruins off the coast of Japan are likewise contentious. Anything discovered that disrupts the prevailing theory will initially be considered controversial and possibly even mocked.[23]

In time, the existence of these underwater sites will cease to be controversial. Knowledge of them will be commonplace, and what is known about the history of humankind and the history of this planet will be updated and corrected. Besides the controversial underwater ruins, there are literally hundreds if not thousands of other submerged cities that had been destroyed by rising sea levels in the past. In the Mediterranean alone, there are more than 200 known sunken cities. Some of them, which have been discovered and excavated, are more than 7,500 years old, including a structure resembling a farmhouse that was discovered by Robert Ballard in the Black Sea, Turkey.[24]

The existence of these underwater structures, along with historical texts that describe the destruction of ancient cities by massive floods, lead to the conclusion that many unknown civilizations might have existed in the distant past — civilizations that were destroyed by worldwide or localized deluges. A true analysis of the historical and religious texts of many of the world's cultures indicates that the appearance of a destructive flood was not a singular event. Rather, there seems to be a cycle of creation and destruction. In other words, human civilizations become increasingly more sophisticated. After thousands of years, a natural disaster such as a worldwide flood strikes, destroying almost all evidence that such civilizations had existed. If this is true, our current civilization is not unique. It is just one of many that had existed before.

4. Cyclical Nature of Civilization

Many Worlds

The seas swallowed many ancient cities. Plato explained this in *Critias*:

> Many great deluges have taken place during the last nine thousand years which have elapsed since the time of which I am speaking; and during all this time and through so many changes, there has never been any considerable accumulation of the soil coming down from the mountains, as in other places, but the Earth has fallen away all around and sunk out of sight.[1]

A regularity of floods and other natural disasters have wreaked havoc upon living beings. Every so often, there is a mega-disaster: a natural disaster so catastrophic that it threatens to end all life on this planet. Science has confirmed this, but various civilizations' historical records first revealed it. Often, historical accounts blend with stories of gods and supernatural creatures, so sometimes it is difficult to separate the two. It is difficult to distinguish between historically factual stories and tales passed along to teach some moral or ethical principle.

Ancient civilizations considered them important enough to preserve forever, and they intended to pass the information to future generations. When reading stories that recount the beginning of the current civilization, a pattern emerges. It is clear that this world is nothing new or special. Rather, other worlds existed before this one, worlds that had been created and then destroyed, before this current reality began. Such stories are found in the sacred literature of various civilizations, including the Hopi of the southwestern United States.

The Hopi View of Creation and Destruction

The Hopi, located in northeastern Arizona, claim that they emerged from the Earth at the beginning of this current cycle of existence. "According to their own mythology, the Hopis [sic.] came into being when the people emerged from the Lower World through an opening in the Earth."[2]

They believe that this world is the fourth: that three other worlds had existed before this one. World history as told through Hopi legends is likely a blend of facts and myths. These they combined to convey historical occurrences that had affected humankind, but also to teach lessons to those who heard the tales. According to these legends, the First World did not contain humans as they would be recognized today. Instead, it contained some large, insect-like creatures that lived deep underground in caves. It is possible that they did not need oxygen.

These creatures did not understand the meaning of life, and they fought amongst each other. Their creator, Tawa the Sun Spirit, was displeased. He sent a messenger called Gogyeng Sowuhti (Spider Grandmother) to tell them that things had to change. Following Tawa's orders, she told them that they had to leave their underground homes and enter the newly created Second World. This they did. Led by the messenger, they traveled from the deep caverns that were previously their homes to other caves that were closer to the Earth's surface. The journey was long, and over time, their appearance changed. By the time they emerged into the Second World, they had evolved into furry creatures. Some had tails; others had webbed fingers. These newly evolved creatures could now survive in the new environment of the Second World.

In time, the Sun God grew unhappy once again, and he created a Third World. Again, the creatures were told to leave their old abode and head to the planet's surface. As they traveled, their forms changed again. Evolution took its course, and by the time they arrived in the Third World, they were recognizable as modern humans.

> The people made their villages. They planted corn. They lived on. They were in harmony, and they were grateful to the Sun Spirit who had created them and given them a new world to live in. Yet things were not perfect. There was a chill in the air, and the light was only a grayness. Spider Grandmother came and taught the people how to weave blankets and cloth to keep their bodies warm. She taught the women how to make pots out of clay so that they could store water and food. But the pots could not be baked and they broke easily. And the corn did not grow very well because warmth was lacking.[3]

An analysis of this legend so far reveals some startling facts — facts that have recently been confirmed by science. Numerous mega-disasters that caused mass-extinctions have plagued the Earth. These disasters, whether they brought fire or ice, lasted for long periods. The disasters of fire eventually ceased. The Earth's volcanoes stopped erupting, the ash eventually fell from the skies, and a new Earth that could sustain life once again emerged.

Likewise, huge glaciers that covered the Earth eventually warmed, and they broke apart into the oceans. These caused massive flooding, and many of Earth's landmasses were completely submerged. Eventually, these floodwaters subsided, the Earth continued to warm, and a new Earth emerged that could again sustain life.

In every mega-disaster that has taken place on this planet, there have been survivors. These survivors head to *refugia*: areas that can sustain life during such events. Some might emerge unchanged after the catastrophes, but for the most part, creatures that survive such events change. When they finally emerge again, they have evolved into a form more suited to deal with the new environment. There is a connection between severe climate change and evolution.[4]

The Hopi legends suggest this scientific understanding. The Sun Spirit tells creatures that their world is ending, and they must head to a new world. Because of the oncoming mega-disaster, they head to places in which they can survive. It takes them a great deal of time to get there, and once they arrive, they have to remain there for a lengthy period. They have to remain there until they are able to enter the new world — the world that emerges after worldwide disasters cease and the Earth's surface is once again inhabitable. When they emerge, however, they are not the same. They have evolved. In the First World, there were insect-like creatures. In the Second, there were mammals: creatures that had fur and webbed fingers and tails. In the Third, human beings appeared. Strangely, these perfectly match historical periods and the mass-extinction events that marked their endings.

There was a super-continent called Pangea during the Triassic Period (245 – 208 million years ago), which ended with a mass-extinction event. However, some reptiles and other creatures survived. The continents continued to separate during the Jurassic Period (208 – 146 million years ago), during which the dinosaurs ruled the planet. This period ended with a relatively minor disaster, and there was a partial extinction. At the end of the Cretaceous

Period (146 – 65 million years ago), the second largest extinction ever took place. This marked the end of the dinosaurs — the insect-like creatures to which the Hopi referred. According to the Hopi, this time is the First World.

After this disaster took its toll, mammals emerged. This took place during the Tertiary Period (65 – 1.8 million years ago). This is the Second World. According to mainstream ideas, human beings appeared approximately 100,000 years ago, and the earliest skeletons and fossils of humans came from Africa. Between 1.8 million years ago and 100,000 years ago, there were numerous natural disasters, including a massive ice age and other less extensive yet still catastrophic periods of glaciation. It is likely that one of these events triggered the emergence of human beings, which corresponds to the Hopi's Third World.

The Hopi do not stop their history in the Third World. They believe that we are currently in the Fourth World. In other words, after the creation of human beings, a mass-extinction occurred due to a mega-disaster. This likely led to the partial extinction of human beings and other creatures. After the disaster had ended, the surviving humans emerged into the Fourth World, and they repopulated the Earth.

Worldwide cultures consider flood stories historical. All the stories are about a flood of worldwide proportions that threatened to wipe out living things. In these accounts, some rode out the flood on rafts. Others made large vessels in which they saved not only humans, but also some animals and birds that they considered important. In other examples, humans found refuge on mountaintops, the only land exposed during the flood. (Some of these stories, and their connection to an actual flood, will be dealt with in more detail later in this chapter.) This flood was the last major disaster recorded in Hopi legends. When the waters subsided, human beings emerged from their refugia.

Land hit by massive tidal waves and submerged under salt water for an extended period would look disastrously different once the waters retreated. In addition, salt drying over the land would cause it to look desert-like. According to Hopi accounts, Pokanghoya and Polongahoya, two hero-gods, emerged into the Fourth World, and they looked around.

>Pokanghoya said, "Everything has a sameness. Something needs to be done."

>Polongahoya answered, "Yes, see how it is out there. The ground is soft. It is nothing but mud."

>So they took their buckskin ball and their playing sticks and began to play *nahoydadatsia*, following the ball wherever it went, running all the time. Wherever their feet touched the soft ground it became hard. They gathered the mud into great mounds and turned them into mountains. Wherever they passed, grass and trees came into being. They raced far to the north, and in an instant created Tokonave, meaning Black Mountain, which in later times the White Men called Navajo Mountain. From there they ran to the south, chasing their ball all the while, and created Neuvatikyao, which the White Men later named San Francisco Peaks. They went eastward then, making hills, mountains and mesas everywhere. They arrived at Muyovi, which the White Men came to call the Rio Grande, and near where the Zunis now live they created salt beds, and they also made salt beds at other places.[5]

If the mythological elements — the linking of natural changes to gods and spirits — are removed, we have an account of human beings emerging from safety after the last Great Flood had subsided. They emerged to find that everything had washed away. Everything looked the same, and there was neither grass nor trees. In addition, the ground, which had been underwater, was soft. It was mud. In time, the Earth hardened, and grass and trees appeared. The ocean salt accumulated in beds, and the Earth eventually returned to its former peaceful state.

The Hopi described what the flood did to the southwestern United States. It caused much greater devastation elsewhere, wiping out entire civilizations forever. However, the Hopi account is important because it provides information about the extent of the flood devastation in areas of the U.S. that are nowhere near the ocean. From what science has revealed, the Hopi's account is accurate.

Many Hopi customs indicate that they may have preserved some ancient knowledge not only of the cyclical nature of civilizations, but also of the technological advancements of earlier societies. In fact, the Navajo called them Anasazi. This term means "Ancient Ones," and it was likely used because the Hopi preserved historical knowledge that many other Native American tribes had lost. The Hopi are somehow connected to Native Americans in Mexico and Central and South American countries. This becomes evident by analyzing their creation stories. It is also immediately evident by a linguistic analysis. The Hopi of Arizona speak a Uto-Aztecan language. This is evidence of a cultural and historical connection to other civilizations in Central and South America. The beliefs of the Hopi, especially those that refer to a cyclical nature of creation and destruction, are similar to Aztec and Mayan beliefs.

The Beginning and End of the Mayan and Aztec Cycles

The Aztecs are bound to the Hopi. The languages they speak are both in the same linguistic families, and this familial relationship demonstrates their connection. Besides their languages, other similarities exist, including their beliefs in the cyclical nature of the world. Unlike the Hopi, however, the Aztecs believe that we are currently in the Fifth World, not the Fourth. They believe that four other suns had existed before this current sun. At the end of each age, the sun dies, and the emergence of a new sun is the beginning of a new age.

This story stems from the pre-Columbian Aztec civilization, but it is likely that they did not really think that new suns began a new age. Instead, the analogy between suns and the cycle of creation and destruction explains the phenomenon. Many of the world's pre-Columbian cultures worshipped a sun god. Therefore, this god affects anything that occurs in life, good or bad. For this reason, "sun" is synonymous with "god." The gods' names were used to label different eras, different cycles of existence. They are still used today to refer to units of time. Even in so-called modern cultures, like Europe and the United States, the names of gods are used to refer to times.

The days of the week, for example, immortalize Greek and Roman gods in Romance Languages. The Italian terms lunedì, martedì, mercoledì, giovedì, and venerdì, refer to the gods Apollo, Mars (Ares), Mercury (Hermes), Jupiter (Zeus), and Athena (Venus). The same is true in Spanish, (lunes, martes, miércoles, jueves, and viernes), and the counterparts in French, Romanian, and Portuguese also refer to the same deities. Likewise, the English and German terms also honor gods. Monday refers to the moon god, and Tuesday is named after Tiu, the Germanic god of war who was identified with Tyr, the Norse god. Wednesday is Woden's day or Odin's day. Thursday is Thor's day, and Friday is the day of Freya, the Teutonic goddess of love.

36. Fresco of Apollo from the Augustus Period (27 B.C.E. – 14 C.E.), Rome, Italy

Gods were equated with all sorts of celestial phenomena, and deities' names were used to mark the passage of time. It is for this reason that modern researchers have mistaken some astronomical observations and historical phenomena as myth alone. Consideration of these connections can help historians and anthropologists to recognize ancient texts for what they really are. According to the Aztec account, they too emerged from the ground into this current cycle of existence. Human beings, as they are called today, came into being while they were still beneath the surface, and they emerged from the ground and into the open through seven caves called Chicomoztoc. Eventually, this current era will end, and a new era (a new sun) will emerge.

According to the Aztecs, the First Sun lasted 4,008 years. It was during this period that large humans lived, whom they referred to as giants. At the end of the cycle, water destroyed the age. The devastation itself was called *Apachiohualiztli*, which meant "flood" or "deluge." Supposedly, seven couples survived this deluge, and they repopulated the world after it had ended. The Second Sun lasted for 4,010 years, but something called *Ehecoatl* destroyed it. This term can be translated as "Wind Serpent," although it is unknown to what it is actually referring. The Third Sun lasted 4,081 years. At the end of this era, fire destroyed the world. And finally, the Fourth Sun lasted for 5,026 years. It ended with a mass-extinction in which human beings died in a flood of blood and fire.[6] Currently, we are in the time of the Fifth Sun.

The Aztecs used a circular calendar to track time's passage both on small and massive scales, in which the cycles of creation and destruction were mapped throughout thousands of years. The sections of the calendar were called "wheels." This fact alone is indicative of the Aztec view of time. Eventually, everything that occurs will occur again. As the wheel of time turns, eventually it will return to the same position from which it started. This position is the beginning. Opposites exist simultaneously in all forms of creation. Where there is light, there must also be darkness, and where there is life, there must also be death. This principle forms the core belief system of many religious traditions on this planet, including Daoism, which introduced the concepts of Yin and Yang to the world. Likewise, when the Aztec calendar returns to its beginning point, it must also be an end. It is a period in which the current cycle of existence is destroyed and a new one is born.

The Mayans shared a similar view, which their circular calendars also represented. They had three separate calendars, represented as wheels, which interlocked and were connected. The *haab* was a 365-day solar calendar divided into 18 months of 20 days and one month of five days. Each day represented on the calendar was associated with a particular god or spirit associated with the day. Keeping in mind that the names of deities were applied to celestial bodies and events, this calendar mapped the cyclical changes that occurred in the heavens. Used in conjunction with this calendar wheel was the *tzolkin*. This was the sacred calendar, which consisted of 260 days, further divided into 20 periods of 13 days each that were likewise associated with gods and celestial events. The final wheel of the Mayan calendar system was called the *long count*. This portion recorded the beginnings and ends of civilizations. Each cycle of existence, according to the long count, lasts for 2,880,000 days.[7] At the end of this period, the world is destroyed, and a new one begins. The Mayans, like the Aztecs and the Hopi, believed that there had been previous worlds (i.e. suns) before this one, and they had all ended due to mega-disasters. This belief in the cyclical nature of creation is not limited to Native Americans in the Occident. It is also found in the East.

Hindu and Buddhist World Cycles

Hinduism, Buddhism, Jainism, and other faiths likewise share a cyclical view of time. Hinduism is the world's oldest extant religion, and it is seemingly the most complex, as it makes use of various cycles (of time) that are all interconnected. The periods in Hinduism directly relate to cosmology. "Its cycles run from our ordinary day and night to a day and night of Brahma, 8.64 billion years long, longer than the age of the Earth or the sun and about half the time since the Big Bang. And there are longer time scales still."[8]

There are Brahma (periods of the Supreme Universe), Kalpas (eras of the Universe), Manvantaras (cycles of the existence of humankind), and Yugas (periods of dharma). In these units of measurement, the kalpas correspond to the Mayan, Aztec, and Hopi notion of "world" or "sun" most directly, as a kalpa refers to the creation and destruction of worlds. The term refers to cycles of existence. Besides these basic units for measuring time, (Brahma, Kalpas, Manvantaras, and Yugas), there are others, such as a Mahayuga, which means "great age." The system itself is complex, but the *Vishnu Purana* explained the basic lengths of these periods:

> Twelve thousand divine years, each composed of (three hundred and sixty) such days, constitute the period of the

four Yugas, or ages. They are thus distributed: the Krta age has four thousand; the Treta three thousand; the Dvapara two thousand; and the Kali age one thousand: so those acquainted with antiquity have declared. The period that precedes a Yuga is called a Sandhya, and it is of as many hundred years as there are thousands in the Yuga.[9]

Keeping in mind that time itself, as considered in the Hindu tradition, is cyclical, an understanding of the length of these units can not only help individuals to keep track of days, months, and years, but also much longer periods. This system can help to pinpoint the beginnings and ends of different ages in history and into the future. At the end of each cycle, there is some sort of a disaster that not only causes the end of the previous cycle, but also jump-starts the next one. "The closing of one door implies the opening of another. Destruction of the cosmos only portends its re-creation. The entire material world is thus subject to everlasting cycles of creation, sustenance and destruction."[10] According to Hindu beliefs, various calamities cause destruction at the end of each Kali Yuga. The devastation following a Manvantara is more pronounced: "Each Manvantara is followed by a Deluge, which destroys the existing continents and swallows up all living beings, except the few who are preserved for the repopulating of the Earth."[11] At the end of a Kalpa the world is completely destroyed, flooded by water. Finally, at the end of a Brahma (approximately 311 trillion years), all worlds are destroyed, never to begin again.

Based on the Hindu cycle, the current Mahayuga began c. 4 million years ago. This means that the previous one ended at about the same time. If so, there must have been a mega-disaster that ended it. Certainly, an Ice Age gripped the planet at this time. According to Hinduism, humankind emerged approximately 120 million years ago. Mainstream scientists mock this claim, as humankind is not believed to have existed before 100,000 years ago. However, the view that humankind is a modern species causes a number of unsolvable problems, problems that will be dealt with at length in the next chapter. Certainly, one can support an evidence-based argument that humankind is much older than generally believed.

It is insignificant whether the Hindu system for measuring time is correct. It is only presented here to demonstrate that belief in time's cyclical nature is common in many traditions. In Buddhism too, there is an understanding that time is not linear, but cyclical. It is clear from the spiritual teachings of both Buddhism and Hinduism that they view life in general as cyclical. When human beings die, they leave their bodies and are reborn after an indefinite time in a different realm. This view of reincarnation is relatable to the cyclical view of time, and the belief in the never-ending creation and destruction of worlds.

The Mahayana Buddhist tradition holds that another Buddha will arrive at the end of time (right before the next mega-disaster). Adherents believe that Maitreya, the Buddha of the future, will arrive 5,670,000 years after the death of Siddhartha Gautama, after six cycles of existence. Based upon the *Dipavamsa* texts, the Buddha was most likely born c. 485 B.C.E., and he died when he was 80.[12] Therefore, if they are correct, there will be a mega-disaster millions of years from now. Many faiths have predicted this end-time event. Christians call it the Rapture. However, both Buddhist and Christian texts do not mention the other disasters that will take place before this end-time.

When we look at the history of this planet as a whole, there have been certain events, such as meteor impacts, that have changed the planet's climate for hundreds (if not thousands) of years, and Ice Ages that have wiped out almost all living creatures. These are called mega-disasters. Besides such mega-disasters, numerous smaller disasters likewise have caused the extinction of many species. Some of these lesser disasters have nearly caused the extinction of human beings. One of these lesser disasters is the Great Flood, which will be discussed in detail later.

There is a natural cycle of creation and destruction. The minor disasters, which certainly would not seem minor to anyone experiencing them, might occur every 400,000 years or so, while the mega-disasters, which lead to massive extinctions and new life forms, occur millions of years apart. Many cultures share the knowledge that time is cyclical. The scientific evidence also indicates that there is a cyclical pattern of devastation: life is created, destroyed, and then created again. This pattern is a natural part of Earth's history, and it will continue to occur in the future.

Planetary Disasters as a Natural Part of Earth's History

Earth's history is a violent one. Even the creation of the planet was seemingly a disaster, but this disaster eventually led to the formation of life. Although there are other theories regarding how the planet formed, the following is generally accepted by the scientific community: 4.5 billion years ago, the Earth had no water, no oxygen, and was covered in toxic gases. It, along with 19 other planets, circled a new star, our sun. The orbits of these planets were different than they are today, and there was debris everywhere, floating through space. Much of this cosmic debris pounded the Earth, and there are tons of craters, reminders of this violent past, that are still visible. Some of these craters are 966 kilometers (600 miles) across. Then, the Earth struck something that was the size of a planet. Some have speculated that Thea, approximately the same size as Mars, collided with the Earth. The impact was so great that it moved Earth off its axis. This created both the Earth's tilt and the moon, and Earth's atmosphere filled with vaporized rock. In addition, the Earth spun faster due to the collision. Four hundred million years ago, a year was 410 days, and each day was 21 hours. However, soon after Earth's impact with Thea, a day lasted only 6 hours.[13]

Icy comets crashed into Earth's surface. When they melted, the first primordial oceans formed. Carbon dioxide dominated the atmosphere. Acid rain fell, accompanied by 400 mile-per-hour winds. The moon was 10 times closer to the planet than it is today, and therefore, tidal changes were huge; they moved hundreds of miles per hour. These huge waves lapped over land, pulling minerals and other life-sustaining ingredients back with them. This created a so-called primordial soup, from which life emerged. This life began with bacteria alone. To these small creatures, oxygen was poisonous. However, they absorbed sunlight and emitted oxygen, their byproduct or waste product. As oxygen levels rose, some forms of bacteria died. For most of them, the poisonous oxygen was too much, and they did not make it. Others adapted, and life continued. After this violent beginning, the Earth did not have a time of prolonged peace. Instead, regular catastrophes bombarded it, which have played a huge role in the development of life. While they were responsible for the development of life, they were likewise responsible for the extinction of life forms.

Mega-disasters have been the culprit in three major extinctions on Earth. Six hundred and fifty million years ago, the Earth froze. Ice from the poles crept toward the equator, covering the entire planet. Glaciers carried stones and rocks for thousands of miles, and today, evidence of this is found in some of the planet's warmest regions. It is undeniable that ice covered even the warmest areas during this glacial period. What caused it is still unknown, although it is generally believed that extreme changes in worldwide temperatures are primarily caused by changes in the planet's orbit around the sun. Whatever the cause, the landmasses were covered with thousands of feet of ice for 25 million years. Eventually, underground volcanic activity began to rewarm the Earth. Massive eruptions punched holes through the ice, and the ice around the globe slowly melted. Sea levels rose substantially and there were flash floods. To provide an example of what actually occurred, it is useful to consider a modern-day volcanic eruption.

Remnants of a Distant Past

In 1996, the Grimsvotn volcano in Iceland erupted, punching a hole through a glacier that was a half mile in height. The hot gases blew a hole in the glacier, and the heat produced flash floods. These floods lasted for 5 hours and carried 45,000 tons of water per second.[14] This was a small-scale incident. Consider a similar scenario that occurred worldwide on a much larger scale. The ice was thicker and the volcano eruptions were stronger. It was a catastrophic event, but what might seem horrible paved the way for the development of complex organisms. Volcanoes emitted carbon dioxide, which trapped sunlight and heated the atmosphere. In time, the ice melted and the ice age ended. Creatures that had survived this glacial period then changed. A new variety of creatures emerged. Before the ice age began, one percent of the Earth's atmosphere was oxygen. However, a chemical in the ice called hydrogen peroxide released when the ice melted. This changed into oxygen. After the ice age, 21 percent of the Earth's atmosphere was oxygen. Creatures that had previously existed evolved, giving rise to complex organisms.

Evolution continued. Then, another disaster struck. Two hundred fifty million years ago, 95 percent of all living creatures died. It was a massive extinction. All moisture disappeared from the planet, and creatures faced rapid drying and warming. It is unknown exactly what caused the change, but temperatures worldwide spiked 20 degrees Fahrenheit, destroying ecosystems. This caused extensive volcanic eruptions. Millions of cubic miles of magma built up under the Siberian Crust and the entire region bulged upward toward the sky. Eventually, it burst free in tons of explosions, enough to cover the entire United States under a mile of molten rock. The traps erupted for a half million years, producing 3,220,000 square kilometers (2,000,000 square miles) of lava.

The volcanic eruptions also released clouds of lethal sulphur dioxide and carbon dioxide. Atmospheric carbon dioxide was 20 times higher than it is today. This greatly impacted the climate, including rainfall. Near the equator, there was no rain at all. Making the devastation even worse, the Earth's oceans had lost their oxygen.

This led to a secondary temperature spike. Methane gas caused the second jump in temperatures. It is found deep underground. It rises through the Earth's crust and enters the oceans. Then, in the form of gas bubbles, it heads to the water's surface, eventually escaping into the atmosphere. Today on ocean floors there is something called methane hydrate. Thirty trillion frozen tons of it are in the deepest parts of the sea. If temperatures ever rose enough to release this gas, there would be a global catastrophe, like the one that occurred 250 million years ago. During this ancient mega-disaster, the majority of creatures became extinct.

However, some survived. Those that did evolved. There is a correlation between natural disasters, such as global ice ages, and evolution. Somehow, the disasters trigger changes in living creatures. They quickly adapt to changing environments to survive. The last major extinction supposedly brought about the end of the dinosaurs. This occurred 65 million years ago when an asteroid struck the Earth near the Yucatan Peninsula in Mexico, leaving a crater 201 kilometers (125 miles) in diameter. Five hundred billion tons of Earth were displaced and shot into the atmosphere at speeds up to 40,234 kilometers (25,000 miles) per hour, and the impact caused a tsunami 91 meters (300 feet) high. The materials launched into the atmosphere heated up upon reemergence, so that when they hit the Earth, they caused massive fires.

The climate changed suddenly, and temperatures plummeted. This is because the impact released sulfur dioxide into the sky. For six months, no sunlight made it through the atmosphere at all. Eventually, the sun reappeared, and with it, large quantities of acid rain fell. Global cooling turned into global warming. The rocks released carbon dioxide, and its warming effects continued for centuries. The temperature increased by 20 degrees over the next 100 years. Vegetation died and plant-eating dinosaurs starved to death. The meat-eating dinosaurs likewise starved to death as the plant eaters disappeared. However, even in this massive extinction, there were survivors. Along with surviving dinosaurs were small creatures that paved the way for the ultimate creation of human beings: mammals. These burrowers and scavengers emerged victorious after this massive worldwide disaster.

Mega-Disasters and Evolution

Based upon all available evidence, mega-disasters are connected to evolution. The end of an ice age reveals the presence of new species. MacDougall wrote:

> The evolution of modern human beings can be traced back through a number of species, collectively known as the hominids, to a common ancestor with the chimpanzees, our closest living relatives among the primates, some five or six million years ago. As far as we can tell, chimpanzees and other members of the family of "great apes" have not changed radically from that distant ancestor. We, on the other hand, have changed a lot. The interesting questions are "why?" and "how?" Clues to these questions are hard to come by, and we may never know the answers with complete certainty. But the timing at least suggests an interesting connection with climate and the Pleistocene Ice Age. For several million years after our common ancestor, hominids evolved slowly. They developed the ability to move around on the ground with an upright posture, although their body structure suggests that they were still expert tree climbers. Then, right around the time when the Earth's average

temperature plunged downward at the beginning of the Pleistocene Ice Age — about three million years ago — the rate of change accelerated drastically. Hominids quickly evolved away from their ape-like ancestors, developing increasingly sophisticated tools and weapons, hunting, planning, complex language, and eventually agriculture, writing, airplanes, and computers. During that time, there was an increase in brain size by more than a factor of three in less than three million years, a breathtakingly rapid change compared to the normal course of evolution. That change took place entirely within the Pleistocene Ice Age. Is there a cause-and-effect relationship?[15]

There are no answers to some of the questions posed herein. Some historical occurrences cannot be known. General ideas — the things that many people consider facts — are nothing more than educated guesses. They are hypotheses proposed to explain things that truly are inexplicable. Topics such as evolution and when human beings actually emerged on this planet are debated, sometimes heatedly. However, what is known is that dramatic changes in climate or atmosphere are associated with the evolution of species.

It has been posited that evolution occurs when a small group of a species separates and lives in a different environment. For example, during mass-extinction events, some species might head to caves or mountaintops in order to escape the devastation that surrounds them. There, in different living conditions, they change. For example, creatures who mate in a dark environment, like deep caverns, might give birth to children who have larger eyes — eyes more suitable for seeing in the dark. And such changes might not happen gradually, as thought by some proponents of Darwin. Other researchers, such as Niles Eldredge and Stephen Jay Gould have suggested that evolutionary changes occur quickly. In one or two generations alone, children may be born with new and unique features that are more suited to their survival in a new, hostile environment. While some creatures evolve, others survive unchanged. Against all odds, humans and other animals find refugia: areas on the planet that are more hospitable. It is in these places that they ride out the storm, finally emerging when mega-disasters have abated.

Refugia and Survival during Mass-Extinction Events

A mega-disaster supposedly wiped out the dinosaurs at the end of the Cretaceous Period, but this is not true. Many died. Others evolved and became modern birds. Some survived and did not change, and it is possible that certain species are still alive. As strange and as unbelievable as this might seem, a great deal of evidence supports this conclusion.

The term dinosaur was created in 1841, so witnesses who saw these creatures alive before this time would have used different terms to describe them. Often, these animals were called dragons, and it is therefore difficult to separate the historical creatures from the mythological fire-breathing ones. (Other cultures referred to them by other names, such as *nago, ryu, bakunawa, ejderha, coca, zmeg, wyvern, azhdaha*, and there are many more. The presence of these terms, used to describe similar, if not the same creatures, is indicative that people of these cultures had seen them. It is for this reason that terms were created to describe what they had seen.) However, by analyzing historical accounts that include such terms, along with archaeological evidence and witness statements, it becomes clear that many dinosaurs not only survived a mega-disaster, but that some of them might exist today.

References to dragons appear in many historical texts. Although dismissed by some people as mythological accounts, the stories that reference the creatures are accepted as historical. In other words, some believe that the creatures were mythological and simply added to historical accounts. This does not make much sense. If these otherwise historical narratives contain accounts of dragons, it is likely that the writers were describing real creatures that did exist. These creatures are not mythological, but dinosaurs. Providing more evidence that these terms referred to the same creatures, dinosaurs, a.k.a. dragons, were listed in scientific catalogues of known species. The *Historia Animalium*, for example, states that dragons were still extant in the 1500's. The book claims that they were rare and much smaller than their predecessors were. However, other texts, such as the *De Natura Animalium*, written in the second century C.E., stated that dragons were still in Phyrgia, and that the creatures could be as large as ten paces in length.

Other accounts record encounters with dragons. In 1572, a scientist named Ulysses Aldrovandus found one while walking along a road in northern Italy.[16] A farmer struck it on the head and it died. Aldrovandus described it as having a long neck and tail and a large body. He measured the body, made drawings of it, and even had it stuffed for a local museum. The description of the animal, and the drawings that he made, resemble a type of dinosaur known as the tanystropheus. They also resemble descriptions of creatures sighted in various locations, such as Loch Ness in Scotland. Other accounts exist in various cultures. An Irish writer described a run-in that he had with a dinosaur in 900 C.E. He described a large creature that had a head like a horse, a huge body with strong legs, and spikes on its tail. Certainly, these details might indicate that he had witnessed a stegasaurus.[17] Marco Polo described a type of dinosaur seen in Chinese provinces:

Here are seen huge serpents, ten paces in length and ten paces in girth of the body. At the fore part, near the head, they have two short legs, having three claws like those of a tiger, with eyes larger than a fore penny loaf and very glaring. The jaws are wide enough to swallow a man, the teeth are large and sharp, and their whole appearance is so formidable that neither man, nor any other kind of animal, can approach them without terror. Others are met with of a smaller size, being eight, six, or five paces long.[18]

Stories of dinosaurs exist in the Bible, in the written records of Sumer, and in countless other cultures throughout the world. An interesting account in Chinese historical records states that dragons (a.k.a. dinosaurs) survived the Great Flood. Other Chinese records reveal that some individuals kept dragons and raised them to use their blood and body parts for medicinal purposes.[19] Today, snake blood is still drunk, and it is considered highly effective in curing numerous ailments. Stories like this, found all over the world, are indicative that dinosaurs and humans might have lived together. Or at least, it is indicative that humans were aware of the existence of dinosaurs — not as creatures that vanished millions of years ago, but as creatures that were still alive in modern times.

Alexander the Great, reporting his victories over cities in modern-day India, stated that his soldiers were terrified of the large dragons found there, dragons that lived in caves. The Greek historian Herodotus likewise described flying reptiles in Egypt and Arabia. His descriptions match a creature called *ramphorhynchus*, which is a small pterodactyl thought to have been long extinct. Herodotus reported seeing many of them in spice groves and among frankincense trees. It is possible that this creature is still alive today, and that it still lives in Africa.

Flying creatures that resemble pterodactyls have been seen in the United States, South America, Africa, and Papua New Guinea. The sightings are especially numerous in Papua New Guinea, and the natives have names for three different varieties of them: *ropen*, *indava*, and *seki-bali*. The same creature is called *kongomato* in Africa. Nocturnal creatures, they are infrequently seen during the day. However, they occasionally do appear in daylight. The natives of Papua New Guinea describe these creatures as flying reptiles. When shown pictures of various types of dinosaurs, they claim that the ropen closely resembles a pterodactyl. Locals in Africa have described a similar creature. They are featherless, with a wingspan between one and two meters (four and seven feet). Sharp teeth line their beaks. Called kongomato, they are usually seen in jungles, and they occasionally torment human beings. When shown pictures of a pterosaur, "every native present immediately and unhesitatingly picked out and identified it as the kongamato."[20] The pterosaurs are pre-historical flying reptiles, related to pterodactyls.

However, the pterodactyl is not the only kind of dinosaur that is likely still alive in Africa. It has been said that the Likouala Swamp in the Congo Basin is home to various types of dinosaurs. Only 80 percent of it has been explored, but reports by natives indicate there may be other creatures there that are generally thought to have become extinct. Shown pictures of different types of dinosaurs, they claim to have seen the *apatosour* and the triceratops living in this area.[21] The natives call the apatosour Mokele Embembe, and they state that they usually appear in the morning and at dusk in shallow parts of the swamp. They are territorial, and although the natives would typically not choose to engage them, they have killed and eaten the creatures before. The animals' footprints have also been found and catalogued. Natives call the creature that we would call a triceratops a N'Goubou. It has six horns, and it has killed elephants.[22]

Other dinosaurs have also been witnessed in various locations. One of the most common is the plesiosaur, an elusive creature that lives in water. Numerous individuals at Loch Ness in Scotland, Okanagen Lake in British Columbia, and Lake Champlain in the United States have reported sightings of this creature. There have literally been tens of thousands of reports, and witnesses describe the exact same type of creature.[23] Some witnesses are certain that what they witnessed was a dinosaur.[24] One description is the following: "It looked like a huge serpent moving up and down, not side to side like a fish. It was more than 30 feet long."[25] The dinosaurs seen in each of these places have nicknames: Nessie, Ogopogo, and Champ. However, it is unlikely that all of the witnesses have seen the same creature. It is far more likely that multiple dinosaurs are still extant at these locations and in many other locales.[26]

We do not have to rely on witness accounts alone to make a decision about whether or not dinosaurs continue to exist. Some dead ones have appeared. In 1925, one of these creatures washed ashore in California. E. L. Wallace, president of the Natural History Society of British Columbia examined the remains. He said, "My examination of the monster was quite thorough...It had no teeth. Its head is large and its neck full 20 feet long. I would call it a type of plesiosaurus."[27]

Other archaeological evidence confirms that dinosaurs did not become extinct millions of years ago. Vases in Peru, created by a pre-Columbian civilization called the Nazca, have drawings of different species of dinosaurs, depicted as coexisting with humans. In Mexico too, ancient figures of dinosaurs have consistently been unearthed. The majority of these figures are about 4,500 years old.[28] Sculptures of dinosaurs have likewise appeared in many countries in Central and South America. They have also been found in countries in South and Central Asia. Pre-Columbian European artwork also depicts dinosaurs. Sometimes, they were drawn alone, but other works depict humans and dinosaurs together. There are even artistic renderings of humans battling large dinosaurs.

The available evidence suggests that dinosaurs were not all destroyed during a mass-extinction event. Certainly, those who believe dinosaurs evolved into birds already knew that. They could only have evolved if they survived the event. While some evolved, others survived unchanged. They might now be extinct, or at least extremely rare, but it is important to understand that they made it through a mega-disaster.

Periods of Glaciation

Besides massive destructive events that cause extinction and evolution, other less-severe disasters strike regularly. Every 100,000 years or so, the planet experiences a period of glaciation, which ends in massive flooding as ice caps melt and rejoin the seas. Louis Agassiz (1807 – 1873) was the first to suggest the regularity of ice ages. The scientific community initially laughed at the idea, but in time, they came to realize that evidence supports the theory. This is a standard human reaction to unique theories. As Arthur Schopenhauer (1788 – 1860) wrote, "All truth passes through three stages. First, it is ridiculed. Second, it is violently opposed. Third, it is accepted as being self-evident."[29] Now it is accepted that the planet faces intermittent periods of glaciation, and these periods end with massive floods. MacDougall explained:

> At their maximum, the ice caps did hold huge volumes of water, and accumulating evidence shows that there were glacial floods as they melted, some of them catastrophic. In fact, some were so catastrophic that when the claim was first made that flowing water had produced the devastation that they left in their wake, the idea was dismissed as preposterous. This reception was eerily reminiscent of the

initial reaction to Agassiz's ice age theory. Catastrophic flooding associated with melting glaciers is now universally accepted, however, and in recent years, the topic has attracted renewed interest. Not only did the gigantic floods wreak havoc with the landscape, but they may also have been responsible for drastic shifts in climate.[30]

A glacial age is one in which the overall temperature of the planet drops considerably. During these periods, glaciers cover at least part of the planet. Currently, we are still in a glacial age that began at the beginning of the Pleistocene Era and peaked approximately 20,000 years ago. This is true because glaciers still cover Greenland and Antarctica. Historically, this is a rare planetary temperature range. There have been five previous glacial periods. Other than these periods, Earth has been relatively ice-free. So, when the ice caps eventually melt, the Earth will return to its more common ice-free state. Sure, it will wreak havoc. Ocean levels will rise, submerging many coastal cities, but this is a normal planetary occurrence. This cycle of ice ages happens frequently on a geological scale, but since human beings have only been on this planet for a short period, they are not accustomed to such changes. However, our ancestors dealt with glacial periods.

Within each glacial age, colloquially called an ice age, there are intermittent periods of warm and cold temperatures. When the temperature gets colder, the ice sheets creep across landmasses and oceans that they normally do not cover. The Earth is currently in a period called an interglacial. The ice sheets are restricted to the poles of the planet, and they do not stretch across North America and Europe as they once had. We have been in this interglacial period, called the Holocene, for approximately 11,000 years. Many believe that these temperate times within an ice age only last about 12,000 years. After this, the ice caps will once again stretch across landmasses, beginning another period of glaciation.[31]

What actually causes these glacial periods (and ice ages in general) is unknown. Some theories claim that such temperature variations happen because of changes in the Earth's atmosphere. Other theories suggest changing positions of the continents or fluctuations in ocean currents. Likewise, changes in Earth's orbit and variations in the sun's energy output could be culprits. No one knows for sure, but it is now understood that they occur regularly.

The last major period of glaciation began c. 19,000 B.C.E. and ended c. 8,000 B.C.E. The peak of this period was in 16,000 B.C.E., and glaciers miles high covered Europe. Huge ice sheets covered most of the United States and all of Canada. Antarctica was mostly ice free, but areas such as the Alps, the Himalayas, and the Andes were completely covered. Glaciers covered England, Germany, Poland, Russia, and Scandinavia. Due to volcanic eruptions and other factors that mirror the end of the last ice age on a much smaller scale, the glaciers began to melt c. 12,000 B.C.E. Because of temperature variations on the planet, the ice melted at different times in diverse places. In addition, in some places that were heavily inundated with ice, a lag effect took place. MacDougall explained:

> The data suggests that there was a lag of two to three thousand years between the temperature increase and the decrease in ice volume. This is not very surprising — think about how long it takes for a bag of ice cubes to melt, or an old-fashioned refrigerator to defrost, even when the ambient temperature is far above freezing.[32]

This is why diverse cultures' flood stories do not date to the same time. Some of these floods occurred hundreds if not thousands of years apart.

Destruction and Rebirth: Flood Stories and Survival

There are more than 500 flood stories from all over the world. Some refer to lesser floods that have taken place in the last 10,000 years, while others refer to the last Great Flood, otherwise known as the Deluge, which occurred c. 11,000 B.C.E. Still others refer to distant great floods. These pre-historic disasters might relate to the last great one in size and scope, but the truth is, no one knows exactly when these events occurred. There are no written records, although some stories passed down as myths might refer to them. These events happened so far in the distant past that cultures that preserved the stories did not assign them a date. Each culture had its own way of telling time anyway, so such dating was likely impossible. Instead, cultures that preserved tales stated that the catastrophes happened during the Time of the Gods. Sometimes, they even attributed the floods to gods. For example, in the Greek account, Zeus sent a flood to destroy humankind, and Prometheus told his son to build a chest in preparation. The only human survivors found safety on the highest mountains. The similar Roman version states that Jupiter became angry at the evil deeds of humans and decided to destroy them. He flooded the Earth. Using earthquakes, rain, and the power of the seas, the entire Earth was underwater, with the exception of Parnassus, where Deucalion and Pyrrah's ship came to rest. It was on this mountaintop that they were saved, so humankind would not be forever extinguished.

This willingness to attribute great floods to gods has not dissipated in so-called modern religions. The Biblical account claims that God became angry with human beings and decided to kill them all. He is not too decisive, however, and ends up changing his mind. He pities them, but lacks the power to withdraw the water. Instead, he asks Noah to build a vessel that can house two of every species. In a tale that blends history, religion, and pure fantasy, Noah succeeds in finding two of every species and herds them aboard. This account, which people in Europe and the Americas are most familiar, is just one of many. Unfortunately, it has the same weaknesses that most tales have: the events described occurred before known human history, so references to gods and goddesses appear. In addition, some impossible exaggerations have been added. These two facts must be considered if we are to extract truth from these historical tales. When we objectively analyze stories, a clear picture of the flood (or floods) emerges.

The Scandinavian story explains that Oden fought an ice giant named Ymir, and when it died, it melted, creating a huge flood. Eventually, the waters subsided, becoming oceans and lakes. Again, take away the religious aspects, and we have a clear record of giant pieces of ice that were quickly destroyed, thus causing a flood. The Penobscot tribe from Maine has a similar story. It relates how Kuloscap defeated ice giants, which afterward washed into the seas. The following is the tale of an indigenous population known as the Yamanas, located in the Falkland Islands:

> Léxuwakipa, the rusty brown spectacled ibis, felt offended by the people, so she let it snow so much that ice came to cover the entire Earth. This happened at the time of Yáiaasága, when men seized power from the women. When the ice

melted, it rapidly flooded all the Earth. People hurried to their canoes, but many didn't make it, and more perished when they couldn't find sheltered places. Some people reached the five mountaintops, which stayed above the flood. These mountains were Usláka, Wémarwaia, Auwáratuléra, Welalánux, and Piatuléra. The water stayed at its high mark for two days and then rapidly lowered. Signs of the floodwaters still show up on those mountains. The few families which [sic.] survived rebuilt their huts on the shore.[33]

The Samothrace flood story describes a Mediterranean disaster. The barriers dividing the Black Sea from the Mediterranean broke apart, resulting in huge waves that destroyed a major portion of Asia's coast in the Samothrace lowlands. Survivors climbed mountains to escape the oncoming deluge. There they prayed to their gods. The floodwaters abated, and this early civilization assumed that the gods had shown them favor. For this reason, they established monuments and temples.

The Babylonian account (2000 – 1595 B.C.E.) clearly reveals that existence is cyclical, and huge worldwide floods routinely wipe out human beings. It relates that floods occurred three times before their civilization rose to prominence. Rather than attribute the disasters to natural occurrences, they accredited them to divine beings. This seems to be a standard human tendency: anything they cannot explain is attributed to something supernatural or divine. The Babylonians claimed that three distinct disasters occurred 1,200 years apart. The gods saw human overpopulation as problematic, and caused disasters to fix the problem. First, there was a plague followed by a long famine. Finally, the gods formed a great flood to exterminate them. Like the Sumerian version, the decision to exterminate humankind was controversial, and the gods argued. One of them called Enki, who was sympathetic to humankind, advised people to bribe the gods through prayer and sacrifice.

The same deity assisted humankind again when Enlil decided to send floodwaters. Enki knew that many humans would die. She could not prevent this, so she told a man named Atrahasis to build a seafaring vessel to escape. According to legend, he followed her instructions. He loaded the ship with his family, cattle, birds and other wild animals. When the Great Storm approached, the precursor to the Great Flood, he sealed the ship's doors with bitumen and cast off. The storm god Adad turned the skies black, and for seven days, a flood ravished the planet. After a week, the responsible gods regretted their actions and withdrew the water. Atrahasis prayed to them and made offerings, and such floods have not occurred since.

The Assyrian version is similar to the Babylonian: Enlil saw overpopulation as a problem and unleashed a flood. Utnapishtim learned about the oncoming flood while either in meditation or in a dream. He hired skilled builders and they constructed a large vessel that could tumble and turn underwater. It was approximately one acre in area and had seven decks. Once he had completed it, he invited his family inside, along with the D.N.A. of other living creatures. When the flood began, they headed into the sea. It lasted for six days, and was more turbulent than even the gods had expected. More people died than they had wished, and the gods repented and wept. Everything was submerged except for the top of Mount Nisir, where the vessel finally came ashore. Similar to the Biblical and Sumerian stories, Utnapishtim released a dove. It found no place to land other than that mountaintop, so it returned. He then unleashed a sparrow, which also returned. Finally, he unleashed a raven, which did not come back. Upon seeing this, he knew that the floodwaters had abated and the people could come out and live on land once again. In gratitude, Utnapishtim made a sacrifice to the gods. He and his wife were given the gift of immortality, and according to legend, they lived at the end of the Earth.

Many different cultures in Siberia have similar flood stories. Once the mythological elements are removed, the commonalities found in such stories are clear. The Kamchadale tell of a time in which the entire world was covered by waters unleashed in a great flood. The people who survived saved themselves by making rafts out of tree trunks bound together by rope. They carried their possessions with them and used large stones tied to ropes as anchors, thus preventing their rafts from disappearing into the sea. When the floodwaters finally receded, they were left stranded on mountaintops.

The Samoyed people from northern Siberia have an unusual flood story that indicates problems that they faced after the deluge had abated. According to their accounts, seven people survived the flood in a boat. After it had ended, there was a terrible draught, and little food was available. The people dug a deep hole for drinking water. However, five of them died from hunger. The two that survived saved themselves by eating the mice that emerged from the ground. According to the Samoyed legend, humankind is descended from this couple. Another similar account is found in north-central Siberia. The Yenisey-Ostyak culture states that the great flood lasted for seven days. The people survived by climbing on floating logs. They were scattered by the strong winds that likewise blew for seven days. According to the myth, this is the reason why people speak different languages all over the world.

Many of the world's flood stories do not mention the ice, just the flood. This might indicate where the stories originated. Ice covered many areas of the planet, but not all. However, when it melted, it affected all. Consider what melting glaciers in Antarctica would do to coastal cities throughout the entire world today, and you will get an idea of the type of devastation caused by such rapidly melting mountains of ice. The Eskimos, who may have always been accustomed to living in icy environments (at least in modern times), do not mention glaciers or ice melting in its flood tale, but they do mention the presence of ice along with the water:

> The ocean rose suddenly and continued rising until it covered even the tops of mountains. Ice drifted on the water, and

when the flood subsided, ice was stranded to form ice caps on the tops of mountains. The shells and bones of many shellfish, fish, seals, and whales were also left high above sea level, where they may be found today. Many people drowned, but many others were saved in their boats.[34]

Some stories do not discuss dealing with a flood at all. The Zoroastrian story involves a man named Yima, who receives news about an oncoming glacial period from Ahura Mazda, the tradition's creator God. Ahura Mazda gave him these instructions:

> Upon the material world the evil winters are about to fall, that shall bring the fierce, deadly frost; upon the material world the evil winters are about to fall, that shall make snowflakes fall thick even an aredevi deep on the highest tops of mountains. And the beasts that live in the wilderness, and those that live on the tops of the mountains, and those that live in the bosom of the dale shall take shelter in underground abodes. Before that winter, the country would bear plenty of grass for cattle, before the waters had flooded it. Now after the melting of the snow, oh Yima, a place wherein the footprint of a sheep may be seen will be a wonder in the world. Therefore, make thee a Vara.[35]

Yima received even more specific instructions about how to create an underground home for all creatures — a home called a vara. Then, he built it. According to the Vendidad:

> Yima made a Vara, long as the riding-ground on every side of the square. There he brought the seeds of sheep and oxen, of men, of dogs, of birds, and of red blazing fires. He made a Vara, long as a riding-ground on every side of the square, to be an abode for men; a Vara, long as a riding-ground on every side of the square, for oxen and sheep. There he made

waters flow in a bed a hathra long; there he settled birds, on the green that never fades, with food that never fails. There he established dwelling places, consisting of a house with a balcony, courtyard, and a gallery... In the largest part of the place, he made nine streets, six in the middle part, three in the smallest. To the streets of the largest part he brought one thousand seeds of men and women; to the streets of the middle part, six hundred; to the streets of the smallest part, three hundred. That Vara he sealed up with the golden ring, and he made a door, and a window shining within. O Maker of the material world, thou holy one! What are the lights that give light in the Vara which Yima made? Ahura Mazda answered: "There are uncreated lights and created lights. The one thing missed here is the sight of the stars, the moon, and the sun, and a year seems only as a day."[36]

This account is historical documentation of preparations made to survive the "evil winter," the last glacial period. The first section of this text indicates that melting glaciers caused the ensuing worldwide flood. The story's hero created an underground city that offered protection from the cold and ice that covered the planet's surface. Some interesting information in the story indicates that the civilization to which this document refers was technologically advanced.[37] If we are to interpret this document as historical, Yima had access to a food source that never fails. This must mean that it was replenishable; it would never run out. He mentions "green that never fades," which he uses to keep birds alive. Based on our modern knowledge, this food source is likely a type of algae. With the right lighting conditions, this food source could last forever, (and according to the tale, they made use of artificial lighting within). It could perhaps sustain human beings for long periods without other dietary supplements. But it seems that the individuals who inhabited the vara used this foodstuff to feed animals. They likely butchered the animals for their own food and clothing.

Other cultures have glacial survival stories, but the Vendidad is unique in its detail. What actually happened to these people is unknown. Since they have not passed down a flood survival story, they might not have survived it. Others cultural histories mention both the ice and its shift into powerful floods. These cultures likely survived both of these related catastrophes and recorded their plight for future generations. The ones that only mentioned the flood either did not have to deal with the glaciers directly, or they did not know that the two phenomena were connected. This is likely, as it is only in modern times that this connection has been understood.

When the idea of glacial periods was first introduced in the nineteenth century, it was laughed at by the scientific world. Now, it has been accepted and is currently taught to children in schools. The connection between melting ice and rising water levels is also understood, as is the creation of massive tidal waves by the breakup of glaciers. Cultures that passed down flood stories with no mention of ice are consistent. Two types of tales record the event. One kind refers to humans building boats or other types of seafaring craft to save creatures from extinction. The other, more common story involves a couple surviving the flood and then repopulating the Earth.

Regarding the former, two tales can summarize such accounts. The Biblical story tells of a man named Noah who built an ark that could house two of every creature. After a seven-day flood, the ship came to rest on the peak of Mt. Ararat. Eventually, he led the creatures down the mountain, and in this way saved them from extinction. The Babylonian account, written thousands of years before the Old Testament, is remarkably similar:

The gods became angry with humans, who had grown too numerous. One of them, named Enlil, had a solution. He decided to kill them with a flood. Another god, Enki, pitied them. He did not want humans to become extinct. Therefore, he told Atrahasis to build an ark. The man followed Enki's instructions, and he filled the vessel with his family, animals, birds, and cattle. When the flooding began, he sealed the door with bitumen and cut the rope that secured it to shore. After seven days, the flood withdrew. In this way, humans and many animals escaped extinction. Such stories, involving gods and the building of vessels, contain symbolic principles, such as a number that is sacred (or at least important) in many religious traditions: seven.

Although it is possible that the flood lasted for a week alone, it is just as likely that it lasted for much longer, and the number was put into place in order to teach initiates a deep spiritual or secular principle. Considering this combination of history and religion, readers can more adequately discern the truth, which points to the historical occurrence of a worldwide flood and numerous people who managed to survive the event.

The latter type of story, (the survival of a couple who later repopulates the Earth), can likewise be summarized by two stories. An account from Bengali relates that a couple sought refuge from a seven-day flood in a mountain cave. They emerged unharmed, and were known as the first man and woman.[38] The natives of the Adaman Islands tell the following story: After humankind had been created, there was a time of peace, but eventually, they became disobedient and evil. This angered the creator Puluga, and he sent a flood to destroy humans. The only survivors were two people, a man and a woman, who survived the deluge in a type of boat. When the floods finally abated, they landed, and although they found themselves facing difficult conditions, they survived.

There are similar stories with one minor difference: the man and woman did not survive together, but found each other after. On Engano, an island near Sumatra, the following story is told:

> The tide rose so high it overflowed the island. All drowned except one woman, who survived through the fortunate chance that her hair got caught in a thorny tree as she drifted along on the tide. When the flood sank, she came down from the tree and found herself alone. Hungry, she searched

for food and finding none inland, went to the beach hoping to catch a fish. She found a fish, but it hid in one of the corpses left by the flood. She picked up a stone and hit the corpse, but the fish escaped and headed inland. She followed, but soon met a living man. The man told her that he had to return to life as a consequence of somebody knocking on his dead body. The woman told him her story, and they returned to the beach and restored the population by knocking on the drowned people.[39]

Such tales, with small variations only, are abundant. Both of these types of stories: the building of a craft to save living creatures and a couple surviving the flood and then repopulating the world, are combined in the Welsh tale:

The lake of Llion burst, flooding all lands. Dwyfan and Dwyfach escaped in a mastless ship with pairs of every sort of living creature. They landed in Prydain (Britain) and repopulated the world.[40]

The notion that a couple survived the flood and then repopulated the known world is found in all cultural histories. It is the Adam and Eve story of the Bible, and consideration of the cyclical nature of floods provide historical but circumstantial evidence that this happened. Certainly, it is likely that many couples survived in many different areas. For people separated from other tribes or groups of people, their locality truly must have seemed like the entire world. This couple, then, was the couple that repopulated the entire known world. And so we have another possibility regarding the last flood. When the waters began subsiding, some people were alone in isolated, small groups, and they did not know that there were other survivors beside themselves. This is logical, if accounts of the last flood are taken at face value.

A review of flood stories, coupled with geological and archaeological evidence, clearly reveals that many floods have destroyed civilizations. Plato passes along this knowledge in his writings, and it is found in other great historians' written documents. The geological evidence tells us that floods are cyclical. Ice ages come and go, which means worldwide floods come and go. Now that you know this, look around. Miles of ice might one day cover the things you see. Hundreds of years later, the ice will break apart, and floods will finish the destruction begun by the vicious ice giants, glaciers. After centuries, what will remain? The majority of our technical advancements and historical records will be lost forever. Especially in the computer age, where written records are becoming sparse, a disaster of such proportions could erase much of the scientific and historical knowledge amassed. Archaeological sites will once again be buried, and our current cities will be broken apart and buried on top of ancient ruins. After no more than a couple thousand years, almost nothing will remain. In this way, an advanced civilization can be wiped out, and after 12,000 years, there might be no sign that it had even existed.

This is precisely what occurred during the last flood. Almost everything was destroyed, and most stories passed down have made it to the present only by word of mouth. The ancients' knowledge was almost completely destroyed. However, some flood tales reveal that information about advanced antediluvian civilizations might have survived. The following is a story from Tamil, in southern India:

> Half of the landmass Kumari Kandam, which was south of India, sank in a great flood, destroying the first Tamil Sangam (literary academy). The people moved to the other half and established the second Tamil Sangam there, but the rest of Kumari too sank beneath the sea. The lone survivor was a Tamil prince named Thirumaaran, who managed to rescue some Tamil literary classics and swim with them to present-day Tamil Nadu.[41]

This tale indicates that ancient knowledge might have been preserved. Civilizations may come and go, but it is difficult to erase proof of their existence. Evidence shows that advanced societies existed before the Great Flood, in Earth's distant past.

5. Advanced Ancient Civilizations

Mainstream View of Human History

According to mainstream historical accounts, human beings first appeared in Africa approximately 100,000 years ago. They did not migrate to the Americas until about 30,000 years ago. The Darwinian Theory claims that human beings evolved directly from *australopithecine genus*, the first apes that walked upright. The *homo genus* evolved from these apes, and *homo erectus* led directly to modern human beings. From Africa, humans spread to other parts of the world. By the peak of the last ice age, humans inhabited most ice-free areas. It is thought that they initially made and used basic stone and wood tools. Over time, as they developed, their tools became more refined and they used fire. Language also developed, so their communicative capabilities increased.

During the Paleolithic Period, humans were nomadic. They lived together in bands, and they hunted and foraged for food. At the end of this period, approximately 10,000 B.C.E., humans began to live in permanent settlements. Agriculture developed, and the first cities emerged. According to mainstream accounts, the first civilization appeared in Mesopotamia (c. 3500 B.C.E.), and was followed by others in Egypt and the Indus Valley (c. 3300 B.C.E.). With the birth of these civilizations, religions appeared, and shrines and temples were established. Writing systems developed, and some of the earliest texts ever discovered were from these civilizations. The pyramid texts in Egypt, for example, date to c. 2400 B.C.E.

It is believed that while complex civilizations were developing elsewhere, the indigenous populations in the Americas remained simple. Supposedly, complex civilizations did not develop in the Americas until much later. The Mayan civilization, which begun c. 1800 B.C.E. is said to have not reached its highest state of development until the Classic Period (250 – 900 C.E.), while the Zapotec civilization did not begin until the sixth century B.C.E. However, this mainstream version of history does not consider any disconfirming evidence. It is a limited and possibly incorrect view of human history.

The general idea among historians and archaeologists is that human beings have continuously evolved, becoming wiser with each passing generation. This mentality holds that each generation, when it exists, is the possessor of more knowledge and technology than previous generations. Through the ages, new knowledge supposedly appears, knowledge that did not exist previously. New inventions surface, inventions that had not previously existed, and knowledge of the universe expands, so each civilization has a greater understanding of the way things are. This misguided idea has pervaded our educational system, and it forms the basis of mainstream historical and archaeological accounts.

Despite multiple versions of the same historical events, history is typically written from one point of view, and no questions are left unanswered. This accepted practice, designed to provide certainty, causes problems. First, historical accounts are biased. Second, any evidence discovered that does not support or fit into the existing theory is discredited and ignored. This unscientific reaction to evidence that might disrupt the prevailing theory occurs because some archaeologists, scientists, and historians do not view evidence objectively. They view it through a pre-set lens. They already "know" the history of this planet and the history of humankind, so any evidence that contradicts that "knowledge" must not be true. Therefore, they look for ways to cast it out or ignore it.

Some historians ignore archaeological finds that contradict the existing theory of human development. The same pre-existing theory is advanced, and historians claim that they have not yet determined how the anomalous evidence fits into the existing theory. In other words, the theory is upheld no matter how much evidence is discovered to the contrary. The theory is not updated due to newly uncovered finds.

Many archaeologists have been punished in various ways for publishing information about finds that contradicted prevailing theories. For example, individuals mining for gold in California found hundreds of stone artifacts and human fossils in the late 1800's. State geologist J. D. Whitney investigated. Among the unearthed objects were numerous spearheads and a mortar and pestle. These objects were close to the bedrock, 61 – 91 meters (200 – 300 feet) beyond the edge of solid lava, and there were no signs of a fissure or any other disturbance through which the items could have slipped. Therefore, they were likely 33 to 55 million years old. Other objects nearby were more than 9 million years old. He published his finds, and they attracted harsh criticism. Archaeologist William H. Holmes (1846 – 1933) criticized Whitney for publishing information about these finds. He stated, "Perhaps if Professor Whitney had fully appreciated the story of human evolution as it is understood today, he would have hesitated to announce the conclusions formulated, notwithstanding the imposing array of testimony with which he was confronted."[1] In other words, if the facts do not fit the current theory, they must be discarded.

Contradictory Archaeological Evidence

Other finds and their subsequent controversy illustrate the same selective inclusion and exclusion of evidence in order to perpetrate an incorrect historical theory. Stone tools found in Huyatlaco, Mexico are approximately 250,000 years old. This date was determined using three distinct procedures: tephra hydration dating, fission track dating, uranium series dating, and by studying mineral weathering. Despite the consensus reached by geologists, their findings sparked controversy. This is because human beings were not thought to have existed anywhere during this time. Because of the findings, the geologists were shunned. One of them, Virgina Steen-McIntyre, was accused of being dishonest, incompetent, and a number of other negative qualities. To clear her name and save her professional reputation, she wanted to publish the findings in a journal.

She wrote to various editors, explaining what she would like to publish, but such journals are peer-reviewed. If other scientists or archaeologists did not agree with her findings, the report would not be published. Frustrated, she eventually wrote to the editor of *Quaternary Research*:

The problem as I see it is much bigger than Hueyatlaco. It concerns the manipulation of scientific thought through the suppression of "enigmatic data," data that challenges the prevailing mode of thinking. Hueyatlaco certainly does that! Not being an anthropologist, I didn't realize the full significance of our dates back in 1973, nor how deeply woven into our thought the current theory of human evolution had become. Our work at Hueyatlaco has been rejected by most archaeologists because it contradicts that theory, period. Their reasoning is circular. *H. sapiens sapiens* evolved ca. 30,000 – 50,000 years ago in Eurasia. Therefore, any *H.s.s.* tools 250,000 years old found in Mexico are impossible because *H.s.s.* evolved ca. 30,000 – .... etc. Such thinking makes for self-satisfied archaeologists but *lousy* science![2]

It is difficult for some people to objectively view evidence. This is because people always interpret new information based upon pre-existing knowledge and beliefs. Therefore, everyone looks through a pre-set lens. True objectivity is nearly impossible to obtain. Talk or write about topics like religious history or planetary history suggesting anything but standard views and you will see just how angry people can get. Considering alternative viewpoints is frightening to them, and they cannot handle it. They mentally shut down, and they mask their unwillingness to consider alternate ideas with anger or ridicule. However, there are people out there who are open-minded, people who think scientifically and are ready to consider all available evidence before settling on a theory. In truth, a ton of evidence suggests that the existing theory of human evolution is wrong. Likewise, evidence supports the theory that the mainstream view of planetary history is incomplete.

First, human beings are surprisingly more ancient than 100,000 years old. Complete skeletons or the bones of modern-looking humans have been found in various locations and dated to great antiquity. A fossilized femur was discovered near Trenton, N.J., 91 inches below the surface. The strata that surrounded it were undisturbed. It was thereby dated to c. 107,000 years ago, (about the same time that human beings are thought to have first appeared in Africa.)[3]

A full human skeleton was found near London, England. It is about 330,000 years old.[4] Another find just as old is a human jaw, found at Moulin Quignon in Abbeville, France. It too is approximately 330,000 years old.[5] Along with the jaw, other bones and teeth have been discovered. They too are more than 300,000 years old. Another site in France likewise revealed the presence of approximately 330,000-year-old human remains.[6] A human skull, femur, tibia, and some foot bones were found in a quarry on Avenue de Clichy, Paris. They were more than five meters (17 feet) beneath the surface. In Ipswich, England, an anatomically modern human skeleton lay beneath a layer of glacial boulder clay. It was approximately 1.5 meters (5 feet) deep, between the clay and glacial sands. Since these deposits were between 330,000 – 400,000 years old, and the strata were undisturbed, the skeleton also dates to this same period. It is 330,000 – 400,000 years old.[7]

Other sites housed anatomically modern human skeletons or bones that date to the same period: approximately 300,000 years ago. However, there are even older discoveries, including a human skull in Argentina dating to 1.0 – 1.5 million years old, a human jaw in England that is 2.5 million years old, and a skeleton found in Savona, Italy that is between 3 – 4 million years of age.[8] Likewise, a human jaw determined to be 2 – 3 million years old was found in Argentina, and human bones found in the Sierra Nevada Mountains in California range from 9 million to 55 million years old.[9] As if these finds were not shocking enough, other remains found are substantially older. For example, in Illinois, the bones of a man were 27 meters (90 feet) underground, in a bed of coal capped with two feet of slate. The coal is between 286 and 320 million years old.[10]

Besides human bones, other archaeological evidence supports the view that human beings are a much older species than previously thought. Such evidence includes tools and fossilized footprints. Ancient tools disrupt the prevailing theory of evolution as much as anomalous human remains do. The following are some examples: Stone arrowheads were found in Argentina along with intentionally shaped slingstones. Some of them are 2 – 3 million years old. Others are 1.7 – 2 million years old. Likewise, a variety of spearheads and arrowheads were discovered on Manitoulin Island in Lake Heron. They are between 75,000 and 125,000 years old. Older artifacts have also been recovered, including a stone pestle dating to more than 9 million years ago found in the Sierra Mountains, California. All this evidence indicates that human beings are a much older species than generally thought. Ancient human footprints provide even more evidence to support this conclusion.

The discovery of ancient human footprints, which date to times when humans are not thought to have existed, causes major problems for adherents of mainstream historical accounts. One can see such footprints in many places, including Kentucky. An investigator reported, "Each footprint has five toes and a distinct arch. The toes are spread apart like those of a human being who has never worn shoes."[11] It is believed that the prints were made before the sand turned into rock. If true, they are more than 300 million years old. Other ancient human footprints are in Russia, preserved in a 150-million-year-old Jurassic rock, right next to a large dinosaur track.[12]

The investigation of ancient footprints captured in stone gets even stranger. Some fossilized footprints are not barefooted tracks. They are ancient shoe prints. Engineer and geologist John Reid discovered a petrified shoe print in Nevada. It shows the outline of the shoe, an indentation where a heel would have worn down the sole, and a clear line of stitching. The rock in which this was found formed more than 5 million years ago. Reid had an image of the print blown up. He wrote:

The microphoto magnifications are twenty times larger than the specimen itself, showing the minutest detail of thread twist and warp, proving conclusively that the shoe sole is not a resemblance, but is strictly the handiwork of man. Even to the naked eye the threads can be seen distinctly, and the definitely symmetrical outlines of the shoe sole.[13]

Another seemingly modern shoe print was found in Cambrian shale near Antelope Spring, Utah. It is over 505 million years old.[14]

The study of unusual archaeological finds, including human remains, stone tools, and footprints, provides evidence that human beings are a much older species. Perhaps humans existed during the mass-extinction events that have regularly plagued the planet since its inception. Evidence supports this scenario. A great deal of evidence also supports the conclusion that human beings of the distant past were an advanced species. The first notion of this might come from seemingly modern shoe prints found preserved in rocks that are millions of years old. However, even more convincing evidence points to the same conclusion. This evidence comes from archaeological finds and historical texts.

Archaeological Evidence of Advanced Civilizations

A modern-looking nail was found embedded in a sandstone block removed from a Scotland quarry. The nail's head was embedded in the rock, so it is impossible that the object had been hammered into it. Therefore, the rock must have formed around it. This means that the nail was between 360 – 408 million years old.[15] Other objects have likewise been encased in stone, including gold threads. One discovered in England dates to 320 – 360 million years ago. Another, which was determined to be 260 – 320 million years old, was found in Morrisonville, Illinois.[16]

Even more amazing artifacts have been discovered. A construction blast at an old meetinghouse in Dorchester, Massachusetts broke apart large rocks. Within one of the largest boulders was a metal vase, broken in two by the explosion. An article in *Scientific American* reported:

> The body of this vessel resembles zinc in color, or a composition metal, in which there is a considerable portion of silver. On the side there are six figures or a flower, or bouquet, beautifully inlaid with pure silver, and around the

lower part of the vessel a vine, or wreath, also inlaid with silver.[17]

This vase is more than 600 million years old. Mainstream views of the history of the planet hold that life was just beginning to form during this time. However, people cannot dismiss this evidence easily. In conjunction with other archaeological finds, there is ample evidence that human beings are not just older than typically considered, but that they were advanced. Other finds that support this conclusion include a coin-like object found in Illinois that is between 200,000 and 400,000 years old. It has figures and inscriptions in an unknown language on both sides. Due to its uniform thickness, investigators determined that someone must have made it in some kind of machine shop.[18]

Carved human figurines dating to c. 2 million years ago were found in Nampa, Idaho, and ancient concrete walls were found in coalmines in Oklahoma; they are approximately 286 million years old. There are many examples of ancient, artificially created objects around the globe. One of the oldest is a metallic sphere from South Africa. Miners have found many spheres. Some of them are solid, made of bluish metal with white spots, while others are hollow, filled with a spongy substance. At least one of them has three parallel lines that stretch across the center of the sphere. This is one of the oldest artificially created objects discovered thus far. It is over 2.8 billion years old.[19]

Other archaeological finds that do not fit the mainstream theory of human history also exist. Some demonstrate that so-called modern inventions are not modern inventions at all. Ancient, technologically advanced civilizations had used them, and they have only been rediscovered in modern times. Such inventions include sparkplugs, batteries, and clocks.

A sparkplug was found in a geode in 1961 near Death Valley. It is composed of a metal core approximately 2 millimeters in diameter encased in a ceramic collar. Some petrified wood surrounds this. Between the wood and the collar is a bit of copper, suggesting that at one time there was a copper collar between the ceramic and wooden layers. Based on the fossils found in the geode, the object was determined to have been more than 500,000 years old.[20]

An example of an ancient battery is the so-called Baghdad Battery, found outside the city during an archaeological excavation in 1936. They found a six-inch-tall, 2,000-year-old pot made out of clay. Inside was a five-inch copper cylinder. The edge of the copper sheet was soldered with a lead-tin alloy and the bottom of the cylinder was capped by a copper disk and sealed with asphalt. Another layer of asphalt sealed the top. Through the center of it was an iron rod that extended vertically into the pot and through its asphalt top.

In 1940, German scientist Wilhelm König determined that the object was a battery, and that it was possibly used for electroplating gold onto silver objects. Various individuals built replicas. Willard Gray, an engineer at the General Electric High Voltage Laboratory in Pittsfield, Massachusetts, built a replica of this device and filled the pot with a copper sulfate solution in the 1940s. It generated an electrical current.[21] About 30 years later, Egyptologist Arne Eggebrecht did the same thing, but he filled the vessel with grape juice, as he believed the ancient civilizations that used it would have done. This also generated an electrical current, and he was able to electroplate a statuette with gold using the battery.[22]

This battery is not unique. Others were found in the same area. Most of them on display in various museums date from 248 B.C.E. to 226 C.E. However, the oldest intact batteries are more than 2,000 years old. It is likely that civilizations used the battery even earlier than this however — more than 4,500 years ago. Dr. König analyzed some pots excavated at Sumerian sites in Iraq. These pots dated to at least 2500 B.C.E. When he lightly tapped them, a blue patina emerged. This is characteristic of silver electroplated onto a copper base.[23] For this reason, it is possible that the Sumerians used the battery, and later civilizations learned about the technology from them. The battery, considered a new invention in the history of humankind, is actually an ancient invention that has been rediscovered.

Mechanical clocks are likewise thought of as a modern invention, and the mainstream historical accounts state that they did not appear until the fourteenth century in Europe. However, a clock composed of more than 30 interconnected gears was discovered in 1900 in a shipwreck called the Antikythera wreck, located off the Greek coast. It is the oldest known astronomical clock in the world, dating to c. 100 B.C.E. Based upon gear settings and inscriptions, it is likely that this device was created in Greece, or at least by individuals who spoke Greek. A crank was once attached to the object, and by turning the crank, a date could be set. Once set, the device would calculate astronomical information, such as the positions of various planets and stars.

37. The Antikythera Mechanism

The Antikythera Mechanism, as it is called, has three dials. Two are on the backside; the third is on the front. The front dial has two scales, and the outer ring is marked with 365 days of the solar year. Within this is a second dial that has the Greek zodiac signs. The front dial has three distinct indicators that showed the date and relative positions of the sun and moon. Another mechanism indicated the moon's phases. In addition, Mars and Venus appear in the device's inscriptions, and the front dial has a parapegma, which indicates the movement of specific stars. Another dial on the device displays the 235 months of the 19-year Metonic cycle. It is located next to another that has 223 distinct divisions that correspond to the *saros*: the length of time between certain eclipses.[24]

This device is amazing due to its complexity and the miniaturization of gears used in its construction. How such gears were constructed without machinery built to create them is unknown. However, it is quite possible that such machinery also existed. Devices like this were not thought to have existed in the first century B.C.E. Likewise, sparkplugs and batteries, which are thought to be modern inventions, are quite possibly ancient inventions. The technology had been lost in the passing of time, and was only *rediscovered* in modern times.

Archaeological evidence that human beings are not just an ancient species, but also technically advanced, is significant. However, even more evidence (to support this view) is on ancient maps and in the historical and religious texts of many of the world's religions.

Ancient Anomalous Maps

Massive libraries once housed the wisdom of the ancient world. The great library at Alexandria, for example, was a storehouse of world knowledge. It contained a book entitled *The True History of Mankind over the Last 100,000 Years*.[25] Religious zealots burned it in the third century, along with thousands of other valuable texts. They did the same thing in the Americas. When the Mayans did not want to give up their own religion to embrace a foreign one, the missionaries began an inquisition in which they tortured and killed non-believers.[26] They also burned Mayan historical and holy texts. Out of thousands of texts, only a handful survived. Back in Europe, the Catholic Church ordered all books in the Byzantine Empire destroyed, with the exception of the newly edited Bible that it had published.[27]

The Church was not the only organization to destroy historical texts. This atrocity also occurred in East Asia. For example, in 212 B.C.E. the Chinese emperor Qin Shi Huang ordered the majority of historical and scientific texts burned. Some information in these texts was lost forever, but extant records reveal that the ancient Chinese had advanced technology. Chinese records state that Emperor Shun (c. 2258 – 2208 B.C.E.) had a flying machine and parachute.[28] Emperor Cheng Tang likewise had a flying machine made for him c. 1766 B.C.E. by an inventor named Ki Kung Shi.[29] It is likely that some of the texts destroyed contained more detailed information regarding the creation and use of these craft. Only the stories, devoid of scientific explanations, have been preserved. This is what happens when texts are destroyed.

Consider if the same thing occurred today. There are airplanes, helicopters, and a variety of other flying machines. If all scientific and historical texts regarding their creation and use were destroyed during a mega-disaster, survivors would know about such craft. However, they would likely not be able to build them. It is specialized knowledge, and the skills and technology needed would eventually be forgotten. The knowledge that such craft existed would not dissipate, but after hundreds of years, facts would become stories, and history would become myth. To know what the ancient civilizations of this planet knew, historical texts must be studied. Many of the existing historical records were based on older accounts. Likewise, many old maps were based on much older source maps. Some of these maps support the idea that humankind is much older than generally thought. They also support the notion that there were technologically advanced civilizations in the distant past.

According to some views, Antarctica was last *completely* free of ice millions of years ago.[30] In addition, there were supposedly no civilizations in existence. People had not yet appeared. However, some maps show the continent completely free of ice. This signifies that there were people alive before the glaciation began. Phillippe Buache drew one such map in the eighteenth century. He based it on ancient maps that have since disappeared. The map shows Antarctica as it was thousands, if not millions of years ago, when it was completely free of ice. Hancock wrote:

> Basing his cartography on ancient sources now lost, the French academician depicted a clear waterway across the southern continent dividing it into two principle landmasses lying east and west of the line now marked by the Trans-

Antarctic Mountains. Such a waterway, connecting the Ross, Weddell, and Bellinghausen Seas, would indeed exist if Antarctica were free of ice. As the 1958 IGY Survey shows, the continent (which appears on modern maps as one continuous landmass) consists of an archipelago of large islands with mile-thick ice packed between them and rising above sea level.[31]

Like anomalous archaeological finds that suggest humankind is an ancient species, this map cannot be easily explained. Other maps are based upon more recent ancient maps. They depict Antarctica not when it was completely free from ice, but when it was only partially free of ice.

The Oronteus Finaeus Map was created in 1531. It was based on earlier maps, and it shows Antarctica partially free of ice. Based upon available evidence, it is likely that Antarctica was partially ice free more than 6,000 years ago.[32] This seems to make the possibility of an advanced sea-faring culture that mapped this territory more plausible, (compared to a culture who mapped the continent millions of years ago). However, mainstream views hold that no such cultures existed. Still, this map seems to show Antarctica with ice-free shores.

Hapgood wrote:

> As my eyes fell upon the southern hemisphere of a world map drawn by Oronteus Finaeus in 1531, I had the instant conviction that I had found a truly authentic map of the real Antarctica. The general shape of the continent was startlingly like the outline of the continent on our modern maps. The position of the South Pole, nearly in the center of the continent, seemed about right. The mountain ranges that skirted the coast suggested the numerous ranges that have been discovered in Antarctica in recent years. It was obvious, too, that this was no slapdash creation of somebody's

imagination. The mountain ranges were individualized, some definitely coastal and some not. From most of them rivers were shown flowing into the sea, following in every case what looked like very natural and convincing drainage patterns. This suggested, of course, that the coasts may have been ice free when the original map was drawn. The deep interior, however, was free entirely of rivers and mountains, suggesting that the ice may have been present there.[33]

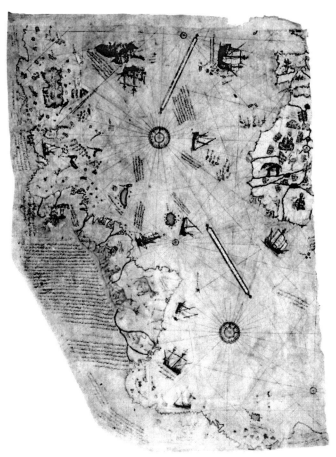

38. The Piri Reis Map

Another famous map that seems to show the same thing is the Piri Reis Map. This map, like many others, stemmed from older documents — some of them older than 400 B.C.E. It was created in Constantinople in 1513, and shows the northern coast of Antarctica when it was free from ice.[34] The map clearly and accurately indicates geographical features, including inlets, small islands, and rivers. The continent, therefore, must have been mapped earlier than 6,000 B.C.E.[35] This map, and the others previously mentioned, are evidence of the existence of at least one, if not multiple ancient human civilizations, that have been forgotten in recent times.

More proof of such civilizations is in ancient historical and religious texts. The accounts have been mistaken as myths, but many historical stories are mistaken as myths until discovered evidence legitimizes the tales. Consider Troy. Before archaeological excavations began, mainstream historians vehemently denied its existence. It was only a myth. Once archaeologists excavated the city, the stories made famous in Homer's books were reinterpreted as historical. Old texts preserve records of ancient yet technologically advanced civilizations. The accounts indicate that cities existed thousands of years before mainstream archaeologists and historians say they did. They also reveal that such civilizations were advanced, using things like electricity, power tools, aircraft, and even nuclear weapons.

Ancient Aircraft described in Judeo-Christian Texts

Many Judeo-Christian texts reveal the possibility that ancient civilizations possessed aircraft. The Kebra Negast, a sacred book from Ethiopia, states that King Solomon had flying machines. He even gave one to the Queen of Sheba:

> And he went into his house and gave unto her whatsoever she wished for of splendid things and riches, and beautiful apparel which bewitched the eyes, and everything on which great store was set in the country of Ethiopia, and camels and wagons, six thousand in number, which were laden with beautiful things of the most desirable kind, and wagons wherein loads were carried over the desert, and a vessel wherein one could travel over the sea, and a vessel wherein one could traverse the air (or winds), which Solomon had made by the wisdom that God had given unto him.[36]

Other texts, including Muslim accounts, relate that Solomon used his flying machine to travel to various places, and he typically landed on mountains. He even traveled to Tibet and spoke with some of the natives there. In Tibet, similar records exist. King Solomon did not just use his craft for joyriding, but also to create maps of the world.

Other accounts describe ancient aircraft, including the Old Testament (the Torah). The Book of Ezekiel describes what many interpret as a UFO sighting. It describes flying craft and pilots, who wore some kind of protective suits that made them look like animals. The following is the account in the English Standard version of the Bible:

> As I looked, behold, a stormy wind came out of the north, and a great cloud, with brightness around it, and fire flashing forth continually, and in the midst of the fire, as it were gleaming metal. And from the midst of it came the likeness of four living creatures....As for the likeness of the living creatures, their appearance was like burning coals of fire, like the appearance of torches moving to and fro among the living creatures. And the fire was bright, and out of the fire went forth lightning. And the living creatures darted to and fro, like the appearance of a flash of lightning.

> Now as I looked at the living creatures, I saw a wheel on the Earth beside the living creatures, one for each of the four of them. As for the appearance of the wheels and their construction: their appearance was like the gleaming of beryl. And the four had the same likeness, their appearance and construction being as it were a wheel within a wheel. When they went, they went in any of the four directions without turning as they went. And their rims were tall and awesome, and the rims of all four were full of eyes all around. And when the living creatures went, the wheels went beside them; and when the living creatures rose from the Earth, the wheels rose. Wherever the spirit wanted to go, they went, and the wheels rose along with them, for the spirit of the living

creatures was in the wheels. When those went, these went; and when those stood, these stood; and when those rose from the Earth, the wheels rose along with them, for the spirit of the living creatures was in the wheels.

Over the heads of the living creatures there was the likeness of an expanse, shining like awe-inspiring crystal, spread out above their heads. And under the expanse their wings were stretched out straight, one toward another. And each creature had two wings covering its body. And when they went, I heard the sound of their wings like the sound of many waters, like the sound of the Almighty, a sound of tumult like the sound of an army.[37]

This is most-likely a description of an encounter with advanced flying machines and their pilots. However, the person who witnessed them did not know what he was seeing, as such technology was unknown. He clearly describes circular craft. They appeared as wheels within wheels, and the edge of these wheels, "the rims" according to the text, were lined with lights. The craft themselves were metallic, the color of beryl. They darted back and forth without seeming to turn. As they moved, they emitted a humming sound, the sound of a motor, which Ezekiel described as similar to both the sound of rushing water and the sound of a tumultuous army. This is so similar to other UFO sightings that it is impossible to deny that this story records a similar interaction with not just the flying objects, but also the creatures that piloted them, dressed in special suits.

Ancient Indian Aircraft

The Kebra Nagast, the Old Testament, and other Muslim texts indicate that flying machines existed, but do not provide many details about the craft themselves. Ancient Indian accounts provide more information. The *Mahabharata*, for example, is a huge text, more than 5,000 pages in length. Written between 540 – 300 B.C.E., it is an account of ancient Indian history, and it describes a civilization that existed thousands of years ago. This civilization, called the Rama Empire, supposedly existed 12,000 years ago, but it was probably flourishing earlier than this; it is likely that this civilization existed until the Great Flood (c. 11,000 B.C.E.), which destroyed many ancient cities. It is likely that it existed more than 13,000 years ago.

This ancient civilization was technologically advanced, and texts such as the *Mahabharata*, written 2,500 years ago, contain numerous references to these flying machines. They are called *vimanas*:

> "Vimanas, decked and equipped according to rule, looked like heavenly structures in the sky... borne away they looked like highly beautiful flights of birds."[38]

"And on this sun like, divine, wonderful chariot, the wise disciple of Kuru flew joyously upward. When becoming invisible to the mortals who walk the Earth, he saw wondrous airborne chariots by the thousands."[39]

"Bhima flew along in his car, resplendent as a sun and loud as thunder... the flying chariot shone like a flame in the night sky of summer... it swept by like a comet... it was [as] if two suns were shining. Then the chariot rose up and all the heavens brightened."[40]

"The vimana had all necessary equipment. It could not be conquered by the gods or demons. And it radiated light and reverberated with a deep rumbling sound. Its beauty captivated the minds of all who beheld it. Visvakarma, the lord of its design and construction, had created it by the power of his austerities, and its outline, like that of the sun, could not be easily delineated."[41]

"When the Daityas were being slaughtered they again took to their vimana and, employing the Danava science, flew up into the sky... I [Arjuna] assaulted their vimana... Wounded by the flight of the deadly-accurate missiles, the Asura vimana fell broken to the Earth... Metali swiftly descended Earthward, as in a steep dive, on our divinely effulgent car."[42]

Other accounts of vimana are found in another ancient Indian text called the Ramayana, which is even older than the Mahabharata. Here are some examples:

"When morning dawned, Rama, taking the celestial car Puspaka had sent to him by Vivpishand, stood ready to depart. Self-propelled was that car. It was large and finely painted. It had two stories and many chambers and windows, and was draped with flags and banners. It gave forth a melodious sound as it coursed along its airy way."[43]

"Beholding the vimana coming by force of will Rama attained to an excess of astonishment. And the king got in, and the excellent vimana, at the command of Raghira, rose up into the higher atmosphere. And in that vimana, coursing at will, Rama greatly delighted."[44]

"The Puspaka Vimana, that resembles the sun and belongs to my brother, was brought by the powerful Ravan; that aerial and excellent car, going everywhere at will, is ready for thee. That car, resembling a bright cloud in the sky, is in the city of Lanka."[45]

The following are other accounts from the *Bhagavata Purana*, dated to the ninth century or earlier, and the *Siva Purana*:

"He traveled in that way through the various planets, as the air passes freely in every direction. Coursing through the air in that grand and splendid vimana, which could fly at will, he surpassed even the Devas."[46]

"Then the highly intelligent Asura Maya built the cities... There were many palaces with gems. Aerial cars shining like the sun, set with Padmaraga stones, moving in all directions and looking like moonbeams, illuminated the cities."[47]

Not all references to vimanas in ancient Indian epics refer to flying machines. In fact, the term vimana describes a variety of transportation. An account in another ancient Indian text called the *Ghatotrachabadma* describes one of these:

"A huge and terrible black vimana made of black iron, it was 400 yojanas high and as many wide, equipped with engines set in their proper places. No steeds nor elephants propelled it. Instead, it was driven by machines that looked like elephants."[48]

A thorough analysis of Indian texts indicates that there were various types of vimanas. Some were used to travel across land, others to travel underwater. Regarding the ships that travel in the skies, there were three distinct kinds: one that could travel close distances, another that could travel between countries, and another capable of interstellar travel.[49] Other texts, such as the *Samarangana Sutradhara*, written by the Paramara King Bhoja of Dhar (1000 – 1055 C.E.), contain more information about the creation of these craft:

> Strong and durable must the body of the vimana be made, like a great flying bird of light material. Inside one must put the mercury engine with its iron heating apparatus underneath. By means of the power latent in the mercury which sets the driving whirlwind in motion, a man sitting inside may travel a great distance in the sky. The movements of the vimana are such that it can vertically ascend, vertically descend, move slanting forwards and backwards. With the help of the machines human beings can fly in the air.[50]

As if this is not enough, the *Vymaanika Shaastra*, (*The Science of Aerodynamics*), written by Maharshi Bharadwaaja in the fourth century B.C.E. provides even more detailed information. According to this scientific text, there were two types of flying vimana. One was the shape of a cylinder. The other was a saucer-shaped craft. The latter was typically a two-storied flying machine that had numerous windows. It could move quickly and emitted a humming noise. The technological capabilities of vimanas surpass those that exist in this present cycle of existence. The vimanas could move in any direction through the sky, and could come to a dead stop. They could also cloak themselves, becoming invisible at will. The temperature and air within the vimanas were regulated, and the ships had weapons.

The pilots of these ships had to be skilled in the variety of maneuvers that the craft were capable of performing. The *Vymaanika Shaastra* explains:

> The pilot should have had training in *maantrica* and *taantrica*, *kritaka* and *antaraalaka*, *goodha* or hidden, *drishya* and *adrishya* or seen and unseen, *paroksha* and *aparoksha*, contraction and expansion, changing shape, look frightening, look pleasing, becoming luminous or enveloped in darkness, deluge or *pralaya*, *vimukha*, *taara*, stun by thunderstorm, *din*, jump, move zigzag like [a] serpent, *chaapala*, face all sides, hear distant sounds, take pictures, known enemy maneuver [sic.], know [the] direction of enemy approach, *stabdhaka* or paralyse, and *karshana* or exercise magnetic pull.[51]

Not all skills and capabilities mentioned are completely understood today, but some of these terms were explained in more detail in the text. Goodha, for example, explained how the vimana could become invisible. The technology involved using the atmospheric layer of the Earth to harness the "dark content" of the sun, which could be used as a cloaking device.[52] A similar technology is referred to as drishya. This refers to a technology that uses electrical energy and the power of the wind while the craft is in flight. Somehow, the combination of these two things creates a glow, the reflection of which appears in the mirror, located at the front of the craft. By manipulating this mirror, the pilots can camouflage the vimana.[53]

The *Vymaanika Shaastra* also contains complex instructions regarding what pilots need to eat and wear. It also discusses the metals needed for the craft's construction, the metals and lenses required on board, and how to protect the craft from the elements. The text also includes "information on steering, precautions for long flights, protection of the airships from storms and lightning, and how to switch the drive to solar energy or some other free energy source, possibly some sort of gravity drive."[54] Other information provided in the text (and in other ancient sources) describes the type of engine used to power the device. The *Samarangana Sutradhara* contains the following information:

> Four strong mercury containers must be built into the interior structure. When those have been heated by controlled fire from iron containers, the vimana develops thunder power from mercury. At once it becomes like a pearl in the sky.[55]

This type of mercury-based engine is today called a mercury vortex engine. It is an ancient technology that is now being rediscovered. Mercury has some unusual characteristics. If it is put onto a plate and heated from underneath with a naked flame, the mercury reacts. When the flame moves in a circle, the mercury rotates in the opposite direction. This reaction gets even more interesting: without changing the rotational speed of the flame, the metal continues to increase its speed. It ends up spinning much faster than the movement of the flame.

The ancient Indian texts *Samarangana Sutradhara* and *Vymaanika Shaastra* both clearly state that the mercury in these machines has to be heated by "controlled fire from iron containers." "Inside one must put the mercury engine with its iron heating apparatus underneath." It is apparent that there is something to this technology; something that the ancients knew. This technology has been lost in the modern age. The properties of this metal should be actively explored, as it might hold the key to unlock some planetary mysteries, including a full understanding of gravitational forces and its connection to electromagnetic forces. There may be other substances that behave in a similar way, and if the heat sources were beside or above the substances, much different reactions could occur. These could include the creation of vortices or other kinds of anomalous atmospheric conditions. They could also be related to geomagnetism, electromagnetism, or other phenomena that might not be completely understood.

Mercury was likely used in vortex engines to power some of the earliest aircraft used by human beings in the current cycle of existence. Besides spinning quickly when heated from beneath, it also has other unusual characteristics. When it is put into a gyroscope and charged with electricity, some of the effects produced include levitation, lights, and more. The ancient texts of the *Mahabharata* and the *Vymaanika Shaastra* indicate that vimanas were built and operated by means of several gyroscopes with mercury vortexes. Hopefully in the near future, we will rediscover the technology. These old accounts are not myths. They are too specific. The only logical conclusion is that ancient aircraft did exist in an ancient Indian civilization. More evidence supports the notion that ancient aircraft existed, including archaeological finds from various cultures.

Archaeology and Ancient Aircraft

Consider what would occur today if an alien spaceship crashed. Armies would spring into action to take forceful possession of the wreckage, as knowledge gained by studying debris is a source of power. Once the craft has been secured, they would use reverse engineering to either duplicate the craft (to the best of their ability), or to create something similar. This scenario is most likely what occurred in ancient times. According to the old Indian texts, a civilization that existed 12,000 years ago had flying machines. They had those that could fly close distances, those that could fly between countries, and those that were capable of interstellar travel. Although the technology possessed by this and other ancient civilizations was different from modern technology, for the sake of comparison, these flying vimanas can be associated with specific modern aircraft. The first type, which could travel close distances, could be hot-air balloons or single-engine airplanes. The second, which could fly between countries, could be associated with modern jets. The last class of vimana described, which were capable of interplanetary travel, are equivalent to modern space shuttles and perhaps space stations.

Upon reading such ancient texts for the first time, one might wonder where the physical evidence is. Certainly, if such craft existed, there would be physical evidence. Seventeen thousand years ago, ocean levels were 120 meters (400 feet) lower than they are today.[56] This was because of the extensive glaciation in Europe, North America, and other landmasses. The temperature changed, and glaciers melted rapidly, creating flash floods. The ocean levels quickly rose 107 meters (350 feet), burying entire islands and seaside communities forever. Areas that were once prime real estate, with harbors and ports to facilitate trade, vanished. They were gone forever.

Today, we know what happens to airplanes that crash into seas. Saltwater eats the metal and fabrics, and corals stretch out, engulfing them. Animals make their homes in the wreckage, and after only a couple hundred years, such aircraft are nearly impossible to find. One only needs to imagine what would occur after more than 10,000 years underwater. The objects would be completely lost. However, some remnants of these ancient aircraft were likely found by later civilizations that developed after the Great Flood. People who found strange pieces of metal fused together in unusual shapes studied them. They took the remnants apart and learned what they could about them. They wondered what the objects were, and they made wooden models of the discovered craft.

Experimenting and playing with the models, as scientists (aerodynamic tests) and children (model airplanes and gliders) do today, the earliest civilizations of the current age learned about aerodynamics principles from their distant ancestors. Legends of a great flood continued until the present, and distant knowledge of flying machines was passed on in the form of models. Some have been discovered in South America, China, and Egypt.

In recent centuries, Columbia has lured treasure hunters seeking a mythical golden city called El Dorado. In the twentieth century, tomb robbers found some unusual gold objects. Some looked like insects and animals, others like modern aircraft. These objects, created by a pre-Columbian civilization known as Tolema or Kalema, look like unusual airplanes with wings and fuselage. They appear to be models of airplanes seen by ancient people. Contrary to modern aircraft, the most likely place for an engine was on the back of the craft. On jet aircraft, engines are under the wings. However, in this gold model, the engine would have to be in an unusual spot, and it was unknown if this position would work. That changed in 1997, when Peter Benting and Algund Eenboom created a larger replica of the airplane. Although bigger, they used the exact same shape and size relationship between parts of the plane. They added an engine and some landing gear, and they took it for a test spin. It flew. "Subsequent test flights revealed that the plane continued to behave impeccably: Takeoffs and landings were perfect, and its flight path was stable."[57] The shape of the craft was perfect aerodynamically, which indicates that this ancient civilization from South America either had explicit knowledge of aerodynamic principles, or they had created an artistic model of something they had seen: a crashed airplane, otherwise known as a vimana.

Another interesting archaeological find is a model airplane or glider from Egypt. Originally found in 1898, it was sent to the Museum of Cairo where it remained unnoticed for many years. The object was a wooden, bird-shaped figurine found in Sakkara next to an inscription that read, "I want to fly." For years, the object was unnoticed by archeologists. However, in 1969, Dr. Caliil Mesiah noticed that it did not appear to have a bird-like shape. The wings looked just like those on a modern airplane, and the back of the object, which would have had a horizontal appendage if it were a bird figurine, had a vertical one instead. Modern aircraft also have this vertical appendage. The only thing missing was a tail wing, but there is a notch on the tail end of the plane where another piece had broken off. Over thousands of years, the piece likely fell off and was lost in the excavation, being misinterpreted as a random piece of wood, (since birds do not have such an appendage, and the object was initially misinterpreted as a carving of a bird). However, the object looked as though it could fly. To test this possibility, Simon Sanderson built an exact scale model of the craft that was five times larger than the original. He put it through a variety of tests and realized that it was aerodynamically sound. It could fly. This indicates that the ancient Egyptians might have also seen the wreckage of some type of vimana, the one that could travel between countries perhaps.

Consider what would occur today if there were no airplanes — if there were no machines that could soar through the heavens. If the wreckage of an ancient craft were found, some individuals would devote their lives to understanding what the object was and why it was used. They would come up with various theories. Some of the theories might be deemed logical by society and become thought of as fact. Other strange theories, such as it being the remains of a large object that could travel through the sky with people inside it, would be mocked. This is because it is an outrageous idea without scientific proof. However, someone might look at the wreckage, and then watch birds like sea gulls or hawks in flight. It would not take long for him or her to develop a theory that others would find preposterous: that ancient humans had large, bird-like craft that could sail through the skies, carrying people inside.

Although others would laugh at this person, a select few would share his or her views. Eventually, people would create models of the craft and throw them through the air, illustrating that its flight was possible. Exactly how the full size ships were created and how they were powered might never be rediscovered, but they would begin to understand that such a technological creation was possible. This scenario is most likely what had occurred in some societies that flourished during the beginning of the modern age. Remnants from ancient, advanced civilizations were found, and models were created to try to understand this once extant technology. However, some civilizations went beyond mere models.

Chinese records indicate that the ancients built flying machines. According to the old Chinese text *Records of the Scholars*, an engineer made a wooden bird-like craft that had a motor. It was able to travel for approximately a mile.[58] Perhaps there was some sort of a wind-up device that powered propellers, enabling the craft to fly. Other descriptions of helicopters exist in Chinese historical accounts, so this possibility is not far-fetched. A book written by Ko Hung in 320 C.E. describes propellers: "Some have made flying cars with wood from the inner part of the jujube tree, using ox leather straps fastened to revolving blades so as to set the machine in motion."[59] Other Chinese texts indicate that Emperor Shun (2258 – 2208 B.C.E.) created a flying apparatus and a parachute, and that Ki Kung Shi designed a flying chariot more than 3,500 years ago.[60]

Similar accounts are in other ancient texts, including Greek and Roman accounts. All of these diverse records together indicate that modern technological advancements, such as helicopters, gliders, planes, and spacecraft, are not new inventions at all. The ancients used such craft, called vimanas in the ancient Indian civilization. After the destruction of these civilizations during the Great Flood, later civilizations found some aircraft remains once the oceans had calmed and receded. The first civilization to have likely found such wrecks was Sumer, whose culture began c. 4,500 – 4,000 B.C.E. The Great Flood occurred c. 11,000 B.C.E. This means that the craft they had found had been exposed to natural destructive elements for approximately 7,000 years. The fact that they were able to make any sense out of what they witnessed is a testament to the wisdom and imagination that they and other ancient civilizations must have had. As if the possibility of ancient flight were not enough, there is also evidence that some modern weapons were likewise used in the distant past, before c. 11,000 B.C.E.

Ancient Atomic Weapons

Historical texts and archaeological finds indicate that ancient atomic weapons might have also existed. According to the *Mahabharata*, written c. 400 B.C.E., the Rama civilization in ancient India had flying machines and nuclear weapons. In the text, these bombs are called Brahma weapons, and surviving victims lost their hair and nails. They displayed other symptoms that we would today relate to radiation sickness. One of the cities destroyed by this type of weapon is Mohenjo-Daro, located in the Indus Valley in Pakistan. The ruins date to 2600 – 1900 B.C.E., but the site might be much older than that. When excavations began in the 1920's, more than 40 bodies were found in unusual positions in the streets. The body positions indicated that they had died suddenly and violently. Further analysis of the remains also indicated that they were highly radioactive.[61]

The unearthed city also had signs of vitrification, which occurs when stone or sand is heated to such a degree that it actually becomes glass. When this site was first discovered, scientists were unable to explain how the vitrification had occurred, as it was unlike that caused by lightning. It was more severe and covered a larger area. After the first atomic bomb test took place in Alamogordo, New Mexico on July 16, 1945, the phenomenon could be explained.

A nuclear blast causes vitrification, and the vitrified sand at the testing site was comparable to (if not exactly the same as) the sand and stone at Mohenjo-Daro. Other ancient sites display similar characteristics, suggesting that a nuclear disaster had taken place. It is likely that the damage came from above. Ancient Indian texts that reference flying craft and weapons describe the devastation caused. This is an account in the *Mahabharata*:

> Gurkha, flying in his swift and powerful Vimana, hurled against the three cities of the Vrishnis and Andhakas a single projectile charged with all the power of the universe. An incandescent column of smoke and fire, as brilliant as ten thousand suns, rose in all its splendor. It was the unknown weapon, the iron thunderbolt, a gigantic messenger of death, which reduced to ashes the entire race of the Vrishnis and Andhakas. The corpses were so burnt they were no longer recognizable. Hair and fingernails fell out, Pottery broke without cause... Foodstuffs were poisoned. To escape, the warriors threw themselves in streams to wash themselves and their equipment.[62]

Hiroshima survivor Akiko Takakura wrote the following about the atomic bomb:

> Suddenly, a flash. "Ah!" Just as they saw it, people in the houses were shoved over and smashed. People walking on the streets were blown away. People were burned — faces, arms, legs — all over. People were killed, all over the city of Hiroshima by a single bomb. Those who died. A hundred? A thousand? No. Ten thousand? No. Many, many more than that. More people than we can count died, speechless, knowing nothing. Others suffered terrible burns, horrific injuries. Some were thrown so hard their stomachs ripped open, their spines broke. Whole bodies filled with glass

shards. Clothing disappeared, burned and tattered. Fires came right after the explosion. Hiroshima engulfed in flames. Everyone fleeing, not knowing where they were or where to go. Everyone barefoot, crying tears of anger and grief, hair sticking up, looking like Ashura [a demonic-looking deity], they ran on broken glass, smashed roofs along a long, wide road of fire. Blood flowed. Burned skin peeled and dangled. Whirlwinds of fire raged here and there. Hundreds, thousands of fire balls 30-centimeters across whirled right at us. It was hard to breathe in the flames, hard to see in the smoke.[63]

The similarities between the Indian historical account and modern-day nuclear survivor accounts written by citizens of Hiroshima and Nagasaki are undeniable. Robert Oppenheimer, the father of the atomic bomb, was familiar with Indian historical texts. After the Alamogordo nuclear test in New Mexico, he was asked if that was the first atomic bomb ever detonated. His response recognized that the technology had been used in the past. He responded, "Yes. In modern history."[64]

Other Ancient Civilizations

Indian historical texts clearly indicate that an ancient, technologically advanced civilization once existed in southern Asia. This was not the only civilization that possessed such knowledge. Evidence suggests that other antediluvian civilizations were likewise technologically advanced. Many cultures possess legends of ancient, flourishing civilizations that were destroyed, such as Lemuria, Mu, Atlantis, and Eden. Atlantis was popularized in Plato's *Timaeus* and *Critias*, which were written approximately 360 B.C.E. According to these texts, Atlantis was an advanced island nation, a naval power that ruled a large area of Europe. Plato wrote that it existed about 9,000 years before the time of Solon, so c. 9,600 B.C.E.

The following is Plato's description of the nation:

> Many great and wonderful deeds are recorded of your state in our histories. But one of them exceeds all the rest in greatness and valour. For these histories tell of a mighty power which unprovoked made an expedition against the whole of Europe and Asia, and to which your city put an end. This power came forth out of the Atlantic Ocean, for in those days the Atlantic was navigable; and there was an island

situated in front of the straits which are by you called the Pillars of Heracles; the island was larger than Libya and Asia put together, and was the way to other islands, and from these you might pass to the whole of the opposite continent which surrounded the true ocean; for this sea which is within the Straits of Heracles is only a harbour, having a narrow entrance, but that other is a real sea, and the surrounding land may be most truly called a boundless continent. Now in this island of Atlantis there was a great and wonderful empire which had rule over the whole island and several others, and over parts of the continent, and, furthermore, the men of Atlantis had subjected the parts of Libya within the columns of Heracles as far as Egypt, and of Europe as far as Tyrrhenia. This vast power, gathered into one, endeavoured to subdue at a blow our country and yours and the whole of the region within the straits; and then, Solon, your country shone forth, in the excellence of her virtue and strength, among all mankind. She was pre-eminent in courage and military skill, and was the leader of the Hellenes. And when the rest fell off from her, being compelled to stand alone, after having undergone the very extremity of danger, she defeated and triumphed over the invaders, and preserved from slavery those who were not yet subjugated, and generously liberated all the rest of us who dwell within the pillars.[65]

Atlantis was destroyed by natural disasters: earthquakes and floods precipitated by volcanic eruptions. Plato himself informs us that numerous floods have wiped out entire civilizations. He wrote, "Many great deluges have taken place during the [last] nine thousand years."[66] The floods to which he refers were lesser floods, and not the Great Flood that destroyed many great cities.

There is a cycle of creation and destruction on this planet. Civilizations arise, becoming increasingly advanced, and then they are wiped out by global cataclysms. These include earthquakes, volcanic eruptions, and massive floods, which relate to intermittent periods of glaciation and then deglaciation. Some individuals today understand this natural cycle, and they know that this present cycle will eventually end. Conversely, others deny this. Some antediluvian civilizations were likely ignorant that they would be destroyed. Others understood this great cycle of creation and destruction. They knew that anything built of wood or metal would eventually be destroyed, leaving no traces for people who emerge at the beginning of the next age. The only things that survive global cataclysms are large stone structures. For this reason, many ancient civilizations created megalithic structures. Strangely, their existence provides additional evidence of advanced technological capabilities.

Megalithic Structures

Unknown civilizations built many megalithic structures before the Great Flood. They were simply used by subsequent civilizations after the deluge. In other words, later civilizations moved into existing structures, and then built houses, temples, and obelisks around them. This used to be a standard view in archaeology, and it has only recently lost favor among mainstream archaeologists. Some people do not like to have any unanswered questions when dealing with historical artifacts and building. Therefore, they will force answers upon them, sometimes ignoring evidence to do so. For example, many historians now believe that Khafre (c. 2520 – 2494 B.C.E.) built the Egyptian Sphinx. The only evidence for this is that the nearby Valley Temple has been attributed to Khafre, and Khafre's cartouche appears in the Sphinx Stela, erected by Thutmosis IV. Some now take this to mean that Khafre was the builder of the monument. However, along with other evidence found on site, it makes much more sense that Khafre was its restorer. This rush to date the monument to the reign of Khafre is relatively new, as archaeologists once regarded the Sphinx as much older than the pyramids. Sir Wallis Budge wrote that the structure was much older than the reign of Khafre, who built the Second

Pyramid. He suggested that it had been built by a civilization that existed before the Egyptians: a civilization that we know little about. John Ward also stated that it was much older than the pyramids. It is likely that the Sphinx was built thousands of years before the reign of Khafre, by a civilization that existed before the last period of destruction.

39. The Sphinx (Giza Plateau, Egypt)

The Sphinx itself cannot be dated using conventional methods because it was carved out of natural rock. For this reason, a date must be intimated in other ways. The Inventory Stela (c. 678 – 525 B.C.E.) states that the structure had existed since before the reign of Khufu (c. 2589 – 2566 B.C.E.), Khafre's predecessor. During this period, it was considered an ancient structure, not originating during the pre-dynastic period, but from the First Time. Later Egyptians, in the dynastic period, regarded the rulers during this First Time as gods because of their accomplishments and attributes. As is common in all societies, historical accounts are embellished and become legends. Kings become heroes, who in turn are occasionally deified. This is why individuals like Osiris, an ancient Egyptian king who conquered India and other countries, founded many cities, and taught much to his followers, was regarded as a god by later cultures.[67]

40. Khafre's Pyramid and the Great Sphinx

Egyptian texts, which describe his deeds, state that he had brought civilization to Egypt. He also taught the inhabitants agricultural techniques and how to make wine. In Ethiopia, he undertook engineering projects, building canals with floodgates and raising riverbanks to prevent the Nile from overflowing.[68] Most importantly, Osiris abolished cannibalism and taught people to live peacefully with their neighbors. Various scholars have tried to link him to flesh-and-blood kings. Frazer suggested that Osiris was Khent, and that the name Osiris was applied to him posthumously.[69]

In time, storytellers magnified his deeds and gave him god-like attributes. Stories about the gods of ancient Egypt, and those found in various cultures, might refer to ancient kings who existed before the Great Flood. If so, some of these individuals might have been responsible for building the Sphinx. It is clear that it existed before the flood: not just because of the Inventory Stela text, but also because of unmistakable signs of water damage on the monument itself. Such exposure to water could not have happened during the early dynastic period (3100 – 2686 B.C.E.). It could only have occurred at the end of the last Ice Age, when the area had a much different climate. It must have already been in existence c. 11,000 B.C.E.

Other evidence points to the same conclusion. Today, if left unattended, sand would completely cover the Sphinx. Throughout the ages, the monument has been completely covered and then subsequently uncovered and restored by various individuals. Khafre was the first known restorer, and Thutmosos IV recorded his name on the Sphinx Stela to commemorate the act. In time, sand covered it again. Thutmosis himself restored the monument again. After, the monument had to be dug out of the sand on three different occasions: in 1818 by Caviglia, in 1886 by Maspero, and in 1925 by the Egyptian Antiquities Service. Hancock points out that building such a monument in a desert with shifting sands would be illogical, as the monument would have to be cleared constantly. It is therefore more likely that the monument was created when the weather in the area was much different. He wrote:

> Since the Sahara is a young desert, and since the Giza area in particular was wet and relatively fertile 11,000 – 15,000 years ago, is it not worth considering another scenario altogether? Is it not possible that the Sphinx enclosure was carved out during those distant green millennia when topsoil was still anchored to the surface of the plateau by the roots of grasses and shrubs and when what is now a desert of wind-blown sand more closely

243

resembled the rolling savannahs of modern Kenya and Tanzania?[70]

When the evidence is put together and reviewed objectively, it seems more likely that the Sphinx is an ancient building: a building that the Egyptians themselves claimed had existed since the First Time. Like many megalithic structures in the world, they were used by countless generations after the floodwaters had abated. These people found huge, sturdy structures, which they themselves lacked the capability to build, and they moved into them. They used them as a base for their new cities, and they made such structures the center of their societies. However, evidence suggests that other structures in Giza are equally ancient.

41. The Pyramids at Giza, Egypt

The Giza plateau pyramids were built with astronomical considerations in mind. The three pyramids, named after Khufu, Khafre, and Menkaure by archaeologists thousands of years after they had been built, perfectly aligned to the star constellation Orion, (which was associated with Osiris), when they were erected. However, this alignment did not occur during the dynastic period. It could only have occurred c. 11,000 B.C.E.[71] This dating procedure, by means of astronomical alignments, is often the only way in which megalithic structures can be dated. This form of dating is in the field of archaeoastronomy, which seeks to understand how ancient cultures made use of celestial phenomena, including the orientation of heavenly bodies. The fascination with astronomical alignments that many civilizations had all over the world makes it possible to date such huge, otherwise undatable structures. According to Geologist Scott Wolter, this is one of the best ways to date ancient structures. In many cases, it is the only way. When this methodology is applied to ancient structures across the globe, it becomes apparent that they are much older than the majority of people believe. In addition, it demonstrates that many of these structures were built by advanced civilizations. The technological capabilities of these ancient societies are still not completely clear, and since there are questions that cannot be answered without rethinking the history of humankind as a whole, such capabilities are ignored in mainstream history textbooks. However, an analysis of ancient megaliths reveals the presence of some technologies that have been just recently rediscovered. It also discloses the existence of technological capabilities that we are just beginning to understand today.

Manufacturing Engineer Christopher Dunn investigated the statues and structures attributed to ancient Egyptians, and has concluded that they must have had advanced tools. He found a granite block that had a deep cut. It could only have been made with a saw that was 11 meters (35 feet) in diameter. This, combined with other evidence, has led him to suggest that giant pits found near pyramids were not boat pits, as mainstream archaeologists suggest, but saw pits.[72] They were pits that held massive saws used to cut granite blocks to exact specifications for use in the building of pyramids and other structures. He studied the perfectly carved faces on statues of Ramses in the Temple of Amun Mut Khonsu, and determined that they were the same: the left halves of the faces were exact mirror images of the right halves and vice versa. He wrote:

> Using computer graphics and comparing the geometry of one side of the crown and head with the other and also with drafting elements such as rectangles and circles, it becomes clear that these statues must have been cut with the assistance of mechanical devices that caused the cutting tool to move along predetermined boundaries to produce an accurate representation in granite of the specified design.[73]

Dunn looked at the precision cutting and shaping that the ancient Egyptians were able to accomplish. He also looked at their mistakes: tool marks left on statue bases and in other locations. He found drill holes and lathe marks on hard stone surfaces. He also found a precisely grooved tubular core of granite. All this evidence put together suggests that ancient Egyptians had advanced tools. Their work represents a high degree of precision: precision that could not be attained without complex tools for measurement, such as metrological instruments. In addition, there are unmistakable signs that ancient Egyptians created some of their statues, temples, and other objects by machining.

According to mainstream archaeologists, the ancient Egyptians did not have such tools. This means one of two things: either they are wrong, and the Egyptians did have such tools, or they are correct. If they are correct, such monuments could not have been built by the Egyptians. Rather, they must have been built by some hitherto unknown ancient civilization.

The monuments in Egypt were created by a civilization that understood geometrical principles such as the Pythagorean Triangle, the Golden Ratio, and the Fibonacci Spiral.[74] Their engineering perfection resulted in exact right angles cut out of the planet's hardest stones. It also resulted in perfect alignments between the stars and pyramids. Such perfection was not just seen on small stone blocks, but on blocks that weighed upward of 200 tons. Many of these large stones were used in the construction of pyramids and temples. The builders of the Valley Temple, for example, lifted stones of this weight 12 meters (40 feet) into the air, and then put them into place among the surrounding stone blocks. To lift just one of these blocks today would be incredible. A specialized, large crane would be needed, and approximately 160 tons would have to be added to it. This would serve as a counterweight, preventing the crane from tipping over. However, only a couple cranes in the entire world are capable of lifting this weight.

 The Egyptians lifted stones this heavy all the time, and they moved the stones around rapidly. Sometimes, the large stones were moved down tight passageways in which only a few people could fit at the same time. In other cases, engineers cut huge blocks, weighing more than 70 tons, that were hoisted up to the upper levels of pyramids. From a modern standpoint, they could have cut them into smaller sizes to make their job easier, but they did not. This suggests that moving around blocks this size was not difficult to them. In addition, there is no mainstream theory proposed that makes much sense regarding how the stones were put into place when building the pyramids. The most widely accepted theory involves the use of ramps and thousands of people to pull the stones up them and into position atop the emerging pyramid. However, an analysis of the weight of the blocks being moved, along with size considerations while keeping in mind the people pulling the blocks, in addition to the counterweights needed to support ramps of this magnitude, makes it impossible that ramps were used. They more likely used a technology that has not yet been rediscovered. The truth is, with all our modern technological capabilities, we are today unable to recreate some of the feats accomplished by ancient builders of megalithic structures.

This is not just the case when considering ancient Egyptians. Megalithic structures are all over the world. Trying to duplicate the ancients' feats, even with modern equipment would still be an impossible challenge today. At the excavated Temple of Jupiter in Lebanon, numerous huge stones were quarried, cut, and then moved into position over uneven terrain and across great distances. There are three stones in particular that weigh an estimated 1,000 tons each, approximately 907,000 kilograms (2 million pounds). Another larger stone is located in a nearby quarry. It weighs an amazing 1,200 tons.[75] To move it today would take 21 heavy-lift cranes working in unison. However, there is no way to get 21 cranes around one single stone. Each crane would be in the way of the others. Even if this problem could be miraculously solved, another problem would surface: how to move the cranes together in the same direction. And it is not enough to have them move in the same direction on flat ground, but up and down the slopes of mountains, as some ancient cultures did.

Trying to duplicate this feat today, with all of the equipment that we currently possess, would be impossible. This is because we do not have the technology that the ancients who built these sites possessed. One megalithic structure called Sacsayhuaman is located north of Cuzco, Peru on a mountaintop. In its creation, stones weighing between 100 and 361 tons were moved from quarries tens of miles away.[76] They were taken up the mountain slope and positioned. According to mainstream archaeologists, the Incans built this site. However, according to the Incans themselves, they did not build it. They only used it. Their predecessors had built the structure thousands of years earlier. One Incan king did not understand the technology possessed by its builders, and he tried to recreate the feat using the knowledge and capabilities that the Inca possessed. It led to disaster.

42. The enormous stones at Sacsayhuaman

43. Close up of perfectly cut megalithic blocks

The king wanted to move a single boulder from a quarry and add it to the preexisting structure at Sacsayhuaman. He assembled more than 20,000 individuals to carry it. "At a certain spot, it fell from their hands over a precipice crushing more than 3,000 men."[77] The Incans did not have the technology to move such large stones. This knowledge was understood by an ancient civilization that existed before the great destruction, and it was lost. Evidence supports the conclusion that many of the megalithic structures are much older than generally believed.

Even the construction of the famous ruins found on the peak of Machu Picchu has not been adequately explained. Exactly how it was built is still unknown. According to mainstream accounts, it was built by approximately 5,000 Incans. This is claimed despite the fact that it could only house between 750 and 1,000 people. However, no more than 250 skeletons or mummies have ever been found. So, there are still major questions left unanswered about who initially built the site, and who first lived there. Any text that deals with the building techniques of the site only reveals how workers quarried, cut and moved stone. That is all. There is no question that the Incans did this. The quarry itself is still visible, there are marks on some of the stones that prove they were rolled into place, and there are still some carved stones that are piled, stones that have not been used in structures. All of these stones are the same shape and size though, which makes one question the accepted beliefs regarding how the Incans cut and shaped stones. Supposedly, they drilled holes into rocks and then filled them with water. Once the water froze, the rocks split. This technique can work to split stone, but it cannot result in precise and consistent cuts. However, the stones cut by the Incans were precise. They were consistent.

44. The ruins at Machu Picchu

45. Machu Picchu at sunrise

Let us back up. Before they utilized the quarry and some lost technique of cutting stones, how did they begin building this site? A walk around the edge of the ruins makes the feat seem impossible. Some agricultural areas are only a few feet wide, joined to the one above it by a staircase only a couple of feet in width. Below that is a 2,438-meter (8,000-foot) drop. It is incredible that they even used such staircases, never mind build them. Visitors will ponder how such a thing was accomplished, and they will always walk away with unanswered questions. Machu Picchu is unfortunately one of those sites that are so incredible that pictures do not do it justice. However, pictures of the ruins in this text will perhaps give readers an idea of the enormity of the project, and the technological advancements that must have been used in its construction. Machu Picchu also might have been built by a civilization more ancient than the Incans, and only used by them later. There is no doubt that they expanded the site, but it is possible that they did not initially build it. This may have occurred with many of the ancient megalithic structures found all over the planet. Strangely, early humans' fascination with celestial events provides a method of dating some of these sites.

46. At the edge of a terrace at Machu Picchu, looking down at the ground, 2,438 meters (8,000 feet) below

For builders of megalithic structures, things in the sky held a special significance. They indicated epochs, and the beginning and end of each era were tracked by stellar and planetary alignments. For this reason, heavenly alignments were important, as was the precession of the equinoxes. Many megalithic structures incorporate alignments to the stars. The pyramids at Giza, for example, are aligned to the star constellation Osiris. The pyramid of Kukulkan, in Mexico, is built so precisely that twice a year, during the spring and fall equinoxes, it casts the shadow of a snake — a representation of the god Kulkulkan — that slithers from the top of the structure to the bottom. Such an obsession with planetary alignments makes it possible to date such structures' creation. This is because Earth's relationship to heavenly bodies changes slightly through the millenia due to the planet's imperfect shape. And it is a good thing that this dating procedure is possible, as other archaeological dating methods are not effective in the dating of megalithic structures.

Using this dating methodology, in which a date can be determined by figuring out when structures matched up to planets and star constellations, many of the world's megaliths are much older than mainstream accounts state. The Tiahuanaco site in Bolivia, for example, has been dated to earlier than 15,000 B.C.E. It is only at this time that planets aligned to the main temple's features. It was built 4,000 years before the Great Flood, although Tiahuanaco itself functioned as a port for years before its creation.[78] Its creators were advanced, and there is evidence of some of their technological advancements still found at high altitudes.

Farming, Detoxification Processes, and Manna

A natural disaster destroyed the site more than 12,000 years ago.[79] Affected by earthquakes and a huge flood, the entire site was submerged. This led to a colder climate that was not conducive to growing crops. Some types of plants survived, but they were poisonous. Since people needed food, they analyzed the chemical composition of the plants, and then put them through a detoxification process.[80] This removed the poison and left the nutritive elements. In the same geographic area, and during the same period, someone created elevated fields that contained alternating high and low strips of Earth. It was a complicated agricultural design that could outperform modern farming techniques. Hancock wrote, "In recent years some of the raised fields were reconstructed by archaeologists and agronomists. These experimental plots consistently yielded three times more potatoes than even the most productive conventional plots."[81]

Many of the advanced ancient cultures decimated by the last great flood had sophisticated scientific and agricultural skills. One food that appears in numerous historical texts is called *manna*. (An archaic spelling of the same term is *mana*.) References to manna appear in the Kebra Nagast, the Dead Sea Scrolls, the Hebrew Bible, the Qur'an, and other texts. Manna is described differently in some of these, and the descriptions even change between translations. Exodus described manna as white, like a coriander seed. Eaten raw, it tasted like wafers coated in honey. In Numbers, it is compared to bdellium. The text describes how Israelites ground it up and made cakes from it. Descriptions of this substance in the Bible contain instructions for how to use it: people should only eat the raw manna that they have collected for each day. Leftover manna will go bad if it is not boiled or baked. In the Qur'an, Muhammad praised the healing power of manna, the juice of which is medicine for the eyes. Other texts state that manna had different flavors. It tasted like honey, bread, and oil.

These discrepancies are normal because the term manna was likely adopted by speakers of diverse languages and used differently. For example, the Chinese city Beijing, which means "southern capital," was romanized using Pinyin, which made use of the Cyrillic alphabet. Beijing became Peking. And now, to many people, asking for Beijing Duck at a Chinese restaurant would sound strange, as the incorrect pronunciation has permeated the United States. Everyone tends to order Peking duck. This romanized version became something even further removed from the original Chinese in the Italian language, which now refers to the city as Pecchino. It is likely that Chinese speakers listening to Italians talk about Beijing would not even recognize the word for the city. These changes in languages occur naturally over time, and the study of such changes is called morphology.

When dealing with historical records of a substance like manna, historians and linguists face inherent problems. First, the same substance had different names in different cultures. This continues today. Foods adopted by the United States from different cultures do not always maintain the original foreign names. Instead, a new name is created for it. Either that, or the original name is anglicized. In addition, once foreign foods are introduced, variations are created in order to satisfy the diverse tastes of the surrounding culture. As an example of all these tendencies, consider the Japanese food known as *sushi*.

Sushi in Japan refers to raw or cooked seafood and egg that is served on top of rice sprinkled with vinegar. Raw fish without rice is known as *sashimi*. Anything in a roll, for example, tuna and rice held together by seaweed, is called *norimaki*. In the United States, many people use the term sushi to refer to all three of these distinct foods. Such people would have a wakeup call if they went to Japan and ordered a sushi roll — something that does not exist. Likewise, the Japanese term *nori* refers to a specific type of seaweed, yet those Americans who use the word seem to think it means seaweed; they use it to refer to all kinds of seaweed. This is not accurate in Japan. As a final example, variations of such Japanese foods have been created in the United States. Here you can find California rolls: a foreign variation of a food that was originally Japanese. Obviously, examples can be found from any culture whose foods and products are used in foreign countries. Considering such examples can clarify problems faced by historians and linguists when dealing with something like manna.

Manna referred to many substances, and some linguistic sharing probably took place between this word and the Egyptian word *mennu*, which simply meant "food." The term for this particular food might have also been borrowed from the Aramaic phrase *man hu*, which meant, "What is it?" This might indicate that the term was applied to any unknown foodstuff: a large variety of foods. However, the real manna had unique properties that other foods did not. This mysterious substance sustained Moses and his followers during 40 years in the desert.

Some other historical texts describe manna, but call the substance something different. For example, the Vendidad, a sacred Zoroastrian account, which describes preparations taken before the last glacial period, describes a super food. The text describes a large underground city built to protect people from the oncoming ice age.

It could house more than 20,000 people, and it had room for livestock, winepresses, and more. The city contained running water and airshafts for air and light during the day. It also contained artificial lighting and beds of water in which their food source could be grown hydroponically. This food was green, and it replenished itself. It could last forever, and it alone could sustain human beings.

Today, this technological advancement is being rediscovered, as NASA and other organizations are exploring the suitability of algae that can sustain human beings for incredibly long periods without any other dietary supplements. One kind of algae being researched is chlorophyta. It is a sustenance that can be used in restricted environments (like space shuttles and submarines) for extended times. Subjected to the right conditions, it continues to replenish itself. Considering the descriptions of manna as an amazing sustainer of life from a variety of ancient texts, it is logical to conclude that the real manna was a type of algae. Either that, or it was another type of prolific plant that has yet to be identified.

Available evidence suggests that ancient civilizations had some technologies that even today would be considered "cutting edge." They had advanced farming technologies, knowledge of aerodynamic principles, and machining technologies. Using these, they were able to create replenishable foods that could sustain human beings for lengthy times. They also were able to create flying machines and other great vehicles. In addition, they were able to move megalithic stones across great distances and then hoist them to great heights — feats we cannot duplicate today. The majority of this evidence, however, is circumstantial. There are gaps in archaeological finds. For example, if some blocks in ancient Egypt show definite signs of machining, why have there not been any machines found? These inconsistencies will likely plague humankind for the next few centuries, until other evidence is unearthed.

Physical Evidence of Ancient Civilizations

So where is the physical evidence? Dr. Arlan Andrews, in the foreword to Chris Dunn's book *Lost Technologies of Ancient Egypt*, explained how advanced objects that may have once existed in Egypt would have disappeared over millennia. He wrote:

> When civilization fails for any reason, metals of all kinds become precious commodities. They become knives, spear points, scrapers, fishhooks, even plows. Ancient Egypt went through many upheavals caused by droughts, earthquakes, civil wars, religious strife, and foreign invasions. During the times of collapse, the advanced metal tools that the ancient Egyptians used were probably disassembled, cut apart, or melted down. What was not immediately used would corrode and disappear after thousands of years. And perhaps some other advanced technology was also employed, the remnants of which we would not recognize today.
>
> Large saw blades and other machine tools, if not secreted away from armies, floods, and mobs, would not endure very

long. Over the millennia, few metal objects from our own time would survive or be recognizable. *Life after People*, a popular cable television show that debuted in 2009, shows example after example of the deterioration of manmade objects after years, merely because of the lack of maintenance. In five thousand years, approximately the timespan estimated in *Lost Technologies of Ancient Egypt*, almost nothing of today's technologies would be left.[82]

If advanced machinery and other objects made from metal would be gone in five thousand years, what would happen to such objects used by a civilization more than 12,000 years ago? Certainly, little if anything would be left today. This is especially true when we consider that many of the ancient great cities were located along coasts, where there were seaports. At the end of the last major glacial period, ocean levels rose substantially, covering many of the largest and most advanced cities in hundreds of feet of water. Saltwater destroys metal.

The difficulty in finding physical evidence is even more substantial, as far as modern archaeological exploration is concerned, because the places where research is conducted are not where people established cities and lived before the last great flood. Seventeen thousand years ago, huge glaciers covered much of the world, and sea levels were more than 115 meters (377 feet) lower than they are today. Alaska and Siberia were one giant landmass, as were all the Japanese islands.[83] Australia, Tasmania and New Guinea were likewise one giant landmass, although it was entirely covered in ice.[84] Near Malaysia, Indonesia, and the Philippines there was a large continent known as Sunda Plains. It disappeared into the ocean between 14,000 and 11,000 years ago.[85] Likewise, the Grand Bahama Banks, which are underwater today, were 120 meters (394 feet) above sea level, and the Florida, Nicaragua, and Yucatan shelves were exposed.[86]

Most of the densely populated places in the world today were uninhabitable in antediluvian times. Areas like Chicago, New York, Amsterdam, Berlin and Moscow, along with most of North America and northern Europe, were completely uninhabitable because they were covered with glaciers more than 3 kilometers (1.86 miles) high.[87] Before the period of the Great Flood, the best places to live on the planet are now uninhabitable. Some of these places are now in the seas, under more than 91 meters (300 feet) of water. Other places have changed from fertile areas surrounded by lakes and lush vegetation into arid, dry areas, such as the Sahara desert.[88] These are the locations in which human beings would have made their homes. Since many of these places are underwater or buried under sand, the chance of finding anything is unfortunately next to nothing.

Hancock explained the devastation caused at the end of the last glacial period by the melting ice:

> Geologists calculate that nearly 5 percent of the Earth surface — an area of around 25 million square kilometers or 10 million square miles — has been swallowed by rising sea-levels since the end of the last Ice Age. That is roughly equivalent to the combined areas of the United States (9.6 million square kilometers) and the whole of South America (17 million square kilometers). It is an area almost three times as large as Canada and much larger than China and Europe combined. What adds greatly to the significance of these lost lands of the last Ice Age is not only their enormous area but also — because they were coastal and in predominantly warm latitudes — that they would have been among the very best lands available to humanity anywhere in the world at that time. Moreover, although they represent 5 percent of the Earth surface today, it is worth reminding ourselves that humanity during the Ice Age was denied useful access to much of northern Europe and North America because of the ice sheets. So the 25 million square kilometers

that were lost in the rising seas add up to a great deal more than five percent of the Earth's useful inhabitable landscape at that time.[89]

The Great Flood nearly wiped out all human beings, but it also destroyed physical evidence of highly advanced civilizations. However, evidence that such civilizations once existed is still extant. There are historical records of ancient aerial craft. Some traveled from city to city, such as modern-day, single-engine airplanes or blimps. Others traveled from country to country, like modern-day jets. The third category described ships that were capable of traveling from planet to planet, like modern-day spacecraft that can take human beings to the moon, and unmanned spaceships that can safely transport robots to other planets. In approximately 11,000 B.C.E., a vicious flood rocked the entire world and destroyed the majority of civilizations. Assume that all these craft were swept away by the floods. Some would be deposited in deep parts of the ocean, where the ocean itself would slowly destroy them. Others, in a dilapidated state, would be washed ashore when the floodwaters retreated.

The Sumerian culture is said to have begun c. 4500 – 4000 B.C.E. Their historical accounts include references to flying craft. Pharoanic rule of Egypt began c. 3100 B.C.E., about 8,000 years after the Great Flood. Although Dr. Andrews noted that almost nothing would remain of technologically advanced machinery after 5,000 years, some objects made from metal could exist longer in the right environment. It is likely that ancient Egyptians saw some remnants of flying machines, such as airplanes. Wooden models of such craft provide evidence of this. Seeing the remnants of a giant bird-like vessel, it would only be a matter of time before some thinker looked into the sky and saw birds flying. From there, the connection would be made. He or she might have sketched the wreckage and then determined what it must have looked like in a working state. The exact nature of the discovery is pure speculation, but this theory explains how Egyptians had airplane models, yet there is no evidence that they ever flew themselves. A similar thing likely occurred in South America as well.

Many of the world's flood stories refer to individuals who survived the deluge by means of boats and other vessels. When the floodwaters began to subside, their rafts grounded on mountaintops. In the Chaldean story, the ship grounded among the Corcyraean mountains in Armenia. In the Hindu version, it came to rest on the highest peak of Mt. Himavat, and in the Biblical account, the ark came to rest on Mt. Ararat. Other flood stories do not mention the names of the mountains, only that the vessels came to rest on high peaks. For example, the Batak story, from Sumatra, explains:

> Debata, the Creator, sent a flood to destroy every living thing when the Earth grew old and dirty. The last pair of humans took refuge on the highest mountain, and the flood had already reached their knees when Debata repented his decision to destroy mankind.[90]

The prolific stories about people surviving floods are indicative of a worldwide deluge that actually took place. And it is likely that many of the survivors actually washed up on high mountains; the floodwaters were that high. It is therefore possible that other things came ashore on high peaks: things like airplanes and other advanced machines. There, survivors saw them. Later, they made models of them. This explains the so-called "gold flyer" found in Columbia. After thousands of years on mountains, these remnants likely rusted away, and today nothing remains of them. However, the evidence that they once existed can still be found in the artifacts of civilizations that had seen such advanced machinery. The only hope of any physical remains being found after so many thousands of years is if some of the aircraft had been frozen after having been deposited on mountaintops. If they had remained frozen, in some of the most remote places on this planet, they still could emerge in years to come. If this ever occurred, it would answer some questions regarding the nature of human history on this planet, and it would change forever the linear view of historical development.

The fact that it is a common view notwithstanding, there is no reason to suppose that historical development is a linear process. Taking into account all of the available evidence, there is more reason to conclude that history is cyclical. In other words, civilizations of the past became increasingly more advanced, until floods or other natural disasters wiped them out, and then the cycle began again. This current cycle too will eventually end. When it does, many of our high-tech inventions will be lost forever. Our cities will crumble, and after being submerged for years, they will be unrecognizable. Then, left unattended for thousands of years, there will be little left that future civilizations would recognize as technologically advanced. Almost all the evidence will have been destroyed. Some vehicles might be found, however; at least what remains of them. Those who find them would likely not understand what they were looking at — pieces of rusted metal in strange shapes — but perhaps someone would come up with a theory and create a model of them. Years later, perhaps they will build the real thing, having reinvented a lost technology.

Progress comes quickly. It is likely that some of the advanced ancient civilizations knew that Earth was plagued by regular natural disasters. They knew about worldwide floods, and they understood that eventually, everything around them would cease to exist. This is why some ancient civilizations created megalithic structures, using stones so large that we would struggle to move today, even with all the technology at our disposal. It is also why they created pyramids that are so precisely aligned to objects in the sky that today it would be nearly impossible to duplicate the feat. These are the types of structures that will survive mega-disasters, and the way in which they were made likely served as a warning to future generations. Certainly, the more these structures are investigated, the more it becomes evident that advanced construction techniques were used. The structures incorporated advanced mathematical understanding and a high-level understanding of celestial bodies and worldwide events, both in the past and in the future. They were built because people knew that only these could remain standing after worldwide disasters such as the last Great Flood.

Antediluvian Survivors

Certainly, some megalithic structures can be accessed today because they are on land, but during the last major glacial period, people lived in different places. The most fertile land of the past is now deep underwater. It therefore stands to reason that many of the most important megalithic structures built by antediluvian cultures are not on dry land today. They are underwater, and many of them have not yet been discovered. Some are currently being investigated by archaeologists and historians. One such monument, previously described, is off the coast of Yonaguni, Japan. It is a huge, megalithic structure resembling a step pyramid. Large blocks weighing approximately 30 tons each were used in its construction. There are also massive statues, staircases, and unusual carvings. Other similar ruins have been found nearby. They have been found off the coast of the Aka and Aguni islands, and off the coast of Chatan, about 30 kilometers (19 miles) north of Naha, Okinawa. These underwater ruins include ceremonial complexes, manufactured walls, step pyramids, and other megalithic buildings. Similar structures, also described previously, have been found off the coast of India, and there are certainly many more waiting to be discovered. Their discovery awaits technological advancements that would allow human beings to explore the deepest areas of the seas, for it is in these locations that antediluvian societies would have flourished.

Physical evidence of technically advanced pre-flood civilizations has been discovered. This evidence, added to historical accounts disguised as myths, leaves no doubt whatsoever that this premise is correct. Historical accounts also inform us that people survived this global catastrophe. The biblical account tells us about Noah, who survived the deluge. In India, it was a man named Manu, and in the Assyrian and Akkadian versions, it was Utnapishtim. The Sumerian tale, the oldest in the world, reveals the heroic actions of Ziusudra. In other civilizations' flood accounts, people survived the disaster on mountaintops or on rafts that were tied down. In all flood stories — more than 500 different tales worldwide — the survivors are considered the progenitors of modern humans.

They are thought of as true heroes. Their stories have been passed down through countless generations to modern times. They have been written about in nearly all languages, and the legends have been shared between cultures and translated into many different tongues. Some cultures think that the survivors were blessed by God. Other cultures believe they actually became gods because of their heroic actions. Such admiration for the deeds of others, and their perceived correlation with divine powers is a natural human tendency. Even today, it has not abated.

In the Catholic Christian tradition, human beings can become saints. In Jewish and Muslim traditions, individuals can also become closer to God. In Islam, these individuals are called awliyā'Allāh. In Buddhism, human beings can likewise become divine. They are called Bodhisattvas in the Mahayana tradition and Arhats in the Theravada. In other religions worldwide, human beings are thought to have the ability to raise their spiritual awareness, thereby changing their true nature. According to such beliefs, as the spirit grows, they become closer to divine beings. It is beyond the scope of this book to provide detailed information about such beliefs; it is only mentioned here so readers can understand that flood stories should not be interpreted with a religious or mythological bias only because such survivors are thought of as superhuman. Sometimes the best explanation for a phenomenon is the simplest. Although religious components may have been added later to teach concepts like self-sacrifice and honoring the gods, these stories, from the beginning, have been historical in nature.

By reviewing these tales, we are assured of one thing: human beings all over the world survived the great deluge. Some who survived were from advanced societies, others from less advanced cultures. Based not only on flood survival stories, but also on historical accounts disguised as myths, we can make some assumptions: Some people survived the flood on its surface. Others survived beneath the water's surface. And once the floodwaters had abated, some primitive societies were taught wonderful things by more advanced survivors. The societies of the world interacted. Survivors of a seafaring, advanced civilization traveled to many places, spreading their knowledge of astronomy, advanced mathematics, building techniques, and legal and moral codes. It is for this reason that many structures throughout the world are built in the same manner, using the same techniques. It is also why ancient people from different parts of the globe shared the same celestial fascination. This worldwide teaching mission carried out by survivors of technically advanced civilizations is not mere speculation. We are told that this occurred. The stories have been passed down in historical documents from many different countries.

6. The Last Great Flood

Cycles of Destruction

Worldwide and isolated natural disasters have destroyed countless civilizations. Stories passed down describe ancient, technologically advanced civilizations that were destroyed. These civilizations include Atlantis, which disappeared into the sea. According to Plato, the Atlanteans were technologically advanced. The civilization of Mu, likewise swallowed by the sea, was also described as advanced. Stories about this great island state that the deluge killed most of its inhabitants. Some miraculously survived, and they eventually traveled to other countries, teaching less advanced civilizations.

Stories about wise people from another world abound in many indigenous cultures, and large, complex megaliths have been attributed to them. An example is on Tinian Island, located in the Mariana Archipelago. Called the House of Taga, the site is composed of large megalithic blocks quarried at a site 1,219 meters (4,000 feet) south of its location. The stones themselves were approximately 4.6 meters (15 feet) in height. When the Spaniards first discovered the location, they asked the local Chamorros about it, who explained that they did not built it — that the "people who had come before" did.

Locals near Machu Picchu, Peru claim something similar. They believe that an ancient culture, possibly the Viracocha, built the site before the Incans used it. Viracocha was an individual god later added to the Incan pantheon of divinities, but it is likely that the term originally referred to a group of people. Viracocha supposedly traveled the world with others, bringing civilization to primitive cultures. He is described as having light-colored skin. The Mayans and Incans relate that people who came from across the sea taught them about mathematics, astrology, and megalithic construction techniques. They described them as Caucasian in appearance, and in some representations they are wearing large hats. Either that, or they had larger heads than most humans.

47. The Incan creator gods Pacha Camac (left) and Pachamama (right)

These people were also described using terms for divinity, and they were thought of as gods. This has led some scholars to posit that the stories are not historical, but mythological. It should be noted that the Spaniards were also thought to be gods when they arrived in the Americas for the first time. The Incans actually believed that the Spaniards were Viracocha and his men, as he had promised to return. Seeing more advanced people, dressed in shiny metal, approach on a sea-faring craft made them believe that they were not human. They thought the visitors were divine. However, the Spaniards were human.

Such cases of extreme mistaken identity (i.e. mistaking humans for gods) have also occurred in modern times. During World War II, U.S. soldiers headed to small islands in the South Pacific to build airfields and other military edifices. They remained there while the war raged. Once it ended, they left. Reinl described what happened next:

> The natives of these islands, isolated from the outside world, lived virtually in the Stone Age until the Americans came and went. Very soon afterward, the natives began making straw and bamboo fetishes resembling airplanes, [and] crude landing surfaces on their islands to tempt the visitors back. The strangers had brought fabulous treasure with them from the skies: tools, fantastic weapons, sky machines they have never dreamed of. What else but gods could possess such superior knowledge? They did not hunt or fish, yet they never lacked food. They came from heaven. They had to be gods.[1]

The island natives prayed for the return of their gods, which were, in fact, only U.S. service members. They established ceremonies, performed sacrifices, and watched the sky, anxiously hoping for the gods to return. Perhaps, if the gods were happy with them, they would come back. If unhappy, they would not. The presence of human beings who have superior knowledge actually spurred the creation of a religion. This included not just a belief system, but religious ceremonies and icons — artistic re-creations of divine machines. This occurred in the twentieth century. We can assume, knowing what we know, that it was only natural for Native Americans to view Spaniards as divine beings when they arrived. When we go further back in time, we see Incan accounts that described divine beings that showed up on their shores and taught them wonderful things. They might have believed that Viracocha and his followers were gods. Mainstream archaeologists support this notion, and they categorized such tales as myths. However, there is no reason to suppose that such stories are fiction.

There is also no reason to presume that Viracocha and his followers were not human. Rather, it is logical to assume that they were members of a hitherto unidentified ancient civilization. Similar accounts are found all over the world. Natives in the Maldives tell stories about the "ancient ones" who had blonde hair and blue eyes. New Zealand stories describes an ancient civilization of fair-skinned people who had great power, and a story from Polynesia describes a group of tall people with incredible knowledge who arrived on great ships from a distant land. These wise individuals, depicted in the histories of various civilizations, are always depicted as coming from the sea. The Sumerian tales indicate that these individuals even lived in the sea.

Sumer's history is problematic for archaeologists and historians who do not like to think outside the box. When they first emerged in our historical record they were already highly advanced, as indicated by their language, artwork, building techniques, and astronomical knowledge, which has only been recently equaled by modern humans. But the Sumerians themselves explained the origin of their civilization, and how they were taught such advanced concepts. According to their historical accounts, their ancestors had five great cities that were all destroyed by the Great Flood. The inhabitants of these large antediluvian cities were visited by wise beings that "emerged from the sea." There were seven of them, and their leader was called Oannes.

He had a human voice, and spoke in a language that they could understand. He wore some type of suit that made him appear fish-like, as modern scuba gear or a deep-water diving suit might appear to someone ignorant of their existence. The men who came from the sea spent their days with human beings, teaching them how to build cities and temples. They also taught them mathematics, a writing system, and how to plant seeds to grow fruits and vegetables. Although they spent their days on land with other humans, they returned to the sea at night, where they presumably slept. To the less advanced Sumerians, these wise beings seemed amphibious; they were able to live on both land and water, and hence they could not have been human beings. For this reason, they are described using terms for divine or semi-divine beings.

If this same tale were reported today, such individuals would not be described using terms reserved for divinity. Many wealthy individuals who enjoy life on the seas might "island-hop." They visit beaches on shores, buy things in stores, and eat at restaurants, only to return to their yachts in the evening to sleep. From a military standpoint, individuals living in a submarine could reemerge from the ocean depths and come ashore using wetsuits and scuba tanks. Keeping this in mind, it is likely that these individuals were not divine or holy beings. They were just more advanced humans. These individuals taught many civilizations across the globe, and they may have provided the spark that ignited human advancement.

According to oral tradition, Easter Island was also visited by the same foreigners who had pale skin and light, reddish hair. They lived on the island for a while and taught the natives many things. It is likely that the *moai* are representative of these people. The moai are large statues, approximately 18 meters (60 feet) tall, which weigh up to 30 tons. They were quarried from a site called Raku Raraku, carved, and then carried up to ten miles. Then, they were put atop stone platforms, where final decorations were added. These included red tufts of hair and white face paint.

48. Moai on Easter Island

China has similar stories in some of its oldest texts. Tales describe tall people with green eyes and reddish hair who interacted with the Chinese.[2] Many scholars initially dismissed such stories as myths. Why? Because their existence did not match up with the standard version of history taught in schools. However, new finds make people reconsider such historical accounts. Besides religious and historical stories of tall, light-skinned individuals who imparted knowledge to various societies, unexplained graves have been discovered. In 1895, Marc Aurel Stein came across the mummified bodies of some Caucasians when unearthing Central Asian texts in the Tarim Basin.[3] Then, Chinese archaeologists found more of these inexplicable bodies in the 1970s. Pringle explained:

> Chinese archaeologists happened upon hundreds of the parched cadavers in Xinjiang while surveying along proposed routes for pipelines and rail lines. Most of these mummies were very Caucasian looking. They had blond, red, and auburn hair. They had deep-set eyes, long noses, thick beards, and tall, often gangly, frames. They wore woolens of Celtic plaid and sported strangely familiar forms of Western haberdashery: conical black witches' hats, tam-o'-shanters, and Robin Hood caps."[4]

Some of them wore Western style robes, decorated with what appeared to be Greco-Roman gods. Others wore more simple clothing. The archaeologists who found the bodies subjected them to radiocarbon testing and found that they were from the twenty-first-century B.C.E.[5] Who they were, however, is still unknown. If they were around c. 2100 B.C.E. in China, their ancestors were likely from the same area. If we were able to look back far enough, we might see that such people were the descendants of individuals from Mu or another lost continent. Although the great flood destroyed the landmass, burying cities and towns forever, some people survived. The survivors' descendants might very well be some of the Caucasian mummies found in China. Other graves that house similar tall, light-skinned individuals have been found in other places throughout the world, including the United States. These bodies by themselves provide no answers, only questions. But once we accept that our historical knowledge is limited and perhaps downright wrong, they begin to tell a story. The existence of such bodies, along with stories of wise Caucasians who traveled across the seas and imparted knowledge to more primitive civilizations, provides evidence of early advanced civilizations. Other evidence is found in petroglyphs all over the world, including the American Southwest.

In the Canyonlands National Park, located in southeastern Utah, there are some drawings credited to the Ancestral Pueblos, otherwise known as the Anasazi. This name means "ancient people." Their depictions, found in Barrier Canyon, are of tall figures with wide shoulders and large eyes. One particular figure, which is much taller than those around it, is represented differently than the rest. While four figures on both sides of it are black with featureless faces, the one in the center is white. It has broad shoulders and a large head. On its face are two parallel lines where the mouth and nose should be, and above that, two black squares with giant white pupils represent its eyes. Why this figure with white skin was drawn much larger the rest is unknown, but its existence might support the notion that Caucasian travelers from an unknown land continued north after visiting South and Central America. Perhaps they taught some of the most ancient Native American tribes, such as the Anasazi.

Other petroglyphs in Utah and surrounding states likewise depict these beings. The Palatki, Canyon de Chelly, and Honanki sites in New Mexico depict humans with helmets and devices strapped to their heads. Some found in Moab, Utah likewise portray humans with unusual devices attached to their heads. Taken singularly, this evidence could point to different conclusions. When all of it is viewed together, it points to one conclusion: there were technically advanced civilizations on this planet before the time of the great flood. Despite the near extinction of human beings, some survived the deluge and passed on knowledge to more primitive global societies.

49. Barrier Canyon Petroglyphs

50. Petroglyphs at Honanki

During the height of the last glacial period, sea levels were 183 meters (600 feet) lower than they are today. Given human beings' tendency to establish their cities and towns on the shores of lakes, rivers, and seas, it is logical that the majority of them were destroyed when the ice broke apart and melted. Sea levels rose 183 meters (600 feet); in some places even more than that. We know this happened. We also know that some people survived the great deluge. Stories from across the planet describe people who survived it by building rafts or seeking refuge on mountaintops and in mountain caves. Some stories describe people of advanced civilizations riding out the storm beneath the water's surface. The Sumerian, Babylonian, and Akkadian versions of deluge survival stories described individuals who entered submarines, carrying with them anything they might need to repopulate the Earth. It is at this point that we herein begin to speculate; the best way to consider what could have happened to technologically advanced people in a submarine during the worldwide super flood is to think about what would happen today.

Tebitu: Submarines in the Deep

Remember that people who survived the deluge did not write flood stories. Later civilizations wrote them. They were stories about ancient, antediluvian civilizations. Most likely, they were passed down orally for centuries before being recorded in written form. There are many flood survival stories, explaining various ways in which human beings made it through this tumultuous event. Several of the accounts are so similar that they likely refer to the same civilization's deeds. These are the Sumerian and Akkadian flood stories, which also happen to be the oldest. According to these tales, human beings gathered the D.N.A. of living creatures, and then boarded a craft. In the Sumerian version, it is called magurgur, a "vessel that can tumble and turn." The Akkadian version uses the term tebitu, which translates (in modern English) to "submarine."

Considering the possibility that antediluvian civilizations were as advanced as modern civilizations, this story is much more logical than the Noah's Ark tale. The Genesis account explains how Noah gathered two of every animal, and then sealed them aboard a vessel. The term used in the biblical account is *tevah*. In modern Hebrew, this term means box, crate or case. In other parts of the Bible, the same term (tevah) is used in other scenarios, and it is translated into

English as basket. Most scholars agree that a good translation for tevah, as it is used in the flood account, is just "vessel." Imagining the size of the vessel needed to house one of every animal, and the resources needed to build it, the account seems illogical. It is therefore possible that the Biblical story of the ark is a rendition of the Sumerian and Akkadian accounts, which were written about 1,000 years before the Old Testament. (The Old Testament was written between 1313 – 450 B.C.E., while the Sumerian account was set down between 2100 – 2000 B.C.E.) If so, the authors of the biblical account might have sought words for technology they did not understand. Seeking a theory to explain these accounts, the tale of a submarine that housed D.N.A. alone seems logical. For this reason, let us assume that we are facing the same global catastrophe that the civilizations mentioned in flood stories faced.

We have to imagine a couple other things before proceeding with this mental exercise. Earth's surface was different than it is today: glaciers stretched across much of the globe. There were some beautiful places to live. These are today submerged in the world's oceans, or they are arid deserts. Other inhabitable areas where advanced civilizations likely resided included landmasses in the Pacific and Atlantic alike that no longer exist, landmasses that have become thought of as legendary rather than historical. Based upon the flood stories referred to herein, the survivors who became the progenitors of modern humans knew about the oncoming deluge and prepared for it. The floodwaters destroyed some cities without warning. Once the devastation began, more advanced societies knew it was headed their way. They might not have had much time, but they were able to prepare in some capacity. Assume that we are in this situation. We pack limited items. Entertainment devices, jewelry, and other unnecessary items are left behind. Quickly, we step into one of several submarines that have been prepared to support human beings for an extended time.

Then, it heads deep underwater to escape the tidal waves and huge chunks of ice that make the ocean's surface so dangerous.

According to the Biblical, Sumerian and Akkadian stories alike, the flood lasted seven days. Of course, the sea level at the end of this flood event was much higher than it had been in the past, and the flooding itself lasted much longer than seven days. However, the heroes of these tales stepped back onto solid land after only a week. Assume that we have multiple submarines. Communication links, if they existed, were severed as soon as the disasters accompanying the flood worsened. These included not just tidal waves, but earthquakes and volcanic eruptions. The devastation was incredible. Each submarine was on its own. The current pushed them around, until eventually, one submarine did not know where the others were. The submarine that we are in has some problems. All power is lost. The hull is damaged, leaking. Water seeps through several cracks, although they are quickly repaired. For days, people inside wait. They are afraid.

After seven days, the other submarines surface, looking for land. The Earth's surface looks different than it had previously. Ocean levels are higher, and continents and islands that once existed had vanished. Their homes are gone. With no other options, they head in random directions seeking land. They eventually find some new suitable locations and come ashore. These survivors become the ancestors of modern humans. The world's flood stories, which were initially known as historical, are based on the events that this group of people experienced. Meanwhile, our submarine is still in trouble. It is stuck underwater without power. The darkness is palpable.

It is pushed around underwater by strong ocean currents, and it eventually comes to rest at a depth of less than 7,000 feet. Modern submarines can withstand the pressure at such depths. There, knowledgeable people aboard start working on repairs. First, they restore some power. The engines are not working, but they are able to switch on emergency power for some limited visibility and to support the proliferation of their renewable food *manna*, (a type of algae previously mentioned). Now, although the people aboard might not be comfortable, they can at least survive. In time, some aboard grow to miss the things that they used to enjoy eating, like different kinds of meat. They might miss alcohol, and they yearn for just one more drink. And all of them likely miss their lives the way they used to be, before the floods destroyed the world as they had known it. In time, the world that they miss, and the foods and drinks that they desire, drive them to devote all their energy to fixing the submarine. However, they are unsuccessful. The engines are destroyed and cannot be repaired with the materials aboard. An idea to build escape pods surfaces, and those aboard with this kind of specialized knowledge plan such vehicles' construction. Unfortunately, this exercise is futile. The power that the submarine uses is from the ocean water itself, and a much more powerful energy source is needed in the experimental construction of a technologically advanced smaller craft that can be used to return to the surface.

Years pass, and their efforts are futile. They have managed to strengthen the submarine, so that it can withstand greater pressure, and the people aboard have grown accustomed to eating manna alone. They grow thin, their muscles small. They feel hopeless, and they believe that they might never see sunlight again. Then, another disaster befalls them. Seismic activity violently changes the ocean floors, and the vessel drops into an expanding trench. On the way down it tumbles and turns. Leaks are dealt with right away, and it eventually comes to rest in much deeper water, depths that cannot be reached using present-day technology. Although they are able to strengthen the tebitu so that it can withstand the pressure at such depths, human beings are another story. They feel the pressure, and it bothers them. The pilots and builders of the craft do what they can to alleviate some of the discomfort, but it is still annoying. In time, the humans aboard become used to this uncomfortable feeling. Tumbling into deeper water was initially thought of as something bad, but sometimes, events that seem initially unfortunate turn out to be the impetus for change. The humans aboard discover a powerful energy source in the ocean depths. Volcanic activity and pockets of methane gas on the ocean floor can be used to power auxiliary craft, if they could be built. In addition, such energy sources could be used to facilitate their lives underwater. Ideas flow through their heads; the natural tendency to invent and better their lives had never faded.

There, in ocean depths never before reached, they remain for years. An untapped power source is nearby, and plans are worked out to harness its energy. The pressure is intense and the ocean outside is mostly silent. Occasionally, the silence is broken by unusual sounds in the deep, creatures that have never seen sunlight calling out to others. Luminescent creatures pass by the submarine's windows and break the darkness. Such appearances spark the creativity latent in these unfortunate human beings.

The Development of Surface-Exploring Craft

Trapped thousands of feet underwater, these poor people initially felt uncomfortable. They were afraid. However, considering the cold, volatile climate of the Earth's surface, things could have been worse. They were alive. They had a replenishable source of food, and they could live in the ship's atmosphere. Oxygen was provided by the seawater itself, and the ship was naturally warmed by undersea volcanic activity. At first, those trapped missed their homes. But the planet's surface was not like it is today. Most places were uninhabitable. Huge glaciers covered the continents and the seas. Underground abodes were more sensible. Since this glacial period had begun approximately 19,000 B.C.E., the people in this craft had never known anything else. To them the Earth was a frozen wasteland, and the climate was harsh. It made survival difficult for those living on the surface. In their new undersea home, survival became easier. After many years, the place began to feel like home. They continued to socialize, play music, and live their lives. They reproduced, and they told their offspring about their previous lives on the surface. They may have described the giant blocks of ice and cold temperatures that plagued them. But this new generation never saw the surface for themselves. Their home, the only home they knew, was underwater. They adjusted to low light levels and high pressure much better than their parents had. They felt comfortable. This is the only life they had ever known, and they were at ease. Generation after generation, they grew increasingly more at home underwater. From stories passed down about life on the surface of the planet, they may have even believed that everything that once existed had been destroyed. In truth, almost everything had been. Some survivors started civilization anew, but the majority of buildings and technological advancements had been destroyed. The ship that housed those unfortunate victims on the ocean's bottom was one technically advanced form of transportation that still existed. It was a remnant of a distant past.

The stories of the surface world were once passed down as truth, but as it happens with the transmission of distant historical stories through generations, the tales were eventually regarded as myth, not history. And for hundreds of years, there might not have been any desire whatsoever to visit the planet's surface. In time, a desire to explore the environment immediately outside the craft developed. Humans are naturally curious. They wanted to travel away from the ship, to see what other creatures live nearby. For this reason, they considered ways to build smaller, exploratory ships. While pondering this question, looking out into the water that surrounded them, they saw large creatures that propelled themselves past the ship at incredible speeds. One creature was likely a giant squid, some varieties of which are luminescent. The sight of such a creature, which not only provided its own light but was also equipped with biological thrusters, must have been inspirational.

Consider the technological advancements that have taken place on the surface. From the invention of the car to helicopters and airplanes and even space shuttles, there is no end to our progress. What would occur if we were trapped underwater for thousands of years, rather than residing on the surface? Certainly, technological advancements would continue, but the inventions would be different.

Ingenious ideas would spring from what we saw around us, as they do on the surface. When the humans underwater first saw a giant squid, they must have wondered. They needed to catch one of these creatures, to find out what made it work. So, the first step was to devise some means of trapping one. Virtually no inventions are perfect the first time they are attempted. A process of trial and error must take place before success is found. They may have tried different forms of bait, then different types of nets. Eventually, they were successful, and they caught one. As we would conduct this investigation on the surface, they likely dissected the creature to determine what made it work. How did it move? How did it light up? Once this was determined, they may have tried to make a synthetic version of the materials that made up its body, a version that would be strong and adaptable for human use.

Similar things exist today, such as artificially created exoskeletons and forms of body armor that are liquid, not solid. Liquid body armor, which is currently being researched by the United States Army Research Laboratory (ARL), involves the addition of liquid to solid layers of a Kevlar bulletproof vest. The way a Kevlar vest works is interesting. They are composed of layers of fibrous material. When a bullet hits a vest like this the fibers stretch, expending energy and slowing down the projectile. In other words, the force of the object is spread out and dissipated over a much larger surface. The true efficacy of this vest lies in its ability to move and change shape. The addition of a liquid to this already efficient material makes it even more amazing. The liquid used is made with polyethylene glycol and silica nanoparticles. This liquid is soaked into each individual layer of the Kevlar vest. Under lower, normal pressure, it remains in a liquid state, but when impacted, it becomes solid. High pressure triggers rigidity.

Underwater humans had some initial success in the creation of a synthetic version of the squid's tissue. They created a craft, based on the technology, with which they could explore the surrounding water. However, if the material that they had created was rigid, its use was limited. They needed a flexible material that could morph. The cylindrical body of a giant squid, and its ability to change its body shape, results in the intake and expulsion of water. This creates movement, and these creatures can move incredibly fast. They are powerful. After decades, like humans on the surface, the undersea humans improved their inventions, this exploratory craft being only one of them. To do this, they went back to the drawing board. They captured more squid. They kept them in tanks alive, until eventually, they not only figured out what made them work, but how to create the same materials biologically. If someone who lived 200 years ago on the surface read the previous statement, he or she would have attributed it to imagination. He or she would place it in the realm of science fiction. However, we all know today that such technology is possible. Experiments with D.N.A. have shown that we can grow human limbs and appendages like ears and noses independently. We can create these things away from human bodies to assist humans maimed in accidents.

If undersea humans headed into the deep approximately 12,000 B.C.E., they have been advancing technologically for more than 14,000 years. Consider the progress we have made in only 1,000 years. They are much more advanced than we are, not because they are from a different planet, but only because they have been around longer. And human progress does not end. It would not have taken them long to figure out how to duplicate the body structure of these amazing luminescent creatures. Using this organic material, perhaps in conjunction with other synthetic materials, they created the types of ships that are often reported entering or leaving large bodies of water. They are generally described as cylindrical, cigar-shaped objects. Many witnesses, including some of those claiming to have been abducted, indicated that the ships seemed semi-transparent. They also said that the shape of the ships changed: that its shape was not constant. Many witnesses stated that they saw beams of light issuing from the ships themselves, and the morphing center at times made the craft appear alive.

There are many luminescent sea creatures, but some of these creatures are not luminescent by themselves. There needs to be some kind of trigger that makes them glow. For example, luminescent plankton found in tropical seas only emit light with some sort of stimulus. When boats move through them, a luminous trail of these creatures is seen in their wakes. Other stimuli likewise cause them to glow, including underwater sounds. Some sounds may be outside human beings' audible frequency, but they can still be measured. They affect luminescent creatures.

It is likely that the unidentified objects seen in oceans have been created using biological, not mechanical principles. If so, the lights seen emanating from these objects might not be intentionally activated by the creatures within. Certainly, they would have lights that they can completely control, but some lights on their ships might be a natural byproduct of the biological materials used in their creation. In other words, external stimuli, such as human beings in cars, boats, and other transportation devices, perhaps trigger this luminescence.

When we look at the UFO – USO phenomenon, it seems clear that these creatures do not want to make their existence explicitly known. This is not surprising. A brief peek at the history of humankind reveals that we are violent in nature. The majority of wild animals try to avoid interactions with us. UFO pilots likewise wish to remain hidden from us. Many reports indicate that UFOs quickly disappear after having been seen. Once they realize they have been spotted, they leave. Of course, there are exceptions, such as UFOs actively investigating airplanes and nuclear submarines. But for the most part, they remain cloaked. They hide from us. So why would they use exterior lights if they truly wish to remain hidden? If this were an unstoppable natural reaction of the materials used in the objects' creation, the question would be answered.

Evolutionary Change and Intentional D.N.A. Modification

There is a connection between evolution and ice ages. Human beings can trace their evolution back through various species, collectively called hominids, to a common ancestor, the chimpanzee, which is our closest living relative among primates. It is commonly assumed that this transformation occurred five or six million years ago. Why evolution occurs is technically unknown, and various theories have been proposed to explain the reasons behind the phenomenon. The evolution of modern human beings suggests a connection to dramatic climate shifts, as they emerged during the Pleistocene Ice Age. MacDougall explains:

> For several million years after our common ancestor, hominids evolved slowly. They developed the ability to move around on the ground with an upright posture, although their body structure suggests that they were still expert tree climbers. Then, right around the time when the Earth's average temperature plunged downward at the beginning of the Pleistocene Ice Age — about 3 million years ago — the rate of change accelerated drastically. Hominids quickly

evolved away from their ape-like ancestors, developing increasingly sophisticated tools and weapons, hunting, planning, complex language, and eventually agriculture, writing, airplanes, and computers. During that time, there was an increase in brain size by more than a factor of three in less than three million years, a breathtakingly rapid change compared to the normal course of evolution. This change took place entirely within the Pleistocene Ice Age.[6]

Evolution seems to be triggered by more than just temperature. The temperature's *effect* on the overall environment is what likely leads to evolutionary change. During the height of the Pleistocene Ice Age, ice sheets regularly moved across the continents. The climate was windy and dry, and as the Earth continued to cool, the forests in Africa, which were the natural habitat of hominids, shrank. The amount of trees decreased, and grasslands expanded. "It is this change in vegetation, not the actual temperature variations, that seems to be the key to human evolution."[7] In other words, evolution occurs when creatures are forced to rely upon different foods in a new environment. Human beings accustomed to ingesting meat and vegetables on the surface of the planet, for example, would evolve in a new, deep-sea environment in which they only ate algae.

Ernst Mayr developed a theory:

New species often evolve when some small subset of an existing population becomes isolated from the rest of their species. In such circumstances, change can occur rapidly, especially if some tradable physical characteristic is favored reproductively — in other words, if individuals with those characteristics are more successful breeders. Eventually the isolated population evolves so far from its ancestors that it can no longer interbreed with the parent population and a new species has been born. Sometimes the new species dies out, but often the newcomers eclipse their parents.[8]

It used to be thought that evolution was a slow, gradual occurrence. Ernst Mayr determined that this idea was flawed, and that evolution occurred quickly. Niles Eldredge and Stephen Jay Gould seconded this notion, and they proposed a theory called punctuated equilibrium. According to this theory, evolution occurs in abrupt changes. There were fast appearances of fossil species, which just as suddenly disappeared. For this reason, there is little possibility of actually discovering transitional forms. When the idea was initially proposed, many scientists thought the new idea contradicted Darwin's writings. However, Darwin himself seemed to support this theory. MacDougall explains:

> A careful examination of Darwin's writings shows that he didn't really describe all evolution as a slow and steady process. Instead, he recognized the importance of geographical distribution and isolation, and he realized that small populations are more amenable to rapid change than large ones.[9]

Scientific understanding of planetary changes and evolution is incomplete. There are only theories to explain such phenomena. However, based upon all available evidence, evolution is triggered by three major factors: (1) abrupt climate change, which leads to reliance upon (2) different foods for sustenance, and finally, (3) an isolated population. If the theory proposed in this book is correct, that so-called UFOs are actually piloted by human beings who now live in the deepest areas of the oceans, these humans would have undergone evolutionary changes. As underwater human beings continued to breed, their offspring would look different. Their bodies would become more suited to the new environment in which they lived. In a dark, high-pressure environment, in which their only food source is a type of algae, what would they look like? In time, their eyes would become bigger, so that they could see better in darker environments. In such an underwater habitat, they would not use their muscles much, and even manual labor carried out in water requires much less strength than the same labor on land, due to the buoyancy of the water itself. Therefore, although their skeletal structure might look the same, musculature would decrease. In an initially cramped environment, offspring would likely have been born with smaller bodies. Their heads would look larger in comparison to such bodies, but an increase in head size would also occur — larger eye sockets to hold bigger, more effective eyes.

All these changes might have occurred naturally due to a new environment and diet, but a technically advanced civilization could also initiate such changes on their own. Whether readers believe this theory or not, one thing cannot be argued. The Akkadian version of the flood story specifically talks about individuals who took D.N.A. aboard a submarine. Linguistically, "tebitu" must be translated as "submarine" in modern English. Some choose to translate it as "a ship that can tumble and turn," and they refuse to make use of the term "submarine" only because they claim submarines did not exist in the epoch to which this tale refers. This is a translation problem. Translators are inserting their own preconceived notions to determine a proper translation. This is something that all reputable translators try to avoid. To translate properly, one must remove himself or herself from the process of translation itself, to render the original author's intent to the population at large. Therefore, even when translating texts like the Epic of Gilgamesh, one should never insert his or her own personal beliefs to influence the translation's emergence into a second language. This is an important consideration, and some translators have been caught adjusting the meaning of terms, or revising complete sentences, so that the text more accurately supports their own beliefs. As a result, some famous books are now filled with translation errors, including some of the most important religious texts in use today. Some readers who do not consider the problems inherent in translation end up believing stories that were not in the original versions. If we cast aside our preconceived notions and truly admit that much of human history is a mystery, the Akkadian term tebitu must be translated as "submarine."

The same is true with the term generally translated as "seed." According to this, and other flood stories, the heroes of the tales, whether they be Utnapishtim, Ziusudra, Noah, or Atrahasis, brought aboard the seed of living creatures. In modern English, this must be translated as D.N.A., and as translators, we must remove our own personal prejudice to accurately translate these terms. Advanced human beings from the distant past who made use of submarines and had knowledge of D.N.A. would likely be able to affect change in their own unborn children. We have such capabilities today. We can clone animals, and although it is unknown if some scientist has secretly done this already, we can clone human beings. We also alter the D.N.A. of animals to increase or decrease certain traits. Unfortunately, this is done to animals whose sole purpose in life is to become food for human beings. Genetic modifications are made to increase the amount of meat on such animals, thereby making their sellers more money. This practice is controversial and has ethical considerations, but it is beyond the scope of this book to discuss such issues. It is enough to consider that today we can and do manipulate D.N.A.

Continuing our mental exercise, in which we assume that the Earth is currently covered with glaciers, and that we are in the lost submarine that is now stuck underwater, it is only natural to assume that in time we would begin to modify D.N.A. to improve our childrens' lives. Once it became clear that we could not return to the surface, we would begin improving our lives underwater. We would try to fix the submarine. When this did not work, we would try to make other craft. We would improve our living environment as much as possible. For this reason, intentional D.N.A. modification might have been carried out. Such modifications might have made newborns smaller, so that they would have comparatively more room in the underwater vessel. Changes in their eyesight and body structure may also have been made, so that the children could see more easily in darkness, and so they could live without discomfort in a high-pressure environment.

Whether it was evolution, intentional D.N.A. manipulation, or a combination of the two, it is likely that, after decades if not hundreds of years, the poor individuals trapped underwater eventually looked radically different. And as their bodies became suited to this new environment, they were no longer suited for life on the planet's surface. The ocean depths had become their new home.

Exploring the Surface

By the time ships had been created with which they could explore the surface, there was no longer an instinctual desire to return to it. The surface was no longer home. Their home was underwater, in the oceanic trenches in the Atlantic, within the Bermuda Triangle, and in the Pacific, within the Dragon's Triangle. Over thousands of years, they expanded their underwater bases, created various types of transportation, and they became increasingly more advanced from a technological standpoint. UFO sightings in the last seven hundred years support this conclusion. Today, such craft are described as triangular, with maneuverability that surface-dwelling humans have yet to develop. Although reports of larger ships exist, the most frequently reported UFOs are smaller, perhaps piloted by two or three humanoids alone. More than five hundred years ago, reports were different. People described less technologically advanced aircraft. For example, the thirteenth century book *Otto Imperialia* by Gervase of Tilbury described an aerial craft traveling above a city in England. According to the text, something resembling an anchor became caught in a church steeple. The craft's door opened, and a man got out to free it. The townspeople who saw this threw stones at him, believing he was some sort of demon.

In time, their technology improved and ships were created with which they could not only explore the planet's surface, but also its atmosphere. Exploratory ships built using the biological principles of deep-sea creatures make perfect ocean-faring vessels. These ships also work perfectly in the sky. The sky's atmosphere is similar to the ocean's. Deschaine wrote, "Tons of water in many forms moves through the sky at all levels. Minerals drift and drop in from space and swirl up from surface soil. Energy constantly crackles around the globe. Our atmosphere is a habitat."[10] Human beings are naturally curious creatures. For this reason, we explore the heavens by developing rockets and other spacecraft. We explore the seas by creating deep diving vessels and submarines. And we explore what lay underground by unearthing and then cataloging ancient archaeological sites. Humankind's curiosity has led to great discoveries and technological advancements. Human beings who might have found a new home in the deepest oceans still possess this inherent curiosity. The ships they created serve not only to simplify their lives by providing a means to travel between underwater bases, but also to explore the surface of the planet and the creatures that live there.

Historical records aboard the ships and in oceanic bases confirm that their ancestors once lived on the planet's surface. Their ancestors perhaps desired more than anything else to return to the surface — their true home. But for their children and their grandchildren who were born underwater, this desire to return to the surface was absent. Their home, the only home they knew, was underwater. And in time, by processes of evolution, intentional D.N.A. modification, or a combination of the two, their bodies had become perfectly adapted to the dark, high-pressure environment in which they lived. After countless generations, stories about life on the surface were no longer viewed as historical. They became myths, legends that were told by the ancients — those godlike people who could leave their ships at will and survive in an unnatural environment. After thousands of years underwater, these humans could no longer survive for long periods on the surface. And their eyes could not adjust well to the high light levels that characterize surface life.

Within the ships, they are fine, as the technology aboard allows them to filter out the blinding sunlight, and the atmosphere in the ships approximates that found in their underwater bases. Based on UFO reports, the pilots occasionally exit their vehicles. This appears to only occur at night, when it is dark. Some witnesses who claim to have seen such creatures exiting aircraft also claim to have been abducted. As explained previously, many abductees state that the creatures who took them performed experiments, most of which centered upon human reproduction. Some women claimed to have been impregnated, only to have the child taken from them later. Men have described these creatures taking their sperm. On the surface, we humans do this to animals for experimental purposes (and to manipulate their D.N.A. for gastronomic reasons). It is possible that underwater humans are doing the same thing: that their sampling is for nonspecific experimental purposes. However, it is much more likely that they have a specific goal in mind. Perhaps they are trying to alter their D.N.A. so that they can return to life on the surface. If so, perhaps these creatures can end all speculation about their existence in person.

All of this is, of course, pure speculation. There is no way to prove any of it. When dealing with a phenomenon like this, it is important to create a theory that makes use of all available evidence, without casting anything out. There is substantial evidence of antediluvian civilizations that were technically advanced. Other evidence points to a regularity of cataclysmic floods. The last major one, which Plato claimed sunk Atlantis, happened 11,600 years ago.[11] Other evidence points to major floods that occurred 15,000 years ago, then 11,000 years ago, and finally the most recent, 8,000 years ago.[12] Pinpointing an exact date for such floods is impossible, a futile exercise. But we can state with certainty that massive floods like this have occurred, and will occur again in the future. We also know that many of the world's flood survival stories are about people who were assisted by wise gods that instructed them to build craft. Remember that many less advanced cultures initially believed that more advanced people were deities.

Native Americans referred to the Spaniards as gods, since they wore shiny suits and traveled across the ocean's surface. Some Pacific islanders likewise thought U.S. soldiers were gods. So although flood survival stories refer to interventions by gods, this is not necessarily what occurred. More advanced cultures assisted less advanced cultures, and instructed certain people to develop craft that could be used to survive the deluge. The Akkadian version of the flood survival story specifically mentions a submarine. Tebitu cannot be translated any other way. The same is true in the Sumerian version, which uses the term magurgur. It has been translated, like the Akkadian term tebitu, as a "ship that can tumble and turn." But this is verbose. The proper translation of both of these terms is submarine. Based on all available evidence, the theory proposed herein makes much more sense than the theory that UFOs come from outside Earth's atmosphere.

Remnants from a Distant Past

As a mental exercise, I previously asked you to put yourself aboard a submarine that was lost — a submarine that became trapped underwater and never returned to the surface. Continuing this exercise, I would like you now to assume that you did return to the surface, coming to rest on one of the many mountaintops described in flood stories. Noah's Ark came to rest on Mt. Ararat. Other vessels landed on mountains in the Himalayas. Some cultures did not create seafaring vessels at all, but survived the deluge in caves high up on mountainsides. No matter what, after seven days, the floodwaters abated and ships worldwide came ashore. These survivors were the ancestors of modern surface-dwelling humans.

Assuming for a moment that one of the theories proposed in this book is true — that technologically advanced civilizations existed on this planet in antediluvian times — let us move forward in time to the present. Since Earth regularly experiences worldwide floods, consider what would occur today if such a flood covered most major landmasses. Billions of people would die. Inventions like automobiles, airplanes, computers, and cell phones would be lost in the waves. Some survivors would board submarines, others would board specially designed ships. Still others would seek shelter on the highest mountains.

When the waves finally recede, ocean levels are much higher than they ever had been. Nearly all of the technological advancements would be underwater. After hundreds of years, they would literally cease to exist. Covered by rocks and sand, under thousands of feet of water, they would lose their place in history. Parents may tell their children about steel, bird-like craft that could carry human beings through the skies. They may tell them that humans of the past used technology based on quartz crystals to speak to each other through handheld devices, though they were thousands of miles apart. The children, having never seen such things, may not believe them. They are fanciful stories alone, devoid of historical truth. And although they might have passed the stories down to their own children, they were called myths.

The remnants of an airplane or car might be found somewhere, preserved in ice or other materials. Such discoveries would cause people to think and wonder. Some might create models from wood or other materials of the things they found. Ancient Egyptians likewise created wooden models of airplanes. Ancient cultures in South America made such models from gold. This is a common human tendency. Although the remnants of aircraft or seafaring vessels would eventually be reduced to nothing, people would continue to make models. Children would try to duplicate the models made by their parents, and eventually, future civilizations would find them.

These people of the future, upon discovering the models, would wonder if perhaps ancient humans had seen such technologically advanced craft. But of course, such a thing is not possible. So a theory that suggested this would be mocked. Instead, mainstream archaeologists and historians would claim that they are simply artistic representations of birds. Even though they have aerodynamically sound wings and fuselage, they would be chalked up as unusual bird carvings. History books would be written, ignoring such anomalous finds. No mysteries would remain. Human beings would begin to think that they know everything about planetary and human history.

When things are found that contradict this idea, the theory will not be changed. The finds will simply be trivialized and ignored. And in this way, human beings will always believe that no culture of the past could ever have matched their ingenuity and technical advancements. They will believe that they are the epitome of all previous civilizations. This cyclical nature of creation and destruction plagues human beings. Unfortunately, the cycle will not end. It will continue forever.

Conclusion

Stephen Jay Gould said, "The most erroneous stories are those we think we know best, and therefore never scrutinize or question." When Louis Agassiz first proposed the idea of ice ages, others dismissed it as nonsense. "Some theologians and other prominent in society thundered 'blasphemy' at the idea of an ice age. Even if they did not have strict theological objections, when the idea that northern Europe had once been buried beneath a huge glacier was first proposed, many contemporary scientists summarily dismissed it."[1]

This is a common human reaction. Anything that contradicts the current theory is summarily dismissed. "Galileo was interrogated by the Inquisition for his heretical proposal, based on observation, that the Earth moved in an orbit around the sun and was not the center of the universe."[2] In the past, people who made contradictory statements were either killed or imprisoned. In modern times, their punishment might not be as severe, but they are still mocked or discredited. This is because people as a whole do not like to think critically. They do not like to question their own pre-existing beliefs.

In the third century B.C.E., the Alexandrian scholar Eratosthenes correctly calculated the circumference of the Earth, and Posidonius created a revolving model of the solar system in the first century B.C.E.[3] However, once the Christian Church gained control, thus initiating the Dark Ages, this information was banned.[4] It was heretical to disbelieve that God positioned the stars in the sky, and to believe the Earth was round.[5] For centuries after this, the knowledge that the Earth was round was lost, and it became common knowledge that it was flat.

This did not change until Columbus had a different idea: an idea contrary to the widespread beliefs of the time. Educator John Dewey explained this:

> Men thought the world was flat until Columbus thought it to be round. The earlier thought was a belief held because men had not the energy or the courage to question what those about them accepted and taught, especially as it was suggested and seemingly confirmed by obvious sensible facts. The thought of Columbus was a reasoned conclusion. It marked the close of study into facts, of scrutiny and revision of evidence, of working out the implications of various hypotheses, and of comparing these theoretical results with one another and with known facts. Because Columbus did not accept unhesitatingly the current traditional theory, because he doubted and inquired, he arrived at his thought. Skeptical of what, from long habit, seemed most certain, and credulous of what seemed impossible, he went on thinking until he could produce evidence for both his confidence and his disbelief. Even if his conclusion had finally turned out wrong, it would have been a different sort of belief from those it antagonized, because it was reached by a different method. Active, persistent, and careful consideration of any belief or supposed form of knowledge in the light of the grounds that support it, and the further conclusions to which it tends constitutes reflective thought.[6]

Keep in mind another interesting phenomenon: ancient cultures and people who were alive before Columbus knew without doubt that the Earth was round. This knowledge was lost, only to be later rediscovered. People considered intelligent generally dismiss ideas as nonsense that run contrary to public opinion. It is for this reason that critical thinking is so difficult to teach and learn.

As strange as it might seem to open-minded individuals, critical thinking is often not encouraged. This is because the process runs contrary to established social order.[7] Education today follows the path of least resistance. Students are not given information that runs contrary to standard historical accounts.[8] This is because such inquiry could threaten the established social order.

To encourage critical thinking skills, teachers must present historical accounts that run contrary to mainstream versions. Hufford wrote, "A teacher should be encouraged to doubt, to recognize and build upon discontent, and to actively question, rather than passively accept, officially-sanctioned, transmitted knowledge."[9] Such questioning could be viewed as radical, but it is this questioning that leads to forward progress.[10] For people to attain the ability to think critically, they must be presented with conflicting ideas. In addition, open-mindedness and open-ended dialogue must be encouraged.[11] Keeping this in mind, the key to forward progress is simply to consider alternate possibilities for things that are regarded as unquestionable facts. One must remain open-minded and consider alternatives.

The UFO phenomenon has been around for hundreds of years, yet it has only been spoken about publicly as the UFO phenomenon since the 1940s. Before this, unidentified flying objects were generally explained from a religious perspective. For anyone to have suggested otherwise in the thirteenth or fourteenth century would have been heretical. This same type of closed-minded thinking has carried over to the modern age, but it is different. Today it is heretical to doubt that aliens pilot such craft. Some people still connect the UFO phenomenon with religion; for various people, the idea of extraterrestrials and UFOs is so integrated with religious and new age ideas that it has become akin to a new type of spirituality. To create a hypothesis for this phenomenon that truly takes into account all available evidence, it is first necessary to strip away all preconceived notions about UFOs. Only then can one consider the phenomenon with an open mind.

A theory about the UFO phenomenon is presented in this text. However, it is important to understand that there are no answers proposed, only possibilities. This theory should be considered as a possible explanation. If it is, then further research must be conducted. Some individuals have spent decades attempting to contact species outside our own atmosphere. Perhaps, if they turned their attention to the deepest oceans, they would find signs of intelligent life.

You should not believe the theory presented in this text based only upon the information within. In fact, if history is a guide, it would be better not to believe such things. In the 1200s, everyone knew the Earth was the center of the solar system, and all planets revolved around it. When Copernicus first came forward stating the Earth revolved around the sun, it sparked immediate controversy. People who believed this heresy were considered evil and ignorant. Likewise, in the 1400s, some people believed the Earth was round. They were disrespected and regarded as unintelligent.

There is a split prejudice when it comes to unidentified flying objects. Some think that anyone who even believes in such a phenomenon is stupid. Others think that such a phenomenon exists, but there is only one explanation: these craft are piloted by creatures from another planet. This belief does not stem from proof, only conjecture, and it is illogical. But just like historical truths, such as the Earth being the center of the universe and the Earth being flat, proof is not necessary for general public acceptance.

If you can keep an open mind, please consider the information presented in this text. A great deal of evidence supports the notion that history is not linear, with the current civilization the result of constant refinement. Rather, it seems that history is cyclical, and that civilizations of the past became increasingly more technologically advanced before being wiped out by mega-disasters like worldwide floods. Evidence suggests that past civilizations were highly advanced, quite possibly as advanced as human beings are today. This evidence includes maps that show the world's coasts as they had existed before the last glacial maximum. It also includes archaeological evidence that ancient cultures had sophisticated astronomical knowledge that has only recently been rediscovered. This knowledge was not only passed down to the present through sacred texts, but also in the undeniable features built into megalithic structures.

Some of the oldest texts in India are technical manuals about how to fly and operate vimanas. They describe aircraft and spacecraft, and no one can deny the age of these documents or the subject upon which they pontificate. This is not the only ancient culture that has records of flying machines. The so-called gold flyer, created c. 300 C.E. in Columbia, is a replica of a jet airplane. It is aerodynamically sound, and it would fly. Likewise, a wooden model of a glider or airplane was found in Sakkara, Egypt near hieroglyphs stating "I want to fly." All this evidence, added to stories about ancient civilizations that were technically advanced, is substantial.

Other evidence has been presented herein, which describes a cyclical nature of creation and subsequent destruction. Ruins of destroyed cities are found underwater. Accounts from more than 500 different cultures describe a deluge that destroyed civilizations. They talk about survivors, the progenitors of modern humans. Based upon all available evidence, it is clear that a massive flood did occur. It may not have been a worldwide flood, but the texts we have today clearly indicate that the people who experienced it *believed* it was a worldwide disaster. Within these flood stories we find the basis of the theory presented herein. The Akkadian, Sumerian, and Babylonian versions of the flood story popularized in the Epic of Gilgamesh, (which may have been the impetus for the Noah's Ark story in the Old Testament), clearly indicate that people survived the deluge by entering submarines. One of these submarines might have suffered damage and been trapped underwater.

This speculation stems from witness reports of UFOs and USOs, which indicate that these craft are connected to water. They are often seen entering or leaving water, and alleged abductees claim that they were brought underwater. This information, considered alongside statements of experts that the shape of these craft is not conducive to interstellar travel, indicates that they must be terrestrial in origin. In other words, these craft must come from Earth. If this is true, where can they be found? The only places on this planet capable of hiding such ships are the deepest oceanic trenches. The unusual occurrences that take place over the trenches in the Bermuda Triangle, Pacific Triangle, and other locations provide further circumstantial evidence that such craft may actually be hiding in these locations.

The available evidence seems to indicate that UFOs are from this planet, and that they have established permanent residences in the deep oceanic trenches that human beings do not have the technology to explore. If this is the case, it leaves one of two options: either creatures from another planet came here in the distant past and were unable or unwilling to leave, or these creatures have always been here. Both of these options are possible, but the second makes more sense for reasons that should be clear by now. Assuming that these creatures have always been here, we have two possibilities: either they are a distinct species, or they are humans who have changed on an evolutionary level due to a severe change in living conditions. Again, both of these are possible, but the latter seems more logical.

We know there is a connection between worldwide disasters and human and animal evolutionary change. And based upon testimonies of abductees, their abductors seem obsessed with human D.N.A. This might be because they wish to alter their own D.N.A., so that they can once again survive on the surface of the planet, which as a whole must be more hospitable than the dark environment in deep oceans. Consider how humans would change in such an environment over the course of more than 12,000 years. In a dark environment, their eyes would become bigger, more capable of discerning movement and change in darkness. In a high-pressure environment, their bodies would become smaller in relation to their heads. And in a small area, their ears and noses would likely become smaller. After millennia, they might look exactly like the grays, who have been seen piloting UFOs.

Certainly, this is all speculation. In time, perhaps they will surface and tell us their own story. When this happens, we will perhaps greet our distant relatives, rather than a truly unique species. This will be interesting, as our treatment of evolutionary relatives, as a whole, is unethical. Human beings treat them poorly, and they regard such creatures (like chimpanzees) as less important than their own species. How will human beings react to other evolutionary ancestors and relatives who are more intelligent? Is respect related to intelligence? Will they show them more reverence, or will they treat them as second-class citizens? Or, will they regard them as non-human, unworthy of respect? How human beings treat other creatures is indicative of how advanced they are, and we as a species are capable of growth. If an eventual meeting between surface-dwelling humans and those who live in the deep oceans occurs, hopefully it would be friendly. If so, imagine what we could learn from each other. It would be an evolutionary jump in human advancement, and the most significant event to ever occur on planet Earth.

Notes

Introduction

[1] Cremo & Thompson, *Hidden History*.
[2] Ibid.
[3] Ibid.
[4] "Tracking Ancient Man-Flight," Retrieved from http://www.ancient-hebrew.org/ancientman/03_vimana.html.
[5] Dunn, *Lost Technologies*.
[6] Ibid.
[7] Cremo & Thompson, *Hidden History*.
[8] Childress, *Technology of the Gods*.
[9] "The Baghdad Battery," Retrieved from http://www.world-mysteries.com/sar_11.htm.
[10] "The Antikythera Mechanism," Retrieved from http://www.bbc.com.uk/news/science-environment-17989915.
[11] Cremo & Thompson, *Hidden History*.
[12] Freke & Gandy, *The Jesus Mysteries*.
[13] Jeremiah, *Christian Mummification*.
[14] "Who Discovered Troy?" Retrieved from http://cerhas.uc.edu/troy/q415.html.
[15] Calvin, *The Ascent of Mind*.
[16] MacDougal, *Frozen Earth*.
[17] Sitchen, *There were Giants upon the Earth*.
[18] Darmesteter (Trans.), *Avesta: Vendidad*, Retrieved from http://www.avesta.org/vendidad/vd2sbe.htm.
[19] Genesis, 7: 19 - 20.
[20] Sandars, *The Epic of Gilgamesh*.

[21] Sitchen, *There were Giants upon the Earth*.
[22] Cremo & Thompson, *Hidden History*.
[23] Ibid.
[24] Ibid.
[25] Ibid.
[26] Friedman, *UFO Propulsion Systems*. Retrieved from http://www.internetarchaeology.org/saufor/otherpapers/ufopropulsion.html.
[27] For more information, see http://ntrs.larc.nasa.gov/search.jsp?R=20040089076&qs=Ns%3DPublicatio n-Date%7C1%26N%3D4294880618.

1. The UFO Phenomenon

[1] Deschaine, *The Sky*, p. 30.
[2] Ibid., p. 32.
[3] Ibid.
[4] http://altereddimensions.net/2012/nuremberg-germany-ufo-battle.
[5] Ibid.
[6] Chierniak, *UFOs*.
[7] Sellier, *UFO*, p. 86.
[8] Ibid., p. 82.
[9] Ibid., p. 82.
[10] Friedman & Berliner, *Crash at Corona*, p. 100.
[11] Quoted in Sellier, *UFO*, p. 83.
[12] Ibid., p. 90.
[13] Ibid.
[14] Birnes, *UFO Encyclopedia*, pp. 70 - 71.
[15] Ibid., p. 78.
[16] Ibid., p. 82.
[17] Ibid., p. 87.
[18] http://www.ufocasebook.com/wales1974.html.
[19] http://www.ufocasebook.com/chihuahuamexico1974.html.
[20] http://www.ufo-blog.com/ufo_crashes/height_611.htm.
[21] http://www.ufocasebook.com/Aurora.html.
[22] Ibid.
[23] There are other "close encounters" beyond the fourth kind. The fifth kind refers to bilateral, intentional contact between non-humans and humans. Close encounters of the sixth kind involve deaths that occur from UFO or

non-human interaction. These deaths refer to animals or humans alone. Cases of cattle-mutilation would fall under this category. The final category, the seventh kind, is used to group instances in which human-alien hybrids are created by sexual or artificial means, such as intentional D.N.A. gene manipulation.

[24] http://www.hyper.net/ufo/abductions.html.
[25] Strieber, *Communion*.
[26] Ibid., p. 25.
[27] Ibid., p. 38.
[28] Ibid., p. 111.
[29] Birnes, *UFO*.
[30] Quoted in Melanson, *Antonio Villas Boas*.
[31] Ibid.
[32] Hatzopoulos, "Alien Abduction Phenomenon."
[33] Ibid.
[34] Ibid.
[35] http://www.ufodigest.com/news/0509/undersea2.php.
[36] MUFON CMS Case #8050 Log # US-10042007-0003.
[37] http://www.waterufo.net/item.php?id=634.
[38] Strieber, *Communion*, p. 206.
[39] Kimball, *Best Evidence*.
[40] Birnes, *UFO Encyclopedia*.
[41] Kimball, *Best Evidence*.
[42] Kean, *UFOs*, p. 179.
[43] Ibid., p. 180.
[44] Guerra, "Circled by a UFO," pp. 47 - 48.
[45] Ibid.
[46] Jafari, "Dogfight," p. 89.
[47] Ibid.
[48] Kean, *UFOs*.
[49] Huertas, "Close Combat," pp. 96 - 97.
[50] Birnes, *UFO Encyclopedia*, p. 296.
[51] Ibid.
[52] Haines, "Unidentified Aerial Phenomena," p. 52.
[53] Ibid.
[54] Ibid.
[55] Kean, *UFOs*.
[56] Bower, "Gigantic UFOs," p. 74.
[57] Ibid., p. 81.

2. USOs

[1] Sanderson, 2005.
[2] Ibid.
[3] Ibid.
[4] Ibid.
[5] Ibid.
[6] Ibid.
[7] Ibid.
[8] Ibid.
[9] Ibid.
[10] Gallo, *Underwater Astonishments*.
[11] Berlitz, *Dragon's Triangle*, p. 95.
[12] Ibid.
[13] Ibid.
[14] Ibid.
[15] History Channel's (Mystery Quest) *Devil's Triangle*.
[16] Ibid.
[17] http://www.maryceleste.net/.
[18] http://www.abovetopsecret.com/forum/thread60876/pg1.
[19] Ibid.
[20] Sanderson, *Invisible Residents*.
[21] Retrieved from http://www.abovetopsecret.com/forum/thread60876/pg1.
[22] Berlitz, *Dragon's Triangle*.
[23] Ibid.
[24] Ibid.
[25] Walz, *UFO Files*.
[26] Berlitz, *Dragon's Triangle*, p. 100.
[27] Ibid., p. 61.
[28] Ibid.
[29] Ibid.
[30] Personal communication.
[31] McKay, *Bringing Life to Mars*.
[32] Pereira, "UFOs in Brazil," p. 204.

3. Underwater Cities

[1] Ryall, *Japan's Underwater Pyramids*.

[2] Ibid.
[3] Ibid.
[4] Ibid.
[5] Hancock, *Underworld*, pp. 9.
[6] Ibid.
[7] Ibid., p. 366.
[8] Joseph, "Archaeological Scandals."
[9] Ibid.
[10] Ibid.
[11] Ibid.
[12] Ibid.
[13] Mosheim, *Ecclesiastical History*.
[14] Hanson, "Was Jesus a Buddhist," p. 86.
[15] http://www.dharmakshetra.com/holy%20land/Dwarka.html.
[16] http://wikimapia.org/17077648/Dwarka
[17] http://sacredsites.com/asia/india/dwarka.html.
[18] Hancock, *Underworld*.
[19] http://www.crystalinks.com/biminiroad.html.
[20] http://www.blavatsky.net/science/atlantis/emails/cuba.htm.
[21] Ibid.
[22] Ibid.
[23] https://cs.uwaterloo.ca/~shallit/Papers/stages.pdf.
[24] http://news.nationalgeographic.com/news/2000/12/122800blacksea.html.

4. Cyclical Nature of Civilization

[1] Plato, *Critias*.
[2] Courlander, *Fourth World of the Hopi*.
[3] Ibid., p. 18.
[4] Gamble, Davies, Pettitt, & Richards, "Climate change and evolving human diversity in Europe during the last glacial."
[5] Courlander, *Fourth World of the Hopi*, p. 26.
[6] Fernandez, A. *Pre-Hispanic Gods of Mexico*.
[7] http://www.timeanddate.com/calendar/mayan.html.
[8] Sagan, *Cosmos*, p. 258.
[9] Wilson, *The Vishnu Purana: A System of Hindu Mythology and Tradition*, p. 21.
[10] Retrieved from http://hinduism.iskcon.org/concepts/111.htm.
[11] Sinha, *Study of the Bhagavata Purana*, p. 433.

[12] Jeremiah, *Living Buddhas*.
[13] This evidence is found in the coral growth rings of ancient oceans. See Harris, S., Stubberfield, T., & Nelson, T. *Prehistoric Disasters*.
[14] Sigmarsson, Karlsson & Larsen, "*The 1996 and 1998 subgalcial eruptions beneath the Vatnajokull ice sheet in Iceland: contrasting geochemical and geophysical inferences on magma migration.*"
[15] MacDougal, *Frozen Earth*, p. 188.
[16] *Forbidden History: Dinosaurs and the Bible*. Retrieved from http://www.forbidden-history.com/dinosaur-movie.html.
[17] Ibid.
[18] The Travels of Marco Polo. Book 2, Chapter 40. Quoted in *Forbidden History*.
[19] *Forbidden History*.
[20] Ibid.
[21] Ibid.
[22] Ibid.
[23] Ibid.
[24] Ibid.
[25] Ibid. Statement is by Dr. James Miller, 1983.
[26] Such creatures have also been seen off the coast of Brazil, in China, Russia, Norway, England, and Japan. They have likely been seen in many more locations as well.
[27] *Forbidden History*.
[28] Ibid.
[29] http://theageofreason.org/post/1633692270/all-truth-passes-through-three-stages-first-it.
[30] MacDougall, *Frozen Earth*, p. 89.
[31] Others believe that these interglacial periods last much longer; some think that there could be as many as 10,000 more years before the next glacial advancement.
[32] MacGougall, *Frozen Earth*, p. 174.
[33] Isaak, *Flood Stories*.
[34] Ibid.
[35] Peterson, *Avesta Vendidad*.
[36] Ibid.
[37] Please remember that such documents were written thousands of years after the events that they describe. They were likely passed down orally for generations before eventually being recorded in written form.
[38] Note the similarities between such stories and the Biblical and non-Biblical Adam and Eve stories.

[39] Isaak, *Flood Stories*.
[40] Ibid.
[41] Ibid.

5. Advanced Ancient Civilizations

[1] Cremo & Thompson, *Hidden History*, p. 100.
[2] Ibid., p. 92.
[3] Ibid.
[4] Ibid.
[5] Ibid.
[6] Ibid.
[7] Ibid.
[8] Ibid.
[9] Ibid.
[10] Ibid.
[11] Ibid., p. 151.
[12] Ibid.
[13] Ibid., p. 116.
[14] Ibid.
[15] Ibid.
[16] Ibid.
[17] Ibid., p. 106.
[18] Ibid.
[19] Ibid.
[20] Childress, *Technology of the Gods*.
[21] http://www.thelivingmoon.com/43ancients/02files/Ancient_Electricity_01.html.
[22] Ibid.
[23] Ibid.
[24] http://www.antikythera-mechanism.gr/.
[25] Childress, *Technology of the Gods*.
[26] http://religionvirus.blogspot.com/2008/12/one-catholic-priest-destroyed-entire.html.
[27] Childress, *Technology of the Gods*.
[28] Tomas, *We Are Not the First*.
[29] http://www.bibleufo.com/ufos.htm.
[30] http://www.badarchaeology.com/?page_id=560.
[31] Hancock, *Fingerprints of the Gods*, p. 18.

[32] http://www.world-mysteries.com/sar_1.htm.
[33] Hapgood, *Maps of the Ancient Sea Kings*, p. 79.
[34] http://www.maproomblog.com/2007/02/the_piri_reis_map_of_1513.php.
[35] Hancock, *Fingerprints of the Gods*.
[36] *Kebra Nagast*, p. 36.
[37] Ezekiel 1: 1-1: 24.
[38] http://www.atlantisquest.com/Excerpt.html.
[39] Ibid.
[40] Ibid.
[41] Ibid.
[42] Ibid.
[43] Ibid.
[44] Ibid.
[45] Ibid.
[46] Ibid.
[47] Ibid.
[48] Ibid.
[49] Sutherland, *Vimanas*.
[50] http://www.bibliotecapleyades.net/vimanas/esp_vimanas_8.htm.
[51] Sutherland, *Vimanas*.
[52] Ibid.
[53] Ibid.
[54] Childress, *Technology of the Gods*, p. 167.
[55] Sutherland, *Vimanas*.
[56] Hancock, *Fingerprints of the Gods*.
[57] Coppens, *Ancient Alien Question*, p. 188.
[58] Silverburg, *Wonders of Ancient Chinese Science*.
[59] Quoted in Childress, *Technology of the Gods*, p. 147.
[60] Ibid.
[61] http://www.beforeus.com/indusa.htm.
[62] Roy, *Mahabharata*.
[63] Takakura, "The children who don't know the Atomic Bomb," pp. 101 - 102.
[64] http://www.bibliotecapleyades.net/ancientatomicwar/esp_ancient_atomic_10.htm.
[65] Plato, *Critias*.
[66] Ibid.
[67] Jeremiah, *Christian Mummification*.
[68] Mosjov, *Osiris*.

69 Frazer, *Adonis, Attis, Osiris.*
70 Hancock, *Fingerprints of the Gods*, p. 346.
71 Ibid.
72 Although the mainstream theory holds that these pits were used to house wooden boats, symbolic and necessary vessels for the journey through the afterlife, no evidence has ever been unearthed to suggest that they once contained wooden boats.
73 Dunn, *Lost Technologies.*
74 Ibid.
75 Hancock, *Fingerprints of the Gods.*
76 Ibid.
77 Vega, *Royal Commentaries*, p. 237.
78 Posnansky, *Tiahuanacu: The Cradle of American Man.*
79 Ibid.
80 Ibid.
81 Hancock, *Fingerprints of the Gods*, p. 91.
82 Andrews, Foreword to *Lost Technologies*, p. xii.
83 Hancock, *Underworld.*
84 Ibid.
85 Ibid.
86 Ibid.
87 Ibid.
88 Ibid.
89 Ibid., p. 53.
90 Gaster, *Myth, Legend, and Custom*, p. 100.

6. The Last Great Flood

1 Reinl, *Chariots of the Gods.*
2 Pringle, *Mummy Congress.*
3 Ibid.
4 Ibid., p. 141.
5 Ibid.
6 MacDougal, *Frozen Earth.*
7 Ibid., p. 194.
8 Ibid., pp. 191-192.
9 Ibid., p. 192.
10 Deschaine, *The Sky*, p. 30.
11 Hancock, *Underworld.*

[12] Ibid.

Conclusion

[1] MacDougall, *Frozen Earth*, p. 3.
[2] Ibid., p. 17.
[3] Dewey, *How We Think*.
[4] Freke & Gandy, *Jesus Mysteries*.
[5] Ibid.
[6] Dewey, *How We Think*, pp. 5 - 6.
[7] Hufford, "Teacher Education."
[8] Hein & Selden, *Censoring History*.
[9] Ibid., p. 96.
[10] Lyutykh, "Practicing Critical Thinking."
[11] Canestrari & Marlowe, "From Silence to Dissent."

Bibliography

Alley, R. B. *The Two-Mile Time Machine: Ice Cores, Abrupt Climate Change, and Our Future.* Princeton, NJ: Princeton University Press, 2000.

Andrews, A. Introduction to *Lost Technologies of Ancient Egypt* by C. Dunn (Bear & Company, 2010), ix-xv.

Bahn, P. & Renfrew, C. *Archaeology: Theories, Methods and Practice.* New York, NY: Thames and Hudson, 1996.

Bellamy, H. S. *Built before the Flood: The Problem of the Tiahuanaco Ruins.* London: Faber & Faber, 1943.

Berlitz, C. *The Dragon's Triangle: The Fascinating Examination of One of the World's Greatest Mysteries.* Hammersmith, London: Grafton Books, 1991.

Beyer, B. "How to teach thinking skills in social studies and history." *Social Studies,* September/October (2008): 196-201.

Bharati, A., "Anthropological approaches to the study of religion: Ritual and belief systems," *Biennial Review of Anthropology,* 7, 230 - 282, 1971.

Birnes, W. *The UFO Magazine UFO Encyclopedia.* New York: Pocket Books, 2004.

Bower, R. "Gigantic UFOs over the English Channel, 2007." In *UFOs: Generals, Pilots, and Government Officials Go on the Record*, edited by Leslie Kean, 73 - 81. New York: Three Rivers Press, 2010.

Bramley, W. "UFO cults: A brief history of religions," in *Exposed, Uncovered, and Declassified: Lost Civilizations & Secrets of the Past* (Kindle Edition), eds. M. Pye and K. Dalley (Pompton Plains, NJ: New Page Books, 2012).

Brookfield, S. *Developing Critical Thinkers*. San Fransisco, CA: Jossey-Bass, 1987.

Brown, H. *Cataclysms of the Earth*. New York: Twayne Books, 1967.

Budge, E. (Trans.). *The Kebra Nagast*. New York: Cosimo Books, 2004.

—. (Trans.). *The Book of the Dead: The Paprys of Ani*. Sacred Texts, 1895. http://www.sacred-texts.com/egy/ebod/.

Calvin, W. H. *A Brain for All Seasons: Human Evolution and Abrupt Climate Change*. Chicago: University of Chicago Press, 2002.

—. *The Ascent of Mind: Ice Age Climates and the Evolution of Intelligence*. New York: Bantam Books, 1991.

Canestrari, A., & Marlowe, B. "From silence to dissent: Fostering critical voice in teachers." *Encounter: Education for Meaning and Social Justice*, 2005.

Cherniak, D. (Director). *UFOs: The Secret History* (DVD). UFO T.V. & Spirit Culture Media, 2010.

Childress, D. H. *Technology of the Gods: The Incredible Science of the Ancients*. Kempton, IL: Adventures Unlimited Press, 2000.

Coppens, P. *The Ancient Alien Question*. New Jersey: New Page Books, 2012.

—. "Atlantis: The Lost Walhalla," in *Exposed, Uncovered, and Declassified: Lost Civilizations & Secrets of the Past* (Kindle Edition), eds. M. Pye and K. Dalley (Pompton Plains, NJ: New Page Books, 2012).

Courlander, H. *The Fourth World of the Hopi: The Epic Story of the Hopi Indians as Preserved in their Legends and Tradition.* Albuquerque, NM: University of New Mexico Press, 1971.

Cremo, M. & Thompson, R. *The Hidden History of the Human Race.* Los Angeles, CA: Bhaktivedanta Book Publishing, Inc., 2008.

Cremo, M. *Forbidden Archaeology's Impact.* Los Angeles, CA: Bhaktivedanta Book Publishing, Inc., 1998.

—. *Forbidden archaeology: The hidden history of the human race.* Los Angeles, CA: Bhaktivedanta Publishing Company, 1996.

Davis, N. *The Ancient Kingdoms of Mexico.* London: Penguin Books, 1990.

Deschaine, S. "The sky is alive." *Fortean Times,* September 2012, 30-35.

Dewey, J. *How We Think.* Boston, MA: D.C. Heath & Co, 1910.

Dunn, C. *Lost Technologies of Ancient Egypt.* Rochester, VT: Bear & Company, 2010.

—. *The Giza Power Plant: Technologies of Ancient Egypt.* Rochester, VT: Bear & Company, 1998.

Erdoes, R. and Alfonso, O. *American Indian Myths and Legends.* New York, NY: Pantheon Books, 1984.

Feldmann, S. *African Myths and Tales.* New York, NY: Dell Publishing, 1963.

Fernandez, A. *Pre-Hispanic Gods of Mexico.* Mexico City, Mexico: Panorama Editorial, 1992.

Frazer, J. *Adonis, Attis, Osiris: Studies in the History of Oriental Religion.* New York, NY: University Books, 1961.

Freke, T., & Gandy, P. *The Jesus Mysteries: Was the Original Jesus a Pagan God?* New York, NY: Three Rivers Press, 1999.

Friedman, S. *UFO Propulsion Systems*, 2002. http://www.internetarchaeology.org/saufor/otherpapers/ufopropulsion.html.

Friedman, T., & Berliner, D. *Crash at Corona*. New York, NY: Marlowe & Co., 1992.

Fullan, M. "Understanding Change." In *The Jossey-Bass reader on educational leadership*, ed. Fullan, M. (San Francisco, CA: Jossey-Bass, 2007), 169-181.

Gallo, D. *Underwater Astonishments*. Monterey, CA: TedTalks, 2007. http://www.youtube.com/watch?v=YVun8dpSAtO.

Gamble, C., Davies, W., Pettitt, P., & Richards, M. "Climate change and evolving human diversity in Europe during the last glacial." *Royal Society Publishing*, 2004: 243-254.

Gaster, T. H. *Myth, Legend, and Custom in the Old Testament*. New York, NY: Harper & Row, 1969.

Giddings, R. W. *Yaqui Myths and Legends*. Tucson, AZ: University of Arizona Press, 1959.

Gifford, D. *Warriors, Gods & Spirits from Central & South American Mythology*. Glasgow, Scotland: William Collins, 1983.

González-Reimann, L. *Tiempo Cíclico y Eras del Mundo en la India*. [Cyclical Time and World Eras in India]. Mexico City, Mexico: Colegio de México, 1988.

Guerra, J. M. "Circled by a UFO." In *UFOs: Generals, Pilots, and Government Officials Go on the Record*, edited by Leslie Kean, 47-51. New York, NY: Three Rivers Press, 2010.

Haines, R. F. "Unidentified Aerial Phenomena and Aviation Safety." In *UFOs: Generals, Pilots, and Government Officials Go on the Record*, edited by Leslie Kean, 52-64. New York, NY: Three Rivers Press, 2010.

Hancock, G. *Underworld: The Mysterious Origins of Civilization*. New York, NY: Three Rivers Press, 2002.

—. *Fingerprints of the Gods*. New York, NY: Crown Publishers, 1995.

Hancock, G. & Bauval, R. *The Message of the Sphinx: A Quest for the Hidden Legacy of Mankind*. New York, NY: Three Rivers Press, 1996.

Hanks, M. "Oppenheimer's Iron Thunderbolt: Evidence of Ancient Nuclear Weapons," in *Exposed, Uncovered, and Declassified: Lost Civilizations & Secrets of the Past* (Kindle Edition), eds. M. Pye and K. Dalley (Pompton Plains, NJ: New Page Books, 2012).

Hanson, J. "Was Jesus a Buddhist?" *Buddhist-Christian Studies, 25*, 75-89, 2005.

Hapgood. C. *Maps of the Ancient Sea Kings*. London, England: Turnstone Books, 1979.

Harris, S., Stubberfield, T., & Nelson, T. *Prehistoric Disasters* (DVD). Discovery Channel, 2012.

Hatzopoulos, D. "Alien Abduction Phenomenon." *Best UFO Resources*, 2012. http://www.hyper.net/ufo/abductions.html.

Hein, L. & Selden, M. *Censoring history: Citizenship and memory in Japan, Germany, and the United States*. Armonk, NY: Sharpe, 2000.

Herodotus. *History*. (Translated by G. Rawlinson). London: Dent, 1920.

Huertas, O. S. M. "Close Combat with a UFO." In *UFOs: Generals, Pilots, and Government Officials Go on the Record*, edited by Leslie Kean, 93-98. New York, NY: Three Rivers Press, 2010.

Hufford, D. "Teacher education, transformation, and an education for discontent." *Journal of Philosophy and History of Education, 58* (2008): 83-91.

Imbrie, J. & Imbrie, K. P. *Ice Ages: Solving the Mystery*. Berkeley Heights, NJ: Enslow, 1979.

Isaac, M. *Flood Stories from Around the World*, 2002. http://www.talkorigins.org/faqs/flood-myths.html.

Jafari, P. "Dogfight over Tehran." In *UFOs: Generals, Pilots, and Government Officials Go on the Record*, edited by Leslie Kean, 86 - 92. New York, NY: Three Rivers Press, 2010.

Jeremiah, K. *Christian Mummification: An Interpretative History of the Preservation of Saints, Martyrs and Others*. Jefferson, NC: McFarland & Co., Inc., 2012.

—. *Living Buddhas: The Self-Mummified Monks of Yamagata, Japan*. Jefferson, NC: McFarland & Co., Inc, 2010.

Joseph, F. "Archaeological Scandals," in *Exposed, Uncovered, and Declassified: Lost Civilizations & Secrets of the Past* (Kindle Edition), Edited by M. Pye and K. Dalley (Pompton Plains, NJ: New Page Books, 2012).

Kida, T. *Don't Believe Everything You Think: The 6 Basic Mistakes We Make in Thinking*. Amherst, NY: Prometheus, 2006.

Kimball, J., (Producer). *Best Evidence: Top 10 UFO Sightings* (DVD). Third Way Productions, Inc., 2007.

Lambert, T., & Gluckman, D. (Directors). *Ice World* (DVD). Discovery Channel, 2007.

Lapple, A. *Inchiesta sui grandi miracoli della storia.* [Investigation of the great historical miracles]. Italy: Piemme, 1990.

Lyutykh, E. "Practicing critical thinking in an educational psychology classroom: Reflections from a cultural-historical perspective." *Educational Studies, 45* (2009): 377-391.

MacDougal, D. *Frozen Earth: The Once and Future Story of Ice Ages*. Berkeley, CA: University of California Press, 2004.

Mason, L., Boldrin, A., & Ariasi, N. "Searching the Web to learn about a controversial topic: are students epistemically active?" *Instructional Science, 38*(6), (2010): 607-633.

McKay, C. "Bringing Life to Mars." *Scientific American*, 1999. http://meteorite.unm.edu/site_media/pdf/BringingLife.pdf.

Melanson, T. *Antonio Villas Boas: Abduction Episode Ground Zero*, 2001. http://www.conspiracyarchive.com/UFOs/boas-abduction.htm.

Meyer, C. *Teaching Students to Think Critically*. San Fransisco, CA: Jossey-Bass, 1986.

Mojsov, M. *Osiris: Death and Afterlife of a God*. Malden, MA: Blackwell, 2005.

Mosheim, J. *An Ecclesiastical History, Ancient and Modern, from the Birth of Christ to the Beginning of the Modern Century*. London, England: A. Miller, 1842.

Muller, R. A. & MacDonald, G. J. *Ice Ages and Astronomical Causes*. New York, NY: Springer, 2000.

Nickerson, R. S., Perkins, D. N., & Smith, E. E. *The Teaching of Thinking*. Hillside, NJ: Erlbaum, 1985.

Noble, D. G. *Ancient Ruins of the Southwest: An Archaeological Guide*. Flagstaff, AZ: Northland Publishing Company, 2000.

Opler, M. E. *Myths and Tales of the Jicarilla Apache Indians*. Dover, 1994.

Ovid. *The Metamorphoses*. Translated by H. Gregory. New York, NY: Viking Press, 1958.

Parrinder, G. *African Mythology*. New York, NY: Peter Bedrick Books, 1982.

Patton, D. W. *The Biblical Flood and the Ice Epoch: A Study in Scientific History*. Seattle, WA: Pacific Meridian Publishing Co., 1966.

Pereira, J. C. "UFOs in Brazil." In *UFOs: Generals, Pilots, and Government Officials Go on the Record*, edited by Leslie Kean, 198-205. New York, NY: Three Rivers Press, 2010.

Peterson, J. (Trans.) *Avesta: Vendidad*, 1995. www.avesta.org/vendidad.

Pinchbeck, D. *2012: The Return of Quetzalcoatl.* New York, NY: Jeremy Tarcher, 2006.

Plato. *Critias.* (Translated by B. Jowett). Internet Classics Archive. http://classics.mit.edu//Plato/critias.html.

Posnansky, A. *Tiahuanacu: The Cradle of American Man.* New York, NY: J.J. Augustin, 1945.

Pringle, H. *The Mummy Congress: Science, Obsession, and the Everlasting Dead.* New York, NY: Hyperion, 2001.

Reinl, H. (Director). *Chariots of the Gods.* (DVD). VCI Entertainment, 1972.

Roy, P. C., trans. *The Mahabharata.* Calcutta, India: Oriental Publishing Co., 1965. http://www.sacred-texts.com/hin/maha/index.htm.

Ryall, J. "Japan's Ancient Underwater Pyramid Mystifies Scholars." *National Geographic News,* September 19, 2007. http://news.nationalgeographic.com/news/pf/5467377.html.

Sagan, C. *Cosmos.* New York, NY: Random House, 1980.

Sandars, N. K. (Trans.). *The Epic of Gilgamesh.* New York, NY: Penguin, 1972.

Sanderson, I. T. *Invisible Residents: The Reality of Underwater UFOs.* Kempton, IL: Adventures Unlimited Press, 2005.

Sellers, J. *The Death of the Gods in Ancient Egypt: An Essay on Egyptian Religion and the Frame of Time.* London: Penguin, 1992.

Sellier, C. E. *UFO.* Chicago, IL: Contemporary Books, 1997.

Sigmarsson, O., Karlsson, H. R., &Larsen, G. "The 1996 and 1998 subglacial eruptions beneath the Vatnajokull ice sheet in Iceland: contrasting geochemical and geophysical inferences on magma migration." *Bulletin of Volcanology,* 61(7), (2010): 468-476.

Silverburg, R. *Wonders of Ancient Chinese Science.* New York, NY: Ballentine Books, 1972.

Sinha, P. N. *A Study of the Bhagavata Purana or Esoteric Hinduism.* Benares: Freeman & Co., 1901.

Sitchen, Z. *There were Giants upon the Earth: Gods, Demigods, and Human Ancestry: The Evidence of Alien DNA.* Rochester, VT: Bear & Company, 2010.

—. *Divine Encounters.* New York, NY: Avon Books, 1995.

—. *The Cosmic Code.* New York, NY: Avon Books, 1998.

—. *The End of Days.* New York, NY: William Morrow, 2007.

Smith, W. R. *Aborigine Myths and Legends.* London: Senate, 1996.

Sproul, B. C. *Primal Myths.* New York, NY: HarperCollins Publishers, 1979.

Strieber, W. *Communion.* New York, NY: Beech Tree Books, 1987.

Sturluson, S. *The Prose Edda,* (Translated by J. Young), Berkeley, CA: University of California Press, 1954.

Sullivan, W. *The Secret of the Incas: Myth, Astronomy, and the War Against Time.* New York, NY: Crown Publishers, 1996.

Sutherland, M. *Vimanas: Ancient Flying Saucers of Atlantis and Lemuria,* 2010. http://www.burlingtonnews.net/files/viminas.pdf.

Takakura, A. "The Children who don't know the Atomic Bomb," In *Eyewitness Testimonies: Appeals from the A-Bomb Survivors.* (Hiroshima, Japan: Hiroshima Peace Culture Foundation, 2003), 100-102.

Tedlock, D. (trans.). *Popol Vuh.* New York, NY: Simon & Schuster, 1985.

Tomas, A. *We Are Not the First.* London, England: Souvenir Press, 1971.

Vega, G. *The Royal Commentaries of the Incas.* New York, NY: Orion Press, 1961.

Wagner, T. *The Global Achievement Gap*. New York, NY: Basic Books, 2008.

Walz, J. A. (Director). *UFO Files: The Pacific Bermuda Triangle*. (DVD). The History Channel, 2006.

Waters, F. *Book of the Hopi: The First Revelation of the Hopi's Historical and Religious Worldview of Life*. New York, NY: Penguin Books, 1963.

Willingham, D. "Critical thinking: Why is it so hard to teach?" *American Educator, Summer* (2007): 8-19.

Wilson, H. (trans.). *The Vishnu Purana: A System of Hindu Mythology and Tradition*. Calcutta, India: Punthi Pustak, 1972.

Wolf, M. (Director). *UFO Secret: The Roswell Crash*. UFO TV, 2006.

Zell, O. "Paradises Lost," in *Exposed, Uncovered, and Declassified: Lost Civilizations & Secrets of the Past* (Kindle Edition), eds. M. Pye and K. Dalley (Pompton Plains, NJ: New Page Books, 2012).

Index

abductee. *See* abduction
abduction, 45, 46, 47, 50, 51, 53, 54, 55, 56, 58, 59, 325
Adam and Eve, 197, 314
Agassiz, Louis, 185, 186, 302
Ahura Mazda, 6, 193, 194
Akkadian, 8, 9, 266, 278, 279, 280, 281, 292, 298, 306
Alamogordo, New Mexico, 234, 236
Aldrovandus, Ulysses, 180
Alexander the Great, 27, 78, 181
algae, 6, 13, 15, 194, 257, 281, 290, 291
Alpha Centauri, 120
Amataní, 128, 129
Anasazis, 162
Andaman, 144
Andrew Demades, 102
Antarctica, 186, 187, 192, 215, 216
Antikythera, ix, 2, 212, 213, 309
Antikythera shipwreck, 2
Apachiohualiztli, 165
apatosour, 182
Apollo, ix, 164
Ararat, 8, 195, 262, 299
Aratake, Kihachiro, 132
Ares, 164

Argentina, 206, 207
Arhat, 266
Arjuna, 145, 223
Arnold, Kenneth, viii, 30, 31, 32, 39
Athena, 164
Atlantis, 10, 151, 152, 237, 238, 269, 297, 320, 327
atomic bomb, 234, 235, 236
atomic weapons, 234
Atrahasis, 8, 191, 195, 293
Aurel Stein, Marc, 275
Aurora, 43, 44, 68, 88, 310
awliyā'Allāh, 266
Aymara, 128
azhdaha. *See* dinosaur
Aztecs, 163, 165, 166
Babylonian, 8, 9, 14, 190, 191, 195, 278, 306
Baghdad battery, 2, 211
bakunawa. *See* dinosaur
Ballard, Robert, 4, 153
Barrier Canyon, viii, ix, x, 112, 276, 277
battery, 2, 53, 211
Bay of Bengal, 144, 147
Bean, Allen, 23
Bengali, 196

Benting, Peter, 231
Bentwaters, 60
Berge Istra, 101
Berlitz, Charles, 85, 99, 312, 319
Bermuda Triangle, 11, 12, 56, 81, 90, 92, 93, 95, 96, 97, 99, 103, 149, 295, 307, 328
Berwyn Mountain Incident, 41
Bhagavata Purana, 143, 224, 313, 327
Bharadwaaja, Maharshi, 1, 225
Bible, 27, 181, 197, 214, 220, 255, 279, 314
Bimini Road, 148, 149
biological principles, 21, 125, 126, 149, 285, 288, 296
bioluminescence, viii, 20, 21, 84, 87, 121, 125
Blanchard, William, 33, 35
Boas, Antonio Villas, 51, 52, 53, 54, 55, 59, 311, 325
Bodhisattva, 266
Bolivar Maru, 101
Bolivia, 253
Bower, Ray, 71, 311, 320
Boyd, Alpha, 37
Brahma, 167, 168, 234
Brazel, Mac, 32, 33, 34, 36, 37, 40
Buache, Phillippe, 215
Buddhism, 5, 167, 169, 266
Budge, Wallis, 240
Cairo, Egypt, 231
California Maru, 102
camouflage, 22, 125, 126, 226
Canyon de Chelly, 112, 276
Canyonlands National Park, 112, 276
Cardenas, Filiberto, 56, 72, 113
Carmacks, 23
cephalopods, 87, 125, 126
Champ, 183
Chicomoztoc, 165
China, 8, 230, 260, 274, 275, 314
chlorophyta algae, 13
coelacanth, viii, 85, 87

Columbia, 86, 182, 183, 230, 262, 306
Columbus, Christopher, 11, 29, 78, 79, 138, 139, 303, 304
Communion, 47, 311, 327
Congo, 182
Constantinople, 218
Coyame, 42
Coyame UFO Event, 42
Cretaceous Period, 119, 160, 179
Critias, 10, 151, 155, 237, 313, 316, 326
Crusades, 11
D.N.A., 191, 279, 280, 287, 289, 292, 293, 294, 296, 297, 307, 311
Darwin, Charles, 177, 291
Darwinian Theory. *See* Darwin
De Natura Animalium, 180
Dei Gratia, 94
deluge, 168, 188
Derbyshire, 102
Derenkuyu, 7
Deschaine, Scott, 19, 20, 296, 310, 317, 321
Devil's Sea. *See* Pacific Triangle
dinosaurs, 85, 119, 159, 174, 179, 180, 181, 182, 183
dogu, viii, 108, 109
dragon, 85, 97, 103, 179, 180, 181
Dragon's Triangle. *See* Pacific Triangle, *See* Pacific Triangle, *See* Pacific Triangle, *See* Pacific Triangle
Dunn, Christopher, 245, 246, 258, 309, 317, 319, 321
Dvaraka. *See* Dwarka
Dvarka. *See* Dwarka
Dwaraka. *See* Dwarka
Dwarka, 143, 144, 145, 146, 152, 313
Easter Island, ix, 273, 274
Eenboom, Algund, 231
Egypt, ix, 181, 201, 230, 231, 238, 241, 242, 244, 245, 246, 257,

258, 259, 261, 306, 319, 321, 326
Ehecoatl, 165
ejderha. *See* dinosaur
El Dorado, 230
Eldredge, Niles, 177, 291
electronic fog, 92, 93
Engano, 196
Enola Gay, 33
Eratosthenes, 4, 302
Erie, Lake, 57, 81, 85
Ethiopia, 219, 242
evolution, 5, 158, 159, 173, 174, 176, 177, 185, 203, 205, 207, 289, 290, 291, 294, 296, 320
Ezekiel, 220, 221, 316
Finaeus, Oronteus, 216
Flying Dutchman, 98, 99
Freya, 164
Garriott, Owen, 23
Genesis, 279, 309
geode, 2, 210
Gernon, Bruce, 92
Gervase of Tilbury, 295
Ghost ships, 98
Gilgamesh, 8, 9, 292, 306, 309, 326
Giza, ix, 241, 243, 244, 253, 321
glacial age. *See* glacial period
glacial period, 7, 10, 13, 14, 141, 172, 173, 193, 194, 256, 259, 260, 265, 278, 284
glacial periods, 5, 6, 160, 185, 186, 187, 215, 230, 239
glaciers, 6, 7, 8, 14, 159, 172, 186, 187, 192, 194, 195, 198, 230, 259, 260, 280, 284, 293. *See* glacial periods
Glaser, Hans, viii, 28
Glenn, John, 22, 38, 39
global cooling, 174
global warming, 88, 174
Gogyeng Sowuhti. *See* Spider Grandmother
Gomati River, 145
Gould, Stephen Jay, 177, 291, 302

Government Point, 74
Gray, Willard, 211
grays, 12, 24, 308
Great Flood, 6, 8, 10, 14, 161, 169, 181, 188, 191, 222, 230, 233, 238, 240, 243, 253, 260, 261, 264, 268, 272, 317
Greece, 2, 212
Grimsvotn, 173
Guerra, Julio Miguel, 65, 66, 311, 322
Gujarat, 144, 146
haab, 166
Haines, Richard, 69, 70, 311, 322
Halt, Lt. Col., 62
Hancock, Graham, 134, 215, 243, 254, 260, 313, 315, 316, 317, 322, 323
helicopters, 20, 42, 78, 81, 215, 233, 285
Hermes, 164
Herodotus, 181, 323
hieroglyphs, 38, 43, 78, 106, 306
Hinduism, 5, 167, 168, 169, 327
Hiroshima, 33, 235, 236, 327
Hiruto no Hama, 106
Historia Animalium, 180
Hokusai, viii, 98
Homer, 4, 218
Honanki, ix, 112, 276, 277
Hopi, x, 5, 109, 110, 111, 156, 157, 159, 160, 161, 162, 163, 166, 167, 313, 321, 328
House of Taga, 269
Hubble Telescope, viii, 118
Huyatlaco, Mexico, 204
Hypogeum, 136
Ice Age, 5, 6, 136, 137, 152, 160, 168, 173, 176, 186, 187, 201, 243, 256, 260, 289, 290, 302, 320
Inca, 248, 250, 252
Incans, 127, 250, 270
Indus Valley, 201, 234
Isla de la Luna, 127

Isla del Sol, 127
Italy, ix, 94, 164, 180, 206, 324
Jafari, General Parviz, 66, 311, 324
Jainism, 167
Japan, viii, ix, 2, 7, 12, 20, 29, 33, 81, 88, 90, 100, 103, 107, 108, 131, 132, 134, 141, 143, 147, 152, 256, 265, 312, 314, 323, 324, 326, 327
jellyfish, viii, 20, 21, 22, 84
Jellyfish, viii, 20
Jomon, 107
Joyce, Frank, 32, 36
Jupiter, 164, 188, 248
Jurassic Period, 119, 159
kachina, viii, x, 109, 110, 111
Kaipara Harbour, 80
Kaiyo Maru, 102, 104
Kalema, 230
Kaufman, Frank, 39, 40
Kebra Nagast, 2, 27, 222, 255, 316, 320
Kebra Negast, 219
Kensington Rune Stone, ix, 138, 139
Kevlar vest, 286
Khafre, ix, 240, 241, 242, 243, 244
Khambhat, 146
Khufu, 241, 244
Ki Kung Shi, 215, 233
Kimura, Masaaki, 132, 133, 134, 142
Kitsukawa Maru, 80
Klondike Highway, 23
Kojiki, 143
König, Wilhelm, 211
Krishna, ix, 144, 145, 152
Kyokutei, Bakin, 107
Lake Champlain, 182
Lasca, Carlos, 78
Lebanon, 248
Lemuria, 151, 237, 327
Loch Ness, 85, 180, 182
Lockheed, 68
Lousma, Jack, 23

luminescence, 90, 285, 287, 288
MacDougall, Doug, 176, 185, 187, 289, 291, 314, 318
Machu Picchu, ix, 250, 251, 252, 269
magurgur, 9, 279, 298
Mahabharata, 143, 145, 222, 223, 228, 234, 235, 316, 326
Mahayana, 169, 266
Maitreya, 169
Malmstrom Air Force Base, 60
Malta, 136, 137
Malthais, Vern, 35
mana, 13, 15, 254, 281, 282
manna, 254, 255, 256, 257
Manna, 254, 255, 256
Marcel, Jesse, 32, 33, 34
Mariana Trench, 83, 84, 88
marine creatures, viii, 21
Mars, viii, 115, 116, 118, 119, 164, 171, 213, 312, 325
Martian, 43, 118
Mary Celeste, 94
Mayans, 166, 214, 270
Mayr, Ernst, 290, 291
McGuire, Phyliss, 40
megalithic structures, 240, 244, 245, 247, 250, 252, 253, 263, 265, 306
megaliths, 132, 245, 253, 269
mercury, 225, 227, 228
mercury vortex engine, 227
Mesiah, Caliil, 231
Metonic cycle, 213
Mindanao Trench, 101
moai, 273
Mohenjo-Daro, 234, 235
Mokele Embembe. *See* apatosour
Montana, 60
Moulin Quignon, 206
Mu, 151, 152, 237, 269, 275
myth, 157, 188, 218, 228, 266, 267, 275, 296, 300, 323
N'Goubou. *See* triceratops
Nagahashi, Matajiro, 106

Nagasaki, 33, 236
nago. See dinosaur
NASA, 4, 13, 257
Naviero, 77
New Testament, 143
Nihongi, 143
Nisir, 9, 191
Noah, 8, 9, 189, 195, 266, 279, 293, 299, 306
Northrop, 68
Nuremberg, Germany, 28
Oannes, 272
oceanic trenches, 83, 88, 89, 118, 124, 127, 295, 307
octopi, 125, 126
Oden, 189
Odin, 164
Ogasawara Island, 99
Ogopogo, viii, 86, 183
Okanagen Lake, 182
Okinawa, 70, 265
Old Testament, 2, 9, 143, 195, 220, 222, 280, 307, 322
Orion, 245, 327
Oronteus Finaeus Map, 216
Osiris, 242, 245, 253, 316, 317, 321, 325
Ouchi, Toru, 133, 142
Pacific Triangle, 11, 12, 85, 90, 95, 97, 100, 101, 102, 103, 108, 131, 307
Pakistan, 234
Palatki, viii, 26, 112, 276
Paleolithic Period, 201
Pangaea, 119
Papua New Guinea, 181
Paris, viii, 109, 206
Pelly Crossing, 23
Penniston, James, 64
Penobscot, 189
Pereira, Jose Carlos, 120, 312, 325
Peru, ix, 57, 67, 81, 130, 183, 248, 269
Pinyin, 255
Piri Reis Map, ix, 217

Plato, 10, 151, 155, 198, 237, 238, 269, 297, 313, 316, 326
Pleistocene, 176, 186, 289, 290
plesiosaur, 85, 86, 182
Pokanghoya, 161
Polo, Marco, 143, 180, 314
Polongahoya, 161
Poompuhur, 147
Posidonius, 3, 302
Pringle, Heather, 275, 317, 326
pterodactyl, 181, 182
pterosaur, 182
pyramid, 132, 133, 135, 202, 247, 253, 265
Qin Shi Huang, 214
radar, 24, 42, 60, 61, 63, 65, 67, 68, 71, 76, 77, 92, 104, 125
ramphorhynchus, 181
Ramses, 246
Rapture, 169
refugia, 14, 87, 159, 160, 178
religion, 141, 167, 189, 196, 214, 271, 304, 319
Rendlesham, 61, 65
rogue waves, 90, 95
Roman Catholic Church, 3, 140
Roswell, 32, 33, 34, 36, 37, 38, 39, 40, 41, 42, 43, 68, 328
Rowe, Frankie, 34, 37, 40
Royal Air Force Base, 60
ryu. See dinosaur
Sacsayhuaman, ix, 248, 249, 250
Santa Catalina Channel, 81
Santa María Huertas, Oscar, 67
Schaden, Hermann, 27
Schopenhauer, Arthur, 17, 185
Scotland, 180, 182, 209, 322
Sego Canyon, viii, 112, 113
sex, 52
Shag Harbor, 74
Siva Purana, 224
Smithsonian Institution, 140
Sofia Pappas, 102
sparkplug, 2, 210

Sphinx, ix, 133, 240, 241, 242, 243, 244, 323
Spider Grandmother, 157, 158
squid, 84
Squid, 20
Stealth, viii, 68, 76, 77, 125
Stealth Bomber, viii, 68, 77
Steen-McIntyre, Virginia, 204
stegasaurus, 180
Strieber, Whitley, 47, 48, 49, 51, 58, 311, 327
submarines, 11, 14, 15, 74, 75, 76, 78, 100, 121, 125, 257, 278, 280, 281, 288, 292, 293, 296, 299, 307
Sumatra, 95, 196, 262
Sumerian, 8, 9, 190, 191, 211, 261, 266, 272, 278, 279, 280, 281, 298, 306
Sumerians, 211, 272, 273
Suriqui, 127
Taki Kyoto Maru, 103
tanystropheus, 180
Tawa, 157
tebitu, 9, 279, 280, 282, 292, 298
The Iliad, 4
The Odyssey, 4
Thea, 171
Theravada, 266
Thor, 164
Thutmosis, 27, 240, 243
Tiahuanaco, 253, 319
Timaeus, 10, 151, 237
Titicaca, Lake, ix, 57, 81, 85, 127, 128, 129, 130, 131
Tiu, 164
Tolema, 230
Triassic Period, 119, 159
triceratops, 182
Troy, 4, 218, 309

Tyr, 164
tzolkin, 166
Uros, viii, 127, 128
Utah, x, 10, 112, 208, 276
Utnapishtim, 8, 191, 266, 293
Uto-Aztecan language, 162
utsurobune, 106
Valentich, Frederick, 70
Velez, John, 56
Venus, 164, 213
vimana, 2, 13, 222, 223, 224, 225, 226, 227, 228, 229, 231, 232, 233, 306, 309, 316
Viracocha, 269, 270, 272
Vishnu Purana, 143, 145, 167, 313, 328
vitrification, 234
Vymaanika Shaastra, 225, 226, 227, 228
Ward, John, 241
Whitney, J. D., 3, 203
Woden, 164
Wolter, Scott, 139, 140, 245
World War II, 29, 97, 100, 121, 271
wyvern. *See* dinosaur
Yenisey-Ostyak, 192
Yima, 6, 9, 13, 193, 194
Ymir, 189
Yonaguni, ix, 131, 132, 133, 134, 136, 141, 142, 265
Yukon, 23
yureisen. *See* ghost ship
Zapotec, 202
Zelitsky, Paulina, 149, 150
Zeus, 164, 188
zmeg. *See* dinosaur
zodiac, 213
Zoroastrian, 6, 7, 9, 13, 193, 256

CPSIA information can be obtained at www.ICGtesting.com
Printed in the USA
LVOW13s1829231013

358281LV00027B/656/P